THE
LENTEN
SOURCEBOOK

THE
LENTEN
SOURCEBOOK

HERBERT LOCKYER

WHITAKER
HOUSE

Unless otherwise indicated, all Scripture quotations are taken from the King James Version of the Holy Bible. Scripture quotations marked (ASV) are from the American Standard Edition of the Revised Version of the Holy Bible. Scripture quotations marked (ESV) are from *The Holy Bible, English Standard Version*, © 2000, 2001, 1995 by Crossway Bibles, a division of Good News Publishers. Used by permission. Scripture quotations marked (RV) are taken from the Revised Version of the Holy Bible. Scripture quotations marked (WEY) are taken from *The New Testament in Modern Speech: An Idiomatic Translation into Everyday English from the Text of "The Resultant Greek Testament"* by R. F. (Richard Francis) Weymouth.

Grateful acknowledgment is given to Moody Press for the use of the quote from *Suffering Savior* by F. W. Krummacher. The quote is used by permission. Moody Press, Moody Bible Institute of Chicago.

THE LENTEN SOURCEBOOK

ISBN: 978-1-60374-732-5
eBook ISBN: 978-1-60374-733-2
Printed in the United States of America
© 1968, 2013 by Ardis A. Lockyer

Whitaker House
1030 Hunt Valley Circle
New Kensington, PA 15068
www.whitakerhouse.com

Library of Congress Cataloging-in-Publication Data (Pending)

1 2 3 4 5 6 7 8 9 10 ⨄ 20 19 18 17 16 15 14 13

*Dedicated to Emil and Ruth Weise of Jacksonville, Florida,
with gratitude to God for their abiding friendship.*

CONTENTS

INTRODUCTION

All the saints who believe that as life advances, lowly penitence, godly fear, and watchful discipline are vital to the health, strength, and simplicity of their Christian faith, discover an ever new significance and value in the spiritual observance of Lent with its tender and glorious climax in the death and resurrection of Christ. From the inception of the Lenten period, the church has always associated this season with the truths and teachings concerning our path of escape from sin, the supreme evil and sorrow of our being, and sin's issue and results. The very word *Lent* is filled with the thought of tears and contrition, vigils and fasts, prayers and penitence, and the discipline of earnest religion.

If ever there was an age when man should be summoned out of his secular, exterior life with all its clamorous speed, stress, and strain to experience the life, depth, and strength of faith in the unseen and eternal, it is in our present nuclear age. Thus, as Lent comes again with its days of persistent appeal to think, kneel down in humble contrition, and rise with the cross on our shoulder, we should learn again the secret of combating the rush of living. In a clear, unmistakable voice, Lent says to every believer, "Remember Jesus Christ." And recalling all He so willingly endured during the Passion Week, we shall find ourselves identifying more closely with Him. Such a remembrance period will lead us to pray,

Lord Jesus, by Thy wounded feet
O guide my feet aright!
Lord Jesus, by Thy wounded hands
O keep my hands from wrong!
Lord Jesus, by Thy parched lips,
O curb my cruel tongue!
Lord Jesus, by Thy closed eyes
O guard my wayward sight!
Lord Jesus, by Thy thorn-crowned brow

O purify my mind!
Lord Jesus, by Thy pierced heart
O knit my heart to Thee!
Lord Jesus, by Thy empty grave
O quicken my dead self.

Yet Lent has its soft as well as stern face; its song as well as sorrow. Jesus went out to His cross singing a hymn. Bishop Handley Moule reminds us that Lent is just the old Teutonic word *Lenz* meaning "spring":

Spring is, to be sure, the time of winds, keen and strong, of showering clouds, and ever and again of snows and the sting of frost. But also it is the time of the birds' blessed voices in the budding trees, and the shining out in the black earth of the beloved flowers under the reviving sun. Not otherwise, Lent is indeed the season of renewed severities with the self-life, of new pains of godly sorrow, deepened and hallowed at the cross. But also it has to do with the vernal growths of the peace and joy of faith, and with the fair beauties of the life of love, and with the song of victory over all temptation in the vital brightness of the slain and living Christ of God.

The recognition of the Lenten season is of little value unless it leaves an impact on our life. As we meditate on all the shame and anguish Jesus suffered during His last week ending in His death, ours must be the resolution to strip ourselves of all known, conscious sin, and penitentially seek the cleansing of His blood. The first, and in some ways the most poignant, of Christ's sufferings was His shame when stripped of His garments. May we discover anew during this Lenten season that it is only by such shame He willingly endured that He is able to clothe us with the garment of His own righteousness which we must promise never to shamefully cast away. With Ignatius Loyola, we must learn to pray,

Teach us, good Lord, to serve Thee as Thou deservest;
To give and not to count the cost;
To fight and not to heed the wounds;
To toil and not to seek for rest;
To labor and not to ask for any reward
Save that of knowing that we do Thy will.

In chapter 4 of this book, we have a section dealing with "Stations of the Cross." Since most Protestants don't use this term, we have entitled this section, "Steps to the Cross," but there is no reason why Anglicans and others may not use this section as "Stations." We would like to arrange this section so that it fits into the preaching or Lenten schedule of every denomination.

1

LENT—ITS ORIGIN AND OBSERVANCE

Lent, as practiced through the centuries, is not taught in the New Testament. Even Roman Catholic sources such as the *Catholic Encyclopedia* 111, 484, confesses that, "Writers of the Fourth Century were prone to describe many practices as 'The Lenten Fast of Forty Days' as Apostolic institutions which certainly had no claim to be so regarded." Fasting, so prominent in the development of Lent is, of course, a biblical truth. Two kinds of fasting are to be distinguished, namely, fasting by necessity and fasting by choice, with the latter being of more common usage. Such a custom involved abstinence from food, either entire or partial, accompanied with humiliation, sorrow for sin, and prayer. (See Isaiah 58.) Days of fasting were proclaimed in times of national calamity and were accompanied by a call for confession of national sins. (See 1 Samuel 7:6; 2 Chronicles 20:3.) *"To afflict the soul,"* is often used for fasting. (See Leviticus 16:29–31 RV.) Moses enjoined a solemn fast on the Day of Expiation (see Leviticus 23:27–29), and he fasted forty days on Mount Horeb (see Exodus 34:28). Elijah likewise fasted for the same period. (See 1 Kings 19:8.) As practiced by the Jews, fasting was a religious duty. (See Joshua 7:6; Judges 20:26.) After the captivity in Babylon, national fasting became common and was ordained as the Day of Atonement. (See Nehemiah 7:73; 9:38.) Fasts were sometimes individual and voluntary, as was David's abstinence when his first child with Bathsheba was dying.

After the Jews returned from their Babylonian captivity, it would seem as if four fasts were recognized. (See Zechariah 7:3, 5; 8:19.)

+ The first—in the tenth month, recollecting the start of the siege of Jerusalem. (See 2 Kings 25:1.)
+ The second—in the fourth month, recalling the fall of Jerusalem. (See 2 Kings 29:3–4.)
+ The third—in the fifth month, recalling the destruction of the temple. (See 2 Kings 25:8–9.)

+ The fourth—in the seventh month, recalling the murder of Gedaliah and remaining Jews. (See 2 Kings 25:25.)

The Jewish calendar came to have twenty-two days of fasting, in addition to those just mentioned. It became the custom to fast, as we have indicated, twice each week, for the reason that Moses received the tables of the Law on Mount Sinai on Thursday and came down on Monday. When the Jews fast on the Day of Atonement, they wear a white shroud and cap, and the fast is called "The White Fast." Black is worn on other days, and they are known as "Black Fasts."

In the New Testament, we find that the Pharisees fasted twice a week (see Luke 18:12); that the disciples of John the Baptist fasted, doubtless inspired by the Baptist's own frugal living in the wilderness. (See Matthew 9:14–15.) Although Jesus fasted in the desert for forty days during His temptation, He did not advocate fasting as a practice, at least for its own sake. (See Matthew 6:16, 18.) He rebuked the Pharisees for their ostentatious and hypocritical fasting. Furthermore, He did not appoint fast days but did predict that His disciples would fast after His death. (See Luke 5:33–35.) The early Christians fasted when they were overtaken by affliction. (See 2 Corinthians 6:5.) The Apostolic Church held fasts before certain solemn occasions. (See Acts 13:2; 14:23.) Abstinence from every pleasure of the senses, as well as from food, characterized a religious fast. (See 1 Corinthians 7:5.) Paul, because of his rigid, Pharisaical background, practiced fasting. (See 2 Corinthians 6:5; 11:27.) Fasting is not obligatory today in Protestant churches but is recommended as a Christian duty. Prayer is coupled with fasting, and both are associated with Lent. (See Daniel 9:3; Matthew 17:21.) Dr. W. Griffith Thomas reminds us that…

Fasting represents an attitude of detachment from the things of time and sense, whether it be food and pleasure or lawful ambition.

Prayer represents the complementary attitude of attachment to the things of God. We shall readily determine, under the guidance of the Holy Spirit, what particular forms our fastings shall take, thus helping our spiritual development.

The word *Lent* itself is from the ancient Saxon word *Leneten*, meaning "spring," which is called *Leneten-tide* because it is the time of year when the days noticeably increase in length. The chief part of the fast received the name *Lenetin-faesten*, meaning "spring-first," which became shortened to *Lent. Leneten* was also the name for March because this month manifested a lengthening of the days. Although some of the early church fathers affirmed that Lent was of apostolic origin, the New Testament is silent as to a specific Lenten period. That the same goes back to a very early date in church history is evident from the writings of Irenaeus and Tertullian. At first, its duration was short and very severe, and appears to have been confined to the forty hours between the time of the crucifixion and resurrection. Gradually, the period of fasting increased until it became forty days in accordance with the forty-day fasts of Moses, Elijah, and Jesus.

Ash Wednesday, the first day of Lent, is supposed to have received its name from the Roman Catholic custom of sprinkling palm ashes burned on Palm Sunday on the heads of those who desired to do penance that day; after repenting, they were received into the church. The sprinkling was in the sign of a cross. Lent, then, extended from Ash Wednesday to Easter. The length of the Lenten Fast and the rigor with which it has been observed have varied greatly at different times and in different countries. In the time of Irenaeus, the Fast before Easter was very short, but very severe; nothing would be eaten for forty hours between the afternoon of Good Friday and the morning of Easter. About the middle of the third century, it had become customary to fast during Holy Week. The first mention of the Lenten Fast, or *Quadragesima*, is in the Fifth Canon of the Council of Nicaea in 325 A.D. During the fourth century, Pope Felix III decreed a thirty-six day fast; then, in 487 A.D., four more days were added to make it correspond to our Lord's forty-day fast in the wilderness. In England, a Lenten Fast was first observed by Earconberht, King of Kent in 640 A.D. During the eighth or ninth century, the period became fixed and has been observed in the Roman Catholic, Greek Catholic, and Anglican churches ever since. In the Eastern Church, the period lasts for fifty calendar days. Lent is still described as "the six weeks of the fast"—Holy Week not being reckoned in. Sundays are part of the Lenten season but because they were reckoned as feast days, they were not included among the forty days of fasting or abstinence.

The character and extent of the fasting varied, but there was almost a universal cessation of everything of a festival nature and the strict observance of religious duties. In the Middle Ages, meat, eggs, and milk were forbidden during Lent by ecclesiastical and statute law. During the religious confusion of the Reformation, the practice of fasting was generally relaxed. After the revolution, Lenten laws fell obsolete though they remained on the Statute Book till repealed by the Statute Revision Act of 1863. During the eighteenth century, the strict observance of the Lenten Fast was generally abandoned, but devout saints like William Law and John Wesley still advocated it. The custom of women wearing and mourning during Lent, followed by Queen Elizabeth I and her court, survived well into the nineteenth century. Around the sixteenth century, Lent was enjoined both upon moral grounds and for the benefit of the fish trade: hence, the French proverb, "Salmon and sermon have their season in Lent." Lay persons were imprisoned for eating flesh during Lent.

The biographer of John Buchan, the Scottish author who became Lord Tweedsmuir and Governor General of Canada, says that this renowned writer always "showed the usual Scots' Presbyterian reaction to Lent." Writing to his mother from Oxford University, he said, "This is the first day of Lent and all the prize idiots here are making a pretense of fasting...I was ill-advised enough to go to chapel, and found a service of nearly twice its proper length."

With the growth of the Oxford Movement in the Anglican Church, the practice of observing Lent was revived and although no hard and fast rules were laid down as to abstinence, the recognition of the period as discipline or as an exercise of self-denial were followed. The extent of fasting is left to individual discretion. In Roman Catholicism, the season retains many of its ancient features, particularly penance and fasting. Among many Protestant churches, Lent is recognized as the last week of our Lord's earthly life, and is known as Passion or Holy Week, covering the days between and including Palm Sunday and Easter Day, when most impressive services are held. Mid-Lent, or the fourth Sunday in Lent, was long known as "Mothering Sunday," an allusion to the custom of girls in Christian service being allowed to go home to visit their parents.

Lenten likewise means "spare," "meager," "frugal," "stunted," as food was in Lent. The word was used in this sense by Shakespeare's "A lenten entertainment" (*Hamlet* Act II, Scene 2); "A lenten answer" (*Twelfth Night* Act I, Scene 5); and "A lentenpye"—pie (*Romeo and Juliet* Act II, Scene 4). Dryden, in *Hind and Panther* (Act III, Scene 27) also used the term in the same way: "With a lenten salad cooled her blood." Other associations of the term are, "A lenten faced fellow," one with a mournful and hungry look. Daffodils are spoken of as "The Lent Lily" because they bloom during Lent. "Guleaggo's Lent" refers to the form of torture devised by Guleaggo Viconti, calculated to prolong the unfortunate victim's life for forty days. "St. Martin's Lent" was so named because it extended from Martinmas, November eleventh to Christmas. Among well-known Proverbs are "After a Christmas Comes a Lent," "Marry in Lent, Live to Repent," and "He Is Welcome as the First Day in Lent."

2

LENTEN PREPARATION

A meditation of Passion Week cannot be undertaken in a cold, formal, or mechanical frame of mind. A sense of sin, guilt, penitence, and a fresh and fuller commitment to the claims of Christ are essential if the season is to yield spiritual profit. A little less food will clear our minds so that we can more clearly understand all that the Savior willingly endured on our behalf. Genuine sorrow for our sin that gave Him His Calvary will deepen our heart's love for Him. The prayerful remembrance of His shame and anguish will lead us into a fellowship of His sufferings, which Paul knew so much about. For many, as they pass by, Easter is only a holiday—not a holy season. But the multitudes must be made to see that it was because of sin that Easter was so essential; the satanic intrusion into God's universe was so vital that Jesus was promised as the seed of the woman to destroy the works of the devil. (See Genesis 3:15.) Those who preach the cross must first understand the cause of it, namely, sin. If sin is to be detected, pardoned, removed, and killed to its very roots, the world has no other way of salvation from the curse and bondage of sin save through the name and merits of the Redeemer. (See Acts 4:12.)

The sin question is so integral a part of Christ's doctrine and death that it is bound up forever with His very name—a large space to which is given in Scripture. An angel whispered to Joseph, *"Mary shall bring forth a son, and thou shalt call his name Jesus: for he shall save his people from their sins"* (Matthew 1:21–25). Salvation from the guilt and power of sin light up from within the peerless name of Jesus. In *Verbum Crucis*, Dr. William Alexander reminds us that,

> Theology has two great chapters—one upon the Nature of God, so far as it is revealed to man; the other upon sin, its essence, its practice, its removal.

It was because "sin was something and somewhere for every man and woman in the world" that Jesus came from heaven and took the likeness of sinful flesh upon Himself. It was for the soul's emancipation from sin that Jesus was manifested and ultimately murdered. At the heart of His teaching was the abolition of the very being, as well as the guilt of sin. "Christ never said that He came to found a school of literature, or logic, or art, or science— though He did all this indirectly"—but that His supreme mission was the provision of a perfect salvation for a sinning race. Even His miracles empha- size this. "To Him there was something more blighting than leprosy; more crippling than paralysis; more melancholy than deafness, or blindness, or loss of speech. A line of light from His lifted finger runs along the whole dark ranks of diseases and enables us to spell out the meaning of His lesson. *'Son thy sins be forgiven thee. Sin no more. Neither do I condemn; go, and sin no more'* (John 8:11)." Thus, the true significance of Easter will be lost unless those who observe it realize that Jesus was nailed to His cross by sin and for sin; that without the shedding of His blood, there is no remission of sin.

Lent has come down to us associated with ideas of tears and contrition, vigil and fast, the judgment seat of the Holy One before whom, *"the heavens are not clean"* (Job 15:15). The forty days annually brought a persistent appeal to think and bow before an offended Maker in contrition who then rose, "ran- somed, healed, restored, forgiven." As discord with a thrice Holy God is at the very base of life, the saints of old gradually instituted the Lenten season for the purpose of exposing the fact and terribleness of sin necessitating the death of God's Son upon the accursed tree where He achieved a glorious vic- tory over the triple alliance—sin, the flesh, and the devil. Therefore, as the preacher prepares his Easter messages in which the pre-eminent thought will be that Christ died for sinners, he will prayerfully prepare his own heart first. As water never rises above its own level, so the preacher cannot lift those he ministers to above the level of his own spiritual experience. This is why he will undertake a thorough examination of his own heart, and bring discovered sin under the cleansing efficacy of the precious blood of Christ. It is only thus that as he goes out to preach the crucified Jesus and His resurrection, such a doctrine will become a dynamic in the lives of those to whom he witnesses. Having bowed before the Lord in the silence of his own study and with the cross before his eyes, crying, "God, be merciful to me a sinner," the preacher, preaching a message he has felt, will witness spiritual results in his Passion Week ministrations. Proclaimed truth unrelated to the life and experience of the herald has a deadening effect upon hearers. *"We also believe, and therefore speak"* (2 Corinthians 4:13). When head of the Cambridge Theological Hall,

Dr. Handley Moule heard a student's eulogy concerning another student. "Ah, he was a consistent gentleman; he had a right to speak for the Lord."

If there has been inexorable self-examination, penitent confession, and a fuller commitment to the claims of the Crucified One on the part of the preacher throughout the days preceding Easter, he can be assured of a season of rich blessing during his ministry in Holy Week. His constant ideal and intercession must be…

> Teach me this day to keep in view,
> The prize Thy followers should pursue;
> To adorn Thy doctrine, and to shed
> Fragrance and light where'er I tread.

Preachers who have entered into the fellowship of Christ's suffering and have proved that "Every thorn upon His brow makes thee more and more His slave" will have no difficulty whatever about entering Passion Week in the right spirit. If his own heart has been broken over his own sin and sorrow or that of others, he will have an impressive tenderness in his voice as he preaches about the broken body and heart of his Master. To quote Bishop Moule again, who, wanting to speak on our Lord's heart as veritably broken as indicated in the Messianic Psalm (Psalm 69:20), came to experience that a broken heart was a great loss, and thus wrote,

> Broken heart, whose nameless pain
> Stranger souls explore in vain,
> There is One, of skill so strong
> He can turn that pain to song.
> Once, by agonies unspoken,
> His own holiest heart was broken;
> Sorer pangs than ever thine
> Wrung that Sufferer divine.
> Now His woe in joy is ended—
> Yet that breach abides unmended;
> For, though suffering pass away,
> To have suffered lasts for age;
> Only, breach 'tis now no more,
> But an always open door!
> There the mourner who would win
> Calm as balm is welcome in,
> In the Lord's kind heart and deep

Holy tears unblamed to weep,
Till new lights and hopes awaken
Trembling through the soul forsaken
Born of sorrow's secret tryst
With a once heartbroken Christ.

If a world broken by its sin is to be moved by the message of the "once heartbroken Christ," there must be more brokenhearted preachers to proclaim such a message. Heart-communion with the crucified Redeemer inspires a man to declare the full truth of the cross and the empty tomb, not only as Lent comes around, but at all times. As he seeks to maintain unbroken fellowship with Him who is the "Immortal Gardener of the flowery place," the preacher comes to experience with Paul that the presentation of the Christ of the cross and the garden is to those who believe the power of God unto salvation.

3

LENTEN PROGRAMS

Long before Passion Week comes around, the devoted pastor prayerfully considers how to use the period for the utmost spiritual profit. He gives much thought to the various ways by which he can bring the impact of the Easter Gospel to bear upon the life of his church. Christ's last days culminating in His death and resurrection will be constantly before him as he plans the programs or services for his congregation. Eschewing all promptings to present a merely dramatic and emotional aspect of the crucifixion, the pastor strives for effective ways to lift Christ up, that the hearts of all to whom he is to minister will be drawn to Him. The sanctification of believers, the restoration of backsliders, and the salvation of lost sinners will be the pastor's objectives as he carefully arranges his schedule for the Lenten season. For loyal pastors who have been in the ministry a long time, experience has taught them how best to set in order the most effective way of observing Easter, and they have no need, therefore, of any guidance from a sourcebook. In the preparation of the one in your hands, the author had in mind young and inexperienced pastors who require help as they come to face Easter Week with its opportunities of declaring the truths such a season represents. It is to be hoped that the following suggestions and examples will be of service to those who endeavor to make full proof of their ministry.

EASTER WEEK ON THE CHURCH CALENDAR

The wise and devoted pastor, eager to exercise a profitable ministry of the Word, should bear in mind the various days and seasons generally recognized among the churches of all denominations. These particular occasions give him an opportunity for emphasizing the several facets of the Christian faith. Christmas and Easter are prominent among the dates on the church calendar. As we are dealing with Easter Week in this volume, pastors, apart from any united Easter services they may engage in, have their own pulpit ministry to maintain and usually plan special messages for Palm Sunday, regular week-night services, and Easter Sunday. Churches having an efficient choir often arrange an Easter musical program during the Holy Week, during which the pastor gives a brief message. To aid a busy pastor we herewith include messages and outlines relevant to his Easter program.

⌣

For Palm Sunday—morning service

Theme: Palms and Willows
Text: "Palm trees…and willows of the brook" (Leviticus 23:40).

Sermon

The contents of the twenty-third chapter of Leviticus are highly instructive to the careful student of Scripture because, like the book as a whole, it is rich in typical teaching. Within this chapter we have outlined the seven feasts of Jehovah which were the seven great religious festivals observed yearly by Israel in response to the divine command. From verse 39 to the end of the chapter, the seventh feast is recorded and was known as "The Feast of Tabernacles," which, like the Lord's Supper, has a backward and forward look. As the Supper looks back to the cross with its deliverance and forward to the return of Christ for our entrance into glory, so "The Feast of Tabernacles" was a memorial of the exit out of Egypt by the power of God and prophetic final restoration of Israel.

In the verse before us, the people had to bring the boughs and branches of certain trees to the tabernacle and there rejoice before the Lord for seven days. Thus visible nature presented itself to Israel as a manifest parable of deep spiritual truths. The fruit of the earth reminded the people that the God of Sinai was the supreme Lord of nature, the God of seedtime and harvest, the Creator and Sustainer of heaven and earth, and therefore the One responsible for their human and spiritual needs. When we acknowledge the goodness of God, the harvest festival season likely had its origin in the Feast of Tabernacles. As we can see, two parts of the tree-world are specifically mentioned, namely, the desert palm tree and the willows of the brook—emblematic as we shall discover of the contrary experiences of life.

1. The Distinctive Meaning of Each

What are the particular and peculiar characteristics of both the palm and the willow?

Take the palm.

Its manifold uses made the palm the most useful of trees to the ancient Israel. In fact, it had no equal when it came to utility. It has been written about as "The king among the grasses," and "The prince of vegetation." The palm grows upright in the sun, and is the emblem of gladness, renown, and victory as seen in victors receiving a laurel of palm leaves. All that is best in life can be likened to the palm tree. Thus, we speak of our good days as our palm days. When the psalmist set out to describe the righteous, he said that because of their rectitude they flourished as the palm tree. (See Psalm 92:12.)

Take the willow.

The willow on the other hand droops as it grows, so we have named it "The Weeping Willow," and it symbolizes sadness, humiliation, captivity, and death—the opposite of the flourishing palm. Yet each year the people had to bring the willows, as well as the palms, and rejoice over them before the Lord seven days.

2. The Close Association of Both

Palms and willows were brought together because they grow together in human life and experience. Irrespective of our calling or culture, life is a strange mixture of palms growing in the sun, and willows drooping alongside the brook. How intriguing is the florist's advertisement, "Bouquets and Wreaths Made Up." What a striking contrast! What extremes! Yet the florist gains his livelihood by providing both. Bouquets speak of the union of hearts at weddings and represent the happy, singing company. Wreaths, on the other hand, betoken the separation of hearts—the funeral procession with its weeping, heartbroken relatives and friends. We go through life with a bouquet in one hand and a wreath in the other, and sometimes the two are never very far apart. Church bells are rung for weddings and funerals, for births and deaths.

Doubtless all of us have felt the velvet touch of the palm—we have had our days of success and sunshine; days when our dreams were realized, our difficulties conquered, and our lives made radiant with the joy of heaven. Yet we are equally familiar with the sting of the thorn and the droop of the willow. There have been days of sickness, sorrow, and sadness. We have our times of gloom as well as gladness. There is a somewhat pathetic phrase in the Isaiah's description of the captivity of his people. He speaks of them carrying the treasures *away to the brook of the willows* (Isaiah 15:7). Is this not a pathetic journey each of us must take? Are willows not our common lot? There are no empty houses alongside the brook where the willows grow.

Our pilgrim life, then, is a remarkable combination of paradise palms and weeping willows. There is a time to laugh, and a time to weep. Our smiles and sighs, our triumphs and tears, our pleasures and pains are providentially inter-mingled. Our feast days and our fast days are often not very far apart. In fact, life is something like an organist who conceived a unique overture—a mixture of *The Hallelujah Chorus* and *The Death March from Saul*. All writers, poets, and singers touching the heart of man are those who see most vividly this dual aspect of life and portray it accordingly. Shakespeare, in *All's Well That Ends Well*, reminds us that "the web of our life is of a mingled yarn, good and ill together." And the Bible is most precious and fascinating, seeing that it mirrors our lot as being made up of sunshine and shadow, delight and darkness, blessing, and blight.

3. The Grateful Offering of Both

On the first day of the last feast the Jews had to bring both their palms and willows before the Lord and rejoice for seven days. Their joy was not merely natural or earthly, but also deeply spiritual. It was *"before the Lord."*

Grateful for palms!

Ah, you say, that is natural and easy. Is it? God is often forgotten in prosperity. Do we not read that Jeshurun waxed fat, but kicked and forsook the One who had blessed him? Too often, the gifts and blessings of life are received in the spirit of vanity and pride. We flourish the palm over our head as if it were homegrown. With conceit we declare that by our own initiative and wisdom we have gotten the good things we enjoy. But what hast thou that thou didst not receive? God is ever the Giver of the blessings of life. (See Ecclesiastes 5:19.) Thus, we must cast our palms where the elders cast their crowns before the Lord! Amid prosperity, no matter in what form it may reach us, when tempted to exalt ourselves unduly may grace be ours to say, "O soul of mine, never forget that the palms growing in the garden of life were planted by the hand divine!"

Grateful for willows!

Do we not find it hard and irksome to praise God for the drooping willow, and to rejoice in tribulation? It is not easy to be glad when pain, sickness, adversity, and grievous separations overtake us. Yet we triumph in life when grace is ours to rejoice before the Lord over our willows, as well as our palms. It was Shelley the poet, a great sufferer himself who gave the world these lines:

> Most wretched men are cradled into poetry by wrong.
> They learn in suffering what they teach in song.

Paul knew all about the combination of palms and willows, for in one of his biographical sketches he brings together visions and revelations of the Lord he could not speak of and his painful thorn in the flesh. (See 1 Corinthians 12.) We must not despise the willow as being unworthy of thanks. Often the noblest life is the product of sanctified tribulation. That palms can change into willows, and willows into palms, is the clear unmistakable teaching of both Scripture and human experience. The greatest of all Gardeners is skillful at transforming weeping willows into beneficent palm trees and vice versa.

Grace must be ours to take the palms and willows before the Lord in the spirit of praise and gratitude. He makes them both to grow in the natural world, and permits them to be ours in the realm of experience. Was this not so with His servant Job? As we read the opening of his story we find that he had palms in abundance, and added to all the good things of life was the reputation that he was perfect and upright—none like him in all the earth. Yet overnight what terrible reverses were his. His found himself stripped bare of all his possessions. Such was his poverty-stricken condition and bodily disease that Job's wife urged him to do away with his life—"Curse God, and commit suicide," as her advice actually meant. But what was Job's reaction to his trials and to his wife's taunt? Magnificent, was it not? What? Shall we receive good—palm trees—at the hand of God and should we not receive evil—willows of the brook? *"Though he slay me, yet will I trust him,"* (Job 13:15). And because Job could rejoice over his adversity as well as his affluence, God blessed His tried yet triumphant servant with twice as much as he had at his illustrious beginning.

Looking back upon his entrance into parliament and thinking of the days of glory, as well as of the grief that followed, Sir Winston Churchill once said,

> The glory of light cannot exist without its shadows. Life is a whole, and good and ill must be accepted together. The journey has been enjoyable and well worth making—once.

George Matheson, the blind preacher and poet, bore a similar testimony. Bitter experiences led him to write,

> My God, I have never thanked Thee for my thorns. I have thanked Thee a thousand times for my roses, but not once for my thorns. I have been looking forward to a world where I shall get compensation for my cross: but I have never thought of my cross as itself a present glory. Teach me the glory of my cross: teach me the value of my thorn. Shew me that I have climbed to Thee by the path of pain. Shew me that my tears have made my rainbow.

If we bring our palms or the best things in life before the Lord in the spirit of holy gratitude, then He will make them richer gifts still. If we bring our willows, or the dark, inexplicable, unwanted experiences of life before the Lord in the same spirit of praise, then He whom Mary mistook to be the Gardener will transform the weeping willow into a palm of peace and blessing. If we cannot be thankful for everything, we can certainly be thankful in everything.

4. The Union of Palms and Willows in the Life of Christ

We now come to the message and meaning of Palm Sunday as observed by the church throughout the world today. As our great High Priest, Christ is touched with the feelings of our physical make-up, and is therefore able to sympathize with us in the varied experiences of life. Having entered our humanity, He has an intimate acquaintance with the gladness and the sadness alternating within the human heart. Although He was anointed with the oil of gladness above any other, He became the Man of Sorrows enduring grief.

Palm Trees—Jesus knew all about these. On that Sunday, as He entered His Passion Week, the people cut down branches of palm trees and carpeted His way, and as He rode in triumph, they shouted *"Hosanna! Blessed is he that cometh in the name of the Lord"* (Mark 11:9). But He was not unduly exalted with such exultation. He knew that the "Hosannas" would give way to, *"Away with him, crucify him!"*

Willows of the Brook—Jesus had these also for His palm-strewn way led to Calvary: palms one Sunday; pangs the next Sunday. Let it not be forgotten that there are only four days between Palm Sunday and Good Friday. That Jesus could rejoice before His Father for palms as well as willows is seen in the fact that He went out to His cross singing a hymn.

Are the palms ours? Then let us not be unduly elated over prosperity and success. We may find the willows at the next turn of the avenue, and when we meet them we must learn to walk humbly with God among the bountiful palms if we are not to fail in the day of adversity. Are the willows ours? Have losses, sorrows, and separations come our way blinding our faith and confidence in God's love and care? Are we cast down in soul because of the trials divinely permitted? Triumph can be ours only if we take up our cross and kiss it and carry it for His sake. Because the darkness and the light are both alike to Him, He can enable us to rejoice always whether we have palms or willows.

In his vision of heaven, John saw the saints with *"palms in their hands"* (Revelation 7:9). Mark that—palms in their hands! Not a palm in one hand and a willow in the other, as we have here on earth as we linger amid the shadows, but a palm in each hand. There are no willows in heaven—no tears, no anguish, no separation. No harps are there hanging on willow trees, but they are ever tuned and used to magnify and extol our matchless Lord. We are still in the flesh, however, and until the last battle has been fought, the last burden borne, and the last tear shed, we must learn how to offer our palms and willows, our songs and sorrows before the Lord in the confidence that He is able to cause all things—palms and willows—to work together for our good if we love Him and are called according to His purpose.

~

For Palm Sunday—evening service

Theme: The Significance of Palm Sunday
Texts: Matthew 21:6–9; Luke 19:39–40

Sermon

In the course of His public ministry, as Jesus went about doing good, He discouraged any acclaim on the part of those He blessed. Popular adulation was suppressed. Those He healed were charged not to make Him known. More than once He resisted the effort to make Him a king, although He was born a king. Had His kingdom been of the world He lived in, He would have embraced the opportunity of kingship, but He asserted that His kingdom was not of the world surrounding Him. Now, on His triumphal entry into Jerusalem, He not only accepts the acclamation of the populace, but also helps to organize it. This was no last desperate bid for recognition as His enemies were closing in upon Him on every side, neither was it a display of hysteria. Because of who and what He was, the life and labors of Christ were characterized by a calm serenity, and His planned entry into the city was thus free from any panic.

What must not be forgotten is the fact that while He had previously refrained from a general statement of His true messiahship and had shunned popular excitement, He never refused the messianic acknowledgment and honors accorded Him from time to time by individuals. How He praised Peter for his recognition of Him as *"the Christ, the Son of the living God"* (Matthew 16:16). What was His purpose, then, in accepting the popular proclamation of His messiahship at this time? Was it not that He so clearly foresaw that the events that were happening had a religious rather than a political significance? Thomas J. Hardy expressed it this way in his unique volume, *The Year with Christ*:

He foresaw that His appearance in Jerusalem so soon after the raising of Lazarus would be hailed with frantic enthusiasm by the crowds attending the feast. He foresaw that His enemies would place a political construction on this popularity in order to deliver Him to the Roman power as dangerous to the public peace. He was determined that this construction would find no support in any action or words of His. He would not even risk the consent of silence. He knew that He must die, but He would not die as a political victim, as a successor of Theudas or Judas of Galilee. (See Acts 5:36–37.) He was about to suffer for the bondage of His people. He was to suffer for their sins and the sins of the whole world. Therefore, He clothed this last entry into Jerusalem with as much as He could of the pomp and circumstance that attended the ancient religion of Israel.

Furthermore, did not His choice of a beast to ride on have a startling religious significance for the orthodox Jew? Riding on an ass was the fulfillment of a prophecy dear to the heart of a son of Abraham. (See Zechariah 9:9.) Had not Jesus come to restore the theocracy which was the direct government of God without the intermediate agency of a political king, and was not this form of direct government in vogue before Solomon introduced the horse as a beast of burden; had not the judges and seers used the ass as the symbol of their divine commission? While such symbolism may appear crude to us, to the Jew of Christ's day, the significance of such symbolism was conclusive. To those who looked for redemption in Israel, the regal Man on that ass was going back to the time when He Himself was *Jehovah-Elohim*, the Monarch and Guardian of His people. (See Judges 9:4; 12:14; 2 Samuel 13:2, 9; 18:9.)

Another aspect of Christ's triumphant procession was that the resurrection of Lazarus was the primary cause of such a jubilant demonstration. Large numbers of pilgrims were going up to the feast and stopped on the way at Bethany to see the man who had been raised from the dead. (See John 12:9.) Thus it was as the Vanquisher of death that Jesus was acclaimed as He rode to His death and became *"the resurrection and the life"* (John 11:25). Those who hailed Jesus and formed His escort, as He set out to cross the slopes of Olivet to the city, were those Jews who saw and believed at Bethany. As Jesus approached the city, the party was joined by a great multitude of curious inhabitants. (See John 12:12; 8:30.) It is John who gives us a clear idea of the beginning and subsequent growth and orderliness of the pageant introducing Christ's passion. (See John 12:9; Matthew 21:8–9; Mark 11:9–10; Luke 19:37–40.)

The spontaneity of the ovation Jesus received was striking. To quote Hardy again,

> If our Lord desired to raise His advent to the highest spiritual significance, to place it forever beyond the petty interpretation of secular governments and party strife, nothing could have realized His purpose like the great Halleldaily chanted on the Feast of Tabernacles, which then arose to gladden the approaches to the City, and to shock the Pharisees into remonstrance against honours which were divine. "The very stones," Jesus replied, "would cry out, should these hold their peace." So high above all worldly concern was the purpose of His coming that nature, whose Lord He was, was ready with her witness as at Calvary, when, in default of other witness, the sun withdrew his light!

The Benediction of the Eucharist was the first Christian hymn, the "Hosanna" as the highest point of praise before the hush of sacrifice. A similar hush fell on Jesus' heart as He beheld the city and wept over it. Nearing His cross, He shed His tears, and on the cross, He shed His blood, and dying, accomplished His mission to earth.

> Give Thou the triumph, O Jehovah, to the Son of David!
> Blessed be the kingdom of our father David, now to be restored in
> the Name of Jehovah!
> Blessed be He that cometh—King of Israel—in the name of
> Jehovah!
> Our peace and salvation, now coming as from God above!
> Praise be His in the highest heavens, for sending them by Him,
> even the Son of David!
> From the highest heaven send Thou now salvation!

FOR PASSION WEEK—EVENING SERVICE

In the majority of cases, Wednesday is usually the night of the church meeting for prayer and meditation upon the Word. Where this is so, the pastor could profitably dwell upon what happened the Wednesday of the Passion

Week. A message could be given on *The Day of Retirement*. There are no records of the events of this day which Jesus spent closeted in the loving home of Mary, Martha, and Lazarus at Bethany. (See Matthew 21:17; Mark 13:3–14:11.) The next morning, *"a great while before it was day,"* Jesus rose and left Bethany for communion with His Father on Mount Olivet. How the Master must have appreciated the peace and refreshment of that Bethany home in the midst of such a turbulent and troubled week! Although the silence of this day was but a prelude to the storm that followed, Jesus took things quietly in the house of His friends, and while there, received from the heart of a grateful woman a pre-anointing against His coming death and burial.

Actually, the Wednesday of His Passion Week was not a rest day, but one devoted to the instruction of His disciples as to how they were to continue His cause after His death and departure to heaven. He had many things to say to them, which if heeded, would enable them to bear the shock to their faith as they saw Him crucified; it would also carry them through the strain of the days following His resurrection. Throughout the day, we can imagine how Mary and Martha did their utmost to ease the inner burden of the Master, and how they would linger longer than usual before retiring. This was His last evening in the home which His visits had sanctified. Tomorrow He would leave them and never visit them again in person. A veil of holy silence is drawn over a blessed conversation that must have lasted far into the night. When Jesus finally retired to His room in that Bethany home, it was to have His last comfortable sleep on earth. Is it not suggestive that Bethany was chosen as the scene of His ascension—*"He led them out as far as to Bethany…while he blessed them, he was parted from them"* (Luke 24:50, 51)? From the home there He went Home.

An inescapable feature of the last days of Jesus before the completion of a God-given task is the evidence of His humanity and His dependence upon His friends for strength and relief. Amid the increasing hatred of His enemies and the ever-mounting sorrow within His own soul, He sought the solace of those who were devoted to Him. After the homeless years when *"he had not where to lay his head"* (Luke 9:58), He permitted Himself the consolation and provision of the home, the three members of which had been so wonderfully enriched by Him:

Mary—He had led into the ways of deeper prayer and contemplation.

Martha—He had taught how to serve in the home without distraction and undue anxiety.

Lazarus—dearly loved and lost, had been recalled to life by His power. Returning from the grave, Lazarus was silent as to where he had been and what he had seen and heard while absent from home and earth.

He told it not; or something sealed
The lips of that Evangelist.

As the Man of Sorrows, then, Jesus bound loyal hearts to Himself by the transforming energy of His love, and revealed Himself on their behalf as God as well as Man. Wherever in the gospels we are reminded of His humanity within the narrative, there is likewise the manifestation of His creative and regenerative power.

Jesus, divinest when Thou most art Man!

Thinking anew of how, on that Wednesday of His final week, He blessed a home with His fragrant presence, what a different world ours would be if only we were willing to afford Him this Easter by the acknowledgment of His claims as the Creator of every family on earth and in heaven, the undisputed Lordship of our home and family life.

FOR EASTER SUNDAY

It is a remarkable testimony to the magnetism of the cross that after almost two millenniums since Christ died and rose again, churches are crowded on Easter Sunday to listen anew to the message of His sacrifice and conquest of sin and death. How the services of this Lord's Day present the faithful pastor with wonderful opportunities of preaching the word of reconciliation, and of experiencing that such preaching is still the power of God unto salvation! Before his Easter services, the pastor must spend much time with Jesus alone, for is He not the One he will extol as he comes to his pulpit? As to preaching material suitable to the occasion, the preacher has many Easter sermons to browse in order to find grist for his mill. We herewith include two messages for Easter Sunday as guideposts.

Sunday Morning

Theme: The Crown of Thorns
Text: John 19:1–3

Sermon

While there are many aspects of the grim cross of our Savior on which we could profitably spend our time, let us concentrate this "memorial day" upon the symbol of our sins and the shame adorning His brow as He died—the sinless substitute for sinners.

The mock crowning of the Savior was only one of the many indignities willingly endured throughout His final days of suffering. Yet how full of spiritual import for our reverent, adoring hearts is the sight of the thorn-crowned victim of Calvary.

That ugly crown plaited by the soldiers was not only a mock one, but was also a circlet of torture, piercing deep into His lovely brow. Already He had experienced severe scourging; now His hands are bound, which meant that they could not apply a softening touch to the place of pain. Sympathetic fingers easing many an aching heart were not able to lift the garland of spikes relieving thereby the smart, the torture of His own bleeding brow.

And since the Master's willingness to wear that crown of sharp, poisonous thorns is the fact that John so graphically depicts, let us endeavor to understand how such a mock coronation adds to His majesty.

His Condescension

To wear such a crown, Christ had to lay aside His crown of past glory. Rich, yet for our sakes He had to become poor. And it is only when we compare the honor He received from the retinue of heaven with the shame and rejection of earth that we realize what was involved in His voluntary surrender.

Think of it! He left a world of glory for one of meanness; one of bliss for one of misery; one of purity for one of crime; one of life for one of death. He who was the eternal King is treated as a criminal, as the off-scouring of the earth. He who created worlds by the word of His power is sold for the price of a common slave. He who came as the blessed emancipator of souls was bound as a felon and led out to die. He who justly possessed the royalties of heaven suffered the ignominies of earth. He who had borne and will yet bear the crown of universal dominion was diademed with a ring of thorns. He who is and ever will be the fountain of bliss died in the anguish of thirst. Truly such condescension enables us to sing with Stephen the Sabite—

> Is there diadem, as Monarch,
> That His brow adorns?
> Yea, a crown in very surety,
> But of thorns!

His Exaltation

Christ's crown of mockery, however, has added greater glory to His eternal crown of honor.

The head that once was crowned with thorns
Is crowned with glory now.

It is not the weight of gold composing a crown, or the costly jewels bedecking it, that determines its value and worth, but the character of the one whose brow it adorns. Judged thus, what dignity is associated with the crown of thorns worn by the purest of the pure! Had these coarse soldiers only known it—every thorn was but a jewel in wrought with that of Christ's divine majesty. The cruel scorn of man He has transformed into the emblem of divine, regal power. Humbled, He has been highly exalted. Treated as a felon, He yet died a King, withal in disguise. The crown He presently wears is more beautiful because of the chaplet of thorns.

An instructive writer has made the following list of honors the blinded people of Israel awarded their long-expected King:

They gave Him a procession of honor Roman Legionnaires, Jewish priests and Himself bearing the cross. This was the only cortege they could award Him who came to overthrow man's dark foe. Cruel taunts were His paean of praise.

They presented Him with wine of honor—instead of the golden cup of generous wine He was offered the stupefying death-drug dealt out to criminals. But He refused it that He might taste the reality of death. Vinegar mixed with gall was all that they thrust into his parched lips. O, what wretched and detestable inhospitality for the King's Son!

They provided Him with a guard of honor—coarse, brutal soldiers who showed their esteem by gambling for His clothes which had been seized as booty. A quaternion of heartless gamblers—what a bodyguard for Him who had been adored of heaven!

They raised Him to a throne of honor—the bloody tree. Truly, the cross is the full expression of the world's feeling toward Christ. Calvary shows us God's best and man's worst.

They bestowed upon Him a title of honor—the King of the Jews. By preferring Barabbas, they virtually called Him the King of thieves. Placing Him between two robbers, they gave Him the position of highest shame, thereby turning His glory to shame.

True honor, however, is His today; and universal sovereignty will yet be His in virtue of His thorns. May we give Him a true coronation and honor Him aright! Let us highly exalt Him in every part of our life! For His wounds, let us give Him worship; for His anguish, adoration; for His sobs, songs of praise.

His Redemption

Several crowns are ours if we care to win them, and not one of them has a thorn entwined therein. Crowns without thorns can adorn our brows, seeing that He was willing to wear a crown with thorns.

Salvation is ours because of the price the Master paid. His sacrifice is the only remedy for our sins, the inspiration of our present life, and the foundation of our future bliss. He was crowned with mockery in death that we might be crowned with life everlasting.

Thorns and briars are the first product of the fall, and by wearing the crown of thorns, He symbolized the bearing of the curse. Such a bloodstained diadem upon His brow indicated that the sin of the world garlanded His head and heart. He bore our sins in His own body on the tree.

His cruel thorns, His shameful cross
Procure our heavenly crowns!
Our highest gain springs from His love
Our healing from His wounds.

His Sovereignty

As the result of that thorny crown worn so silently and bravely, Christ has gained eternal power over souls. His cross has become His throne. He sways our lives by His scars.

Those murderers thought that they ended His claim as King, but they only added to His right to reign as the King of Kings. They had an idea that by placing a reed in His hands and then nailing them to a cross that power had been taken from His palms. In effect, however, they relegated greater authority to His pierced hands.

They thought that by puncturing His holy heart with a spear-thrust that the flow of love would be stayed, but such only added to the richness of the stream.

They believed that His greatness could be ended by placing Him within the tomb, but this last act only gave Him the opportunity of displaying His deathless power.

Christ now reigns from the tree. Those thorns capture our hearts. With sincerity we cry, "O Nazarene, Thou hast conquered our lives by Thine anguish!" His agonies, sufferings, and bloody sweat cause Him to take deep root in our affections. Enduring the cross, and despising the shame of it, He now rejoices as He witnesses in your salvation and mine the travail of His soul.

The earthly life, gracious miracles, and winning words of the Master will ever carry a charm, but He conquers us entirely by His dying love and out poured blood upon the shameful cross! And love so amazing, so divine, demands and must have our soul, our life, our all.[1]

Alas! Men still give Him thorns. He can be crucified afresh.

> With thorns His temple gor'd and gash'd
> Send streams of blood from every part;
> His back's with knotted scourges lash'd
> But sharper scourges tear His heart.

What are some of those sharp scourges tearing His loving heart in this far-off day? How can we grieve His tender Spirit? What thorns can we plait into a crown for His brow? How can we distinguish them?

There is indifference to His sufferings. O may we never lose the wonder and mystery of Calvary!

There is unbelief in His efficacious death. And this is the piercing sin of multitudes around. His anguish is nothing to them as they pass by.

There is the unreality of professed belief. May we be delivered from calling Him Lord and yet fail to do the things He commands!

There is inconsistency of life. What a thorn! And how it hurts the Master. Nothing is more painful for Him to bear.

There is the greed of worldly gain. How carnality grieves Him! Why, He died naked and was buried in a borrowed grave! He had nothing to leave but His clothes.

There is the neglect of others for whom He died. He feels it when we fail to reflect His passion. He stayed upon the cross that He might save others. Is His compassion ours?

Enough thorns were His on that dark day when they furrowed His brow—why give Him more? May our daily prayer be, "O Lord I would not willingly add to Thy sorrows. Help me to give Thee roses instead of thorns!"

Joseph Plunkett, Irish Republican, who died in 1916, wrote these beautiful lines—

---

1. Isaac Watts, "When I Survey the Wondrous Cross," 1707.

I see His blood upon the rose
And in the stars the glory of His eyes.
His body gleams amid eternal snows
His tears fall from the skies.
I see His face in every flower,
The thunder and the singing of the birds
Are but His voice—and carven by His power
Rocks are His written words.
All pathways by His feet are worn;
His strong heart stirs the everlasting sea;
His crown of thorns is twined with every thorn,
His cross is every tree.

⌒

Sunday Evening

Theme: Joy Bells of the Resurrection
Text: 1 Corinthians 15:17

Sermon

A never-ending stream of joy flows from Christ's empty tomb. Gladness quickly followed gloom on the resurrection morn. It is true, as Professor Salmond reminds us, that "All the apostles were at one in making the death and resurrection of Christ the foundation of their own faith and the principle of their doctrine. To all, the death of Christ was the basis of their proclamation of forgiveness and reconciliation, and the life of Christ was the final argument for their immortality. All found in the power of Christ within them here, the assurance of their life with Christ hereafter."

Yet it must be borne in mind that the disciples did not believe that Christ would rise again from the dead. "*They knew not the scripture, that he must rise again from the dead*" (John 20:9). When they went away to their own homes, the disciples were a crestfallen company. (See Luke 24:11.) When the risen Lord met two of them on the Emmaus road, He found them most dejected. (See Luke 24:17.) But once they were gripped by the fact that the Christ they saw crucified and buried was alive again, what a change! Their joy knew no bounds. (See Luke 24:32, 53.) Delight chased all despair out of their hearts. How glad they were when they saw the Lord! (See John 20:20.) The fact of the resurrection soon became a factor in their life and labors, giving a lilt, a gladness, and spiritual hilarity to their witness which was hitherto unknown. This is why the book of Acts, in spite of extreme suffering for Christ's sake, finds joy persisting throughout its dramatic pages.

How could the disciples be sad when—in and with them—was the risen Lord Himself, causing them to experience the power of His resurrection? Pentecost found Peter and the rest who, although they had not believed that Christ had the power to take up His life again, witnessing as God-intoxicated men. The new wine of the resurrection took visible effect. Theirs was a joyous confidence, banishing all cowardice, and girding them with holy audacity for the Gospel's sake. He who had burst the bars of death was at their side, nerving them to hazard their lives for His name. The resurrection, the keystone of the arch of Christianity, provided its heralds with a message of hope and certainty. Easter joy filled their hearts and made them more than conquerors.

With the clearer light of the Spirit, the disciples came to see that the grave of their Master was the highway to triumph.

> Hell and the grave combined their force,
> To hold our Lord in vain;
> Sudden the Conqueror arose,
> And burst their feeble chain.

Several years ago, Dr. James Little of Ireland wrote:

Easter is the day when everything shines in the light of the immortal hope. It comes like a beacon light shining brightly on the hilltop, illuminating all the dark world around. In the present life, the soul is more or less dominated by the body, with the result that hopes are disappointed, plans frustrated, opportunities missed, and ideals unrealized; but in the future life the soul will be supreme; then hope will attain full fruition, spiritual development be continuous, and every aspiration of the spiritual nature reach fulfillment. Amid the dull routine of the world with all its sadness and tragedy, Easter Day dawns for us with a brighter hope of the Eternal Day when the cry of the soul shall be heard above that of the body, and be fully satisfied because we know that when we awake we shall be satisfied with His likeness. (See Psalm 17:15.)

It is not difficult to trace how Easter sets the joy bells ringing in heaven and on earth.

Easter Brought Joy to the Father

As His beloved Son emerged from the tomb, the Father knew that the resurrection was the receipt for Calvary. The debt had been paid, divine justice had been satisfied, and redemption had been secured for a sinning race.

Easter Brought Joy to the Son

The risen One Himself could not be held captive to death, and such a victory testified to the fact that He had kept the Father's will which brought Him joy. Having endured the cross, joy was now set before Him.

Easter Brought Joy to the Holy Spirit

It was through the eternal Spirit that Jesus could offer Himself up without spot unto God. (See Hebrews 9:14.) The same Spirit helped to raise Christ from the dead. (See Romans 8:11.) Now He could rejoice over the empty tomb because He knew that He now had an instrument whereby He could deliver the sin-bound and defeat the powers of hell.

Easter Brought Joy to Heaven

The angelic announcement that He had risen was the signal for anthems of praise to break forth around the throne. When Jesus left heaven, His absence created a vast emptiness above, but the empty grave meant His return to the Father's right hand. And the joybells never cease ringing in heaven. *"There is joy in the presence of the angels of God over one sinner that repenteth"* (Luke 15:10).

Easter Brought Joy to the Disciples

To the first generation of saints, the resurrection meant reunion with the blessed Lord, and empowerment for His service. (See Acts 1:8.) His death and resurrection were to become both a doctrine and a dynamic in their witness. The resurrection became to them the synonym for joy and the source of spiritual blessing. The bitter end became a blessed beginning. On the third day, the Crucified One rises again and faith is reborn.

This story transcends the political feuds of today as supremely as it shone beyond the petty and self-interested rivalries in which it was clothed.

Each Easter the hope is there, if we grasp it: the evidence is there, if we believe. For as they took Him to the hill outside the city and put Him to death, they were forgiven. He came as a man to save man from sin; He came as God to lift man up to Himself.

The agony of Good Friday and the triumph of Easter Day are offered to us again.

Here is the truth, in its cruel and glorious simplicity: the truth of Jesus of Nazareth, master carpenter, who at the last through wood and nails purchased man's whole salvation.

As we read the Acts, the apostles placed this great truth in the forefront of their teaching and preaching, which yielded remarkable results. Belief in such a fact changed the entire face of the world. Within a few decades, it carried to the utmost bounds of the Roman Empire, which was turned upside down by the potent message of Christ as the Conqueror of death.

Easter Brings Joy to All Who Believe

When Socrates was dying, his pathetic cry testified to the lack of the light of resurrection. "I have faith in the future, and I think I see the golden islands, but oh, that we had a stouter vessel or a stronger word." Praise God, Easter provides us with a "stouter vessel" and "a stronger word." *"Because I live, ye shall live also"* (John 14:19).

Are we not privileged to live on the Easter side of Calvary, and to have the bells of joy, hope, assurance, and triumph ringing in our hearts? What multitudinous blessings are ours, all because of Him who died and rose again on our behalf!

We Have the Joy of Reconciliation (See Romans 5:11)

All enmity vanishes through the empty cross and the empty tomb. This is where friendship and trust take their place. This new bond of sonship is ours.

We Have the Joy of Eternal Salvation (See Romans 10:9–10; 1 Corinthians 15:17)

If Christ did not rise again, we are still in (and will ever be in) our sin. If there is no resurrection, there can be no regeneration.

We Have the Joy of Sanctification (See Romans 6:1–6)

Holiness is the fruit of our union with Christ as the risen, glorified Lord. He relives His life in and through our lives. Is ours the joy of living a more abundant life?

We Have the Joy of Immortality (See Job 14:14)

The future to those of us who are Christ's is no unexplored territory full of frightening shadows. Because He passed through the tomb in resurrection triumph, He illumined the valley for us.

We Have the Joy of Reunion (See 1 Thessalonians 4:14)

The empty grave tells us that all the graves of our dead in Christ will likewise be emptied and that our loved ones will be given back to us. (See 1 Thessalonians 4:16–17.) The joy bells ringing in the garden where the sepulcher was will peal out louder and clearer when Jesus comes to gather us home.

We Are to Have the Joy of Seeing Jesus Crowned (See Hebrews 2:9)

The slain Lamb will be in the midst of the throne. Ours is the prospect of seeing Jesus *"crowned with glory and honor"* (Hebrews 2:7). The scepter of universal dominion is to rest in the pierced hand of Him who opened the sealed tomb and came forth robed with life forevermore.

As the joy bells of Easter peal forth their melody again, may God grant that our own hearts will respond with that consecrated living and surrendered service, pleasing to Him who gave us Easter!

> Cling then, brothers, to a lofty promise
> Of a life superior to decay;
> Uttered by the earth in spring's awakening,
> Voiced by the glad rites of Easter Day.

GOOD FRIDAY: ONE-HOUR SERVICE

At an hour convenient to church and community, the preacher could conduct an impressive one hour service along the lines suggested, with the hour being broken up into ten sections of six minutes each. No preaching is necessary. The prayers, passion narratives and passion poems would be sufficient to make the hour a solemn and memorable occasion. For the preacher's guidance, we have adapted an arrangement by Dr. W. J. L. Sheppard, prepared for the "Passion Pamphlets" by the S.P.C.K., London.

First Period

Hymn: "There Is a Green Hill Far Away"

Prayer:

Almighty and everlasting God, who, of Thy tender love toward mankind, sent Thy Son, our Savior Jesus Christ, who took upon Himself our flesh to suffer death upon the cross that sinners might be saved, mercifully grant that as we tarry together throughout this hour, meditating upon the bitter sorrow of Jesus, that loving, tender, and repentant hearts may be ours. May our meditation of Him be sanctifying as well as sweet. In His Name. Amen.

Scripture: Luke 23:26–31.

Poems: Here recite the *Story of the Cross* in poetic form.

The Question

In His own raiment clad—
With His Blood dyed
Women walking sorrowing
By His side.

Heavy that Cross to Him—
Weary the weight—
One who will help Him waits
At this gate.

See! they are travelling
On the same road—
Simon is sharing with
Him the load.

Oh, whither wandering,
Bear they that Tree?
He who first carries it—
Who is He?

The Answer

Follow to Calvary
Tread where He trod
He who forever was
SON OF GOD.

You who would love Him, stand,
Gaze at His face;
Tarry awhile on your
Earthly race.

As swift the moments fly
Through the Blest Week,
Hear the great Story the
Cross will speak.

Is there no beauty to
"You who pass by,"
In that lone Figure which
Marks the Sky?

(Call for silent prayer, asking all present to concentrate upon Christ's shame and humiliation.)

Second Period

Let us continue to follow His blood-red way as we read:
Scripture: Mark 15:22–23
Poem: Recite further poems on the tragic story of the cross.

How He died—

On the Cross lifted up
Thy Face we scan—
Bearing that Cross for us,
Son of Man.

Thorns form Thy Diadem
Rough wood Thy Throne—
For as Thy Blood is shed—
Us alone.

No pillow under Thee
To rest Thy Head—
Only the splintered Cross
Is Thy bed.

Nails pierce Thy Hands and Feet,
Thy side the spear;

No voice is nigh to say
Help is near.

Shadows of midnight fall
Though it is day—
Thy friends and kinsfolk stand
Far away.

Why He Died

Loud is Thy bitter cry,
Sunk on Thy breast
Hangeth Thy Bleeding Head.
Without rest.

Loud scoffs the dying thief
Who mocks at Thee
Can it, my Savior be
All for me?

Gazing afar from Thee,
Silent and alone,
Stand those few weepers
Thou call'st Thine own.

I see Thy title, Lord
Inscribed above—
"Jesus of Nazareth,"
King of Love!

What, O my Savior!
Here didst Thou see,
Which made Thee suffer and
Die for me.

(Call the worshipers to another moment of silent prayer, bidding them dwell upon the loneliness and isolation of Him who died as the lonely Lamb of God bearing the sins of the world.)

Let us continue in prayer:

O Blessed and only Savior, who for our sakes didst offer Thyself as a sacrifice for sin, most precious and well-pleasing in Thy sight O God, give us grace that at the foot of Thy cross we may truly watch with Thee. In these quiet moments be Thou our stay, that we may enter both into a fuller realization of what sin is, and also into a deeper knowledge of Thy love and pardoning mercy. Give us the pure purpose of entire surrender to the service of God and of conformity to His will, that we may be enabled to offer and present unto Him ourselves, both souls and bodies, to be a reasonable, holy, and lively sacrifice, acceptable and well-pleasing in Thee. Grant this, O Lord, for Thy tender mercy's sake. Amen.

Third Period

Scripture: Luke 23:32–38
Poem: continuing the story of the cross,

> Jesu, in Thy dying woes,
> Even while Thy life-blood flows,
> Craving pardon for Thy foes:
> Hear us, Holy Jesu.
>
> Savior for our pardon sue,
> When our sins Thy pangs renew,
> For we know not what we do:
> Hear us, Holy Jesu.
>
> Oh, may we, who mercy need,
> Be like Thee in word and deed,
> When with wrong our spirits bleed:
> Hear us, Holy Jesu.

(Call for another moment of silent prayer urging all present to dwell upon the mediatorial aspect of the cross He died for me.)

Let us continue in prayer:

O loving Savior, who didst plead for Thy murderers their ignorance of their terrible sin, have mercy upon us, we beseech Thee, for all our sins which we have committed in ignorance, unknown to us but all known to Thee. May Thy precious blood there shed for us cleanse us this day from all sin. Give us also that mind which was in Thee, that we too, after Thy great example, may love our enemies and pray for them that despitefully use us and persecute us, that our Heavenly

Father may forgive us our trespasses as we forgive them that trespass against us. Grant this, O Lord, for Thy holy name's sake. Amen.

Fourth Period

Scripture: Luke 23:39–43
Poem:

> Jesu, pitying the sighs
> Of the thief, who near Thee dies
> Promising him "Paradise"
> Hear us, Holy Jesu.
>
> May we, in our guilt and shame,
> Still Thy love and mercy claim,
> Calling humbly on Thy name:
> Hear us, Holy Jesu.
>
> Oh, remember us who pine,
> Looking from our cross to Thine;
> Cheer our souls with life divine:
> Hear us, Holy Jesu.

(Exhort the people to silently pray that grace will be granted to exhibit the spirit of Calvary's forgiveness.)

Let us continue in prayer:

O Blessed Lord, who didst come into this world to save sinners, who didst never break the bruised reed nor quench the smoking flax, and who in Thine own most bitter agony didst speak the promise of pardon and peace to the soul of the dying thief, look in mercy, we beseech Thee, upon us who for our evil deeds do worthily deserve to be punished; look upon us both now and in our dying hour; and remember us, our Lord and our God, for good, that, when we shall depart this life, we too may rest in paradise with Thee: for Thy name and mercy's sake. Amen.

Fifth Period

Scripture: Luke 2:25–35; John 19:15–27
Poem:

> Jesu! loving to the end
> He whose heart Thy sorrows rend

And Thy dear human friend:
Hear us, Holy Jesu.

May we in Thy sorrows share,
And for Thee all peril dare,
And enjoy Thy tender care:
Hear us, Holy Jesu.

May we all Thy loved ones be,
All in one holy family,
Loving for the love of Thee,
Hear us, Holy Jesu.

(Ask for a further brief moment of silent prayer when each worshiper prays for grace to exhibit the same kind, thoughtful considerate attitude of the Master in His loving provision of His widowed mother.)

Let us continue in prayer:

O Lord Jesus Christ, not only Son of God, but also most truly Son of Man, who didst from the cross look down in love upon Thy mother, and care for her in Thy dying pain: make us, we pray Thee, living and gentle, tender and true, to those to whom Thou hast united us in ties of earthly relationship; and grant that all whom we love may be true members of the family of our Father in heaven, that at last we may be united for ever in that blessed home which Thou art preparing for those who love Thee. Hear us, we beseech Thee, for Thy dear Name's sake. Amen.

Sixth Period

Scripture: Psalm 22:1–8; Matthew 27:45–46
Poem:

Jesu, whelmed in fears unknown,
With our evil left alone,
While no light from heaven is shown:
Hear us, Holy Jesu.

When we vainly seem to pray
And our hope seems far away,
In the darkness be our stay,
Hear us, Holy Jesu.

Though no Father seems to hear,
Though no light our spirits cheer,
Tell our faith that God is near:
Hear us, Holy Jesu.

(Call for silent prayer that grace may be given to discover God in the darkness: that although it does seem as if He has no regard to our tears and trials, nevertheless, He knows all about our sorrows and is at hand to succor and relieve.)

Let us continue in prayer:

O Blessed Savior, who didst endure the three hours' darkness on the cross for our sakes, when our sins were laid on Thee, and Thy Father's face was hidden from Thy sight, suffering thus for us that we may never know nor understand, help us to hate the sins which thus came between Thee and Thy God; and in all hours of darkness and desertion, of loneliness of grief, help us the more to cling to Thee.

Teach us, by that bitter cry
In gloom to know Thee night,
For Thy mercy's sake we pray. Amen.

Seventh Period

Scripture: Isaiah 53:1–3; John 19:28–29
Poem:

Jesu, in Thy thirst and pain,
While Thy wounds Thy life-blood drain,
Thirsting more love to gain
Hear us, Holy Jesu.

Thirst for us in mercy still;
All Thy holy work fulfill—
Satisfy Thy loving will:
Hear us, Holy Jesu.

May we thirst Thy love to know;
Lead us in our sin and woe
Where the healing waters flow:
Hear us, Holy Jesu.

(Silent prayer, interceding that ours may be the ever-increasing thirst for righteousness, holiness of life, and likeness to the Master.)

Let us continue in prayer:

O loving Lord, who didst endure for us the agony of thirst, teach us in all time of bodily pain and suffering to follow the example of Thy divine patience. Grant to us evermore that water of life which flows alone from Thee, of which whoso drinketh shall never thirst, even that Holy Spirit whom Thou dolt give to be within us a well of water springing up into everlasting life. Grant us for Thy holy name's sake. Amen.

Eighth Period

Scripture: Psalm 40:4–8; John 19:29–30
Poem:

> Jesu—all our ransom paid
> All Thy Father's will obeyed
> By Thy sufferings perfect made:
> Hear us, Holy Jesu.
>
> Save us in our soul's distress,
> Be our help to cheer and bless,
> While we grow in holiness:
> Hear us, Holy Jesu.

(In silent prayer counsel, the congregation prays that divine strength will be granted to run the race well, and finish life's course with joy and satisfaction.)

Let us continue in prayer:

O Lord Jesus Christ, whose joy and glory it was to do Thy Father's will, and to finish the work He had given Thee to do, who didst on the cross make a full, perfect and sufficient sacrifice, oblation, and satisfaction for our sins, and for those of the whole world: Grant us ever to rest on Thy finished work, Thy perfect atonement, for our peace with God. Help us also, like Thee, to work the works of Him that sent Thee, while it is day, nor to grow weary in well-doing, that at evening time it may be light. Grant this, O Lord, for Thy mercy's sake. Amen.

Ninth Period

Scripture: Isaiah 53:7–12; Luke 23:46–49
Poem:

> Jesu—all Thy labour vast,
> All Thy woe and conflict past
> Yielding up Thy soul at last:
> Hear us, Holy Jesu.

> When the death-shades round us lower,
> Guard us from the tempter's power,
> Keep us in that trial hour:
> Hear us, Holy Jesu.

> May Thy life and death supply
> Grace to live and grace to die,
> Grace to reach the home on high,
> Hear us, Holy Jesu.

(Silent prayer, in which grace is sought to live in the orbit of God's will, and then to be confident of dying grace when the valley of the shadow of death is reached.)

Let us continue in prayer:

Blessed Savior, who didst lay down Thy life for us, and Thyself didst pass through the dark valley of death, that we might fear no evil nor be afraid to die: grant us, by the constraining power of Thy great love, to devote our lives to Thee, who didst so willingly lay down Thy life for us. Grant us no longer to live unto ourselves but unto Thee, so that, when our departure is at hand, we may peacefully and trustfully commit our souls to Thy gracious keeping, and, resting in the gladness of Thy blessed presence, may await our glorious resurrection. Grant this, O merciful Lord, for Thy great name's sake. Amen.

Tenth Period

Scripture: 2 Corinthians 5:14–21
Poem:

An Appeal from the Cross

> Child of My grief and pain—
> Watched by My love

I came to call thee to
Realms above.

I saw thee wandering
Far off from Me:
In love I seek for thee—
Do not flee.

For thee My blood I shed—
For thee alone:
I came to purchase thee
For Mine own.

Weep not for My grief,
Child of My love—
Strive to be with Me in
Heaven above.

Our Response to Christ

Oh, I will follow Thee,
Star of my soul,
Thro' the deep shades of life
To the goal.

Yes, let Thy cross be borne
Each day by me—
Mind not how heavy, if
But with Thee.

Lord, if Thou only wilt
Make me Thine own,
Give no companion, save
Thee alone.

Grant thro' each day of life
To stand by Thee;
With Thee, when morning breaks
Ever to be.

Closing Hymn: "Beneath the Cross of Jesus."
Prayer and Benediction:

Gracious Lord, we praise Thee for this blessed hour we have
spent with Thee at Calvary. We hear Thee saying to our hearts, "I

am he that liveth, and was dead—I am alive forevermore." Enable us to be more fully identified with Thee in Thy death and resurrection, and be found walking in the newness of life. For all Thou hast made us the recipients of, through Thy shame and sacrifice, we give Thee thanks. Because Thou didst die for us, help us by this Spirit to live for Thee.

Now the God of peace, that brought again from the dead our Lord Jesus, that great Shepherd of the sheep, through the blood of the everlasting covenant, make you perfect in every good work to do His will, working in you that which is well-pleasing in His sight, through Jesus Christ: to whom be glory forever and ever. Amen.

GOOD FRIDAY: THREE-HOUR SERVICE

In many communities, the custom has grown for Protestant and evangelical churches to unite for a three-hour service on Good Friday, with the combined religious bodies meeting in the largest and most central part of the city. Broken up into nine periods of twenty minutes, these services can be most impressive. A printed bulletin of the various periods and times could be circulated beforehand among the churches participating in the service so that those who cannot remain for the whole service can come and leave when they desire. Covering the hours from 12:00 to 3:00, the following nine divisions should be closely adhered to—

Noon–12:20:	Preparation
12:20–12:40:	First Word of the Cross
12:40–1:00:	Second Word of the Cross
1:00–1:20:	Third Word of the Cross
1:20–1:40:	Fourth Word of the Cross
1:40–2:00:	Fifth Word of the Cross
2:00–2:20:	Sixth Word of the Cross
2:20–2:40:	Seventh Word of the Cross
2:40–3:00:	Dedication

The nine pastors chosen by the local ministerial association to conduct these respective periods should have their material well-prepared and time themselves before the service, so as not to exceed their prescribed twenty minutes. If any of the participants exceeds his time, the recognized three-hour service will be thrown off schedule. There should be no chairman for the public gathering. Each pastor would come forward, unannounced, to conduct his own period. If an Order of Service is printed, the name of each pastor could be given at each distinct period. We herewith offer suggestions for the nine periods.

First Period: Noon–12:20 p.m.

Preparation

(Name of pastor leading)
Read: Lamentations 1:12
Hymn: "Sweet the Moments Rich in Blessing"
Prayer:

Almighty and everlasting God, who, because of Thy eternal love didst send Thy Son, our Savior Jesus Christ to take upon Himself the likeness of our flesh, and to bear our sins in His own body on the tree, prepare our hearts and minds for these solemn hours of remembrance. May ours be the consciousness of the risen Lord Himself in our midst! For His sake. Amen.

Read: Isaiah 53
Hymn: "O Come and Mourn with Me Awhile"
Brief Meditation: "What Mean You by This Service?"

The purpose of these hours we are to spend together is to enter, as far as we are able, into the fellowship of the sufferings of Jesus during those three dreadful hours He endured on the cross. For those who witnessed the Savior's death, the crucifixion was a sorrowful scene, but we live on this side of the cross, knowing that the crucified One Himself is alive forever. Yet we hear Him saying unto us, "*Weep not for me, but weep for yourselves, and for your children*" (Luke 23:28). Yet drops of grief can never repay the debt of love we owe.

Thus, we approach Calvary—
1. To learn from Him for what we ought to weep.
2. To meditate upon the terrible judgment upon sin Jesus bore, and to be moved by His dying love to repentance.
3. To learn from Him who died, and is now alive forevermore how to live and how to die.
4. To seek grace to live like Him—to be crucified with Him.
5. To know what it means to be resigned to the Father's will even though that will means suffering.

(The pastor will expand these points to fit in with his time limit.)

Closing Prayer: (Call for a moment of silent prayer, then repeat the Lord's Prayer. The pastor will return to his seat, and the next one will come forward without any introduction and so on through all the periods.)

Second Period: 12:20 p.m.–12:40 p.m.

First Word from the Cross: Forgiveness

(Name of pastor leading)
Read: Luke 23:33–34
Hymn: "Rock of Ages, Cleft for Me"
Prayer:

Most gracious Lord, as we continue in Thy presence, watching Thee as Thou didst die upon the cross, cause us by Thy Spirit, who witnessed Thy sufferings, to fully appreciate Thy forgiving love and grace. Remove our ignorance, we beseech Thee, and inspire us to worship and adore Thee for Thy passion. For Thy mercy's sake, amen.

Read: Isaiah 50:5–11
Hymn: "Go to Dark Gethsemane"
Meditation: (We would urge pastors to dwell deep in C. H. Spurgeon's heart-moving volume *Christ's Words from the Cross.*)

As Jesus uttered His first cry, He was entering the pains and anguish of the cross. Although He was silent in the hours preceding it, allowing cruel men to lead Him as a Lamb silent before the shearers, He now speaks, and His word was Father—a usual expression revealing affection for His Father and unquestioning obedience to His will. Excessive suffering did not drive the Savior from His Father's heart.

(Expand these thoughts as time permits.)

1. Man was at enmity with God—in need of His deliverance, remission, and forgiveness.
2. Man, conscious of his sin, must confess his need and trust God for forgiveness—freely given on the merits of Christ's death.
3. Man cannot plead ignorance in a land of Christian light and liberty, yet the sins of ignorance are manifest and salvation can be ours from sins of omission and commission.

Closing Prayer:

Because there is forgiveness with Thee, O Lord, that Thou mayest be feared, we pray Thee, Thou who art faithful and just to forgive us our sin, purge our waiting hearts anew and enable us to forgive others, as Thou dost forgive us, amen.

Third Period: 12:40 p.m. – 1:00 p.m.

Second Word from the Cross: Salvation

(Name of pastor leading)
Read: Luke 23:43
Hymn: "When Wounded Sore the Stricken Heart"
Prayer:

Blessed Lord, Thou who came from heaven, and wrapped around Thy self the garment of our humanity and who lives among men, we praise Thee for the spiritual wealth we have as the result of Thy poverty and pangs. Because Thou hast made us Thine and we are now the heirs of heaven, continue to overshadow us in these remembrance hours. To the praise of Thy holy name, amen!

Read: Luke 23:39–43
Hymn: "Lord, When Thy Kingdom Comes"
Meditation:

The wonder of Calvary is the revelation of the fact that Jesus as the Son of God came from heaven to earth and became the Son of Man that men might go from earth to heaven. Crucified between thieves and numbered with them as a transgressor, Christ was not overwhelmed with His agony as to be unconscious of the spiritual needs of others.

(Expand these features to fit in with allotted time.)

1. How ready Christ is to respond to a sinner's cry.
2. How forgiveness of sin assures the forgiven one of heaven.
3. How today is the day of salvation and Christ seeks to grant to repentant sinners the merits of His all-sufficient grace.

Closing Prayer:

How we praise Thee, O Savior, for bringing immortality to light through Thy redeeming gospel! Grant that each of us bowed in Thy presence may have the assurance of life everlasting with Thee above, through Jesus Christ our Lord. Amen.

Fourth Period: 1:00 p.m. – 1:20 p.m.

Third Word from the Cross: Affection

(Name of pastor leading)
Read: John 19:26–27
Hymn: "At the Cross Her Station Keeping"
Prayer:

Incarnate Lord, born of a woman, and who in the substance of our flesh was nailed to the cross. We bless Thee for the manifestation of Thy tenderness in those grim hours of thirst and pain. In the midst of Thy sufferings Thou didst bear her tenderly in mind, who gave Thee birth, and didst make provision for her future in Thy committal of her to Thy beloved disciple. Because of the sword piercing Thy mother's heart, as well as Thine own heart, we are here before Thee as redeemed sinners in the spirit of worship. May ours be the further unfolding of Thy love! In Jesus' name, amen.

Read: Luke 2:46–55
Hymn: "Beneath the Cross of Jesus, I Fain Would Take My Stand"
Meditation:

After promising the penitent thief the joy of paradise, Jesus speaks to His mother and John, the disciple whom He loved. How moving are the words of Jesus in this act of the drama of Calvary! *"Woman, behold thy son"* (John 19:26).

What a gory sight He was to gaze upon with His visage marred more than any man, and His form more than the sons of men! In effect, the dying Savior was saying, "Woman, thou art losing one Son; but yonder stands another, who will be a son to thee in My absence. Behold thy son!" To John, Christ's word meant, "Take My mother and care for her in My place as if she were your own mother."

(Develop these added thoughts according to time left.)

1. Christ trusts us to care, not only for those of our own flesh and blood, but also for others.
2. Christ said that those who obey God become His brother, sister, and mother, implying a holy family, a communion of saints.

Closing Prayer:

O Savior of mankind, after Thy example we would pray for all who are near and dear to us, that they be found in a state of grace. Grant unto us the Christ-like capacity to fulfill all filial obligations. May we be moved by that compassionate heart of Thine to care for those in need of home and the necessities of life. For Thy name's sake! Amen.

Fifth Period: 1:20 p.m. – 1:40 p.m.

Fourth Word from the Cross: Anguish

(Name of pastor leading)
Read: Matthew 27:46
Hymn: "Thron'd Upon the Awful Tree"
Prayer:

Our merciful God, who coverest the heavens with clouds, and makest Thy sun to shine upon the just and also the unjust, lift upon us, as we tarry before Thee, the light of Thy countenance. Help us to understand what it meant for Thee to surrender Thy Son to the scourges of evil men, and His heart-anguish as He felt Himself forsaken of Thee when He bore the load of human sin alone. We plead anew the merits of the Savior's blood, and beseech Thee to enlighten our minds as to the solemn meaning of the hiding of Thy face from Thy Son's anguish. In His name, amen.

Read: Psalm 22:1–11, 19–22
Hymn: "Abide With Me, Fast Falls the Eventide"
Meditation:

The fourth cry came out of the darkness, the darkness covering the earth, turning day into night, and also out of our Lord's inner darkness as He felt forsaken of God. As Spurgeon expressed it, "I do not think that the records of time, or even of Eternity contain a sentence more full of anguish. Here the wormwood and the gall, and all the other bitterness are undone. Here you may look as into a vast abyss; and though you strain your eyes, and gaze till sight fails you, yet you perceive no bottom, it is measureless, unfathomable, inconceivable." Here we have God forsaken of God.

> Yea once Immanuel's orphan'd cry
> His universe hath shaken—
> It went up single, echoless,
> "My God, I am forsaken.

Truly, this was the climax of the Savior's desolation who was forsaken in that lone hour so that we might have the promise, *"I will never leave thee, nor forsake thee"* (Hebrews 13:5).

Closing Prayer:

O Lord, we pray that we may never by our sins increase the pain of Thy wounds! In our surrender to Thy claims, we would have Thee see of the travail of Thy soul and be satisfied. We commend to Thy tender grace all Thy dear children passing through the valley of the shadow of death this very hour that the smile of Thy countenance may be theirs, for the sake of Jesus Christ our Lord. Amen.

Sixth Period: 1:40 p.m. – 2:00 p.m.

Fifth Word from the Cross: Suffering

(Name of pastor leading)
Read: John 19:28
Hymn: "When I Survey the Wondrous Cross"
Prayer:

As we consider, O Lord, Thy willingness to taste the bitterness of our sins in the cup mingled with gall, and didst by the bitterness of Thy passion purify our taste which by our disobedience became depraved, we realize that death and the curse were in the cup Thou didst drain to its dregs. Create within each of us a deeper thirst for all that Thy cross provided.

Read: Psalm 69:13–21
Hymn: "O Sacred Head, Now Wounded"

Meditation:

While there are two words in our language which express this evidence of our Lord's humanity—"I thirst"—there is only one in Greek. It is a word showing how deeply He could read the meaning of the Psalms into His own life and sufferings.

(The preacher is advised to emphasize the approach C. H. Spurgeon gives on this fifth word—I thirst.)

1. It is the ensign of Christ's true humanity.
2. It is a token of His suffering substitution.
3. It is a type of man's treatment of His Lord.
4. It is a mystical expression of His heart's desire.
5. It is a pattern of our death with Him.

Closing Prayer:

Blessed Savior, who in Thy life and death was a pattern of all meekness, arm us, we pray Thee, with the same mind. Teach us how to overcome evil with good, and how to emulate Thy patience when reviled and reproached for Thy sake. Knowing that Thou dost thirst after our likeness to Thee, empower us to satisfy Thy desire toward us. Because Calvary has every claim upon all we are and have, enable us to live for Thy glory, through Jesus Christ our Lord. Amen.

Seventh Period: 2:00 p.m. – 2:20 p.m.

Sixth Word from the Cross: Victory

(Name of pastor leading)
Read: John 19:30
Hymn: "Man of Sorrows, What a Name"
Prayer:

Gracious Redeemer, we thank Thee for the finished work of the cross. Nothing was left for human ingenuity or effort, for by the thorns, nails, and spear thrust Thou didst provide a perfect salvation for a sinning grace. Naked, we look to Thee for dress. We come to Thee just as we are, without one plea, save that Thou didst shed Thy blood on our behalf. It was for our sakes, O Christ, that Thou didst become obedient unto death. Accept, we beseech Thee, the love of our hearts for all that Thou didst accomplish for a world of sinners lost and ruined by the fall. In Thy name, amen.

Read: John 17:1–10
Hymn: "Not for Our Sins Alone"
Meditation:

The three words, "It is finished," are one word in the Greek, a word speaking of a glorious consummation. The Father's face is no longer hidden, the intensity of bodily thirst is less felt, the bitterness of death is passing, and the Savior has a mind clear enough to make the tongue say aloud—"It is finished," or *tello*. Thus, He died not as a victim but a Victor. Did He not say, *"The things concerning me have an end"*? (Luke 22:37b). What was the end of His travail? Paul tells us. Christ was manifested to destroy the works of the devil. All the Old Testament types, praises, and prophecies of redemption were fully accomplished when He died in our stead. The atoning sacrifice has been offered and man's doings and deeds to gain access to God are useless. Our deadly doing must be cast at the feet of the Redeemer, and we must live beneath His sheltering, efficacious blood. May grace be ours to finish our course with the joy of fulfillment!

Closing Prayer:

Loving Savior, how helpless and hopeless we are apart from Thy grace. Knowing how utterly unable a sinner was to save himself from the tyranny of his sin, Thou wast made sin for a lost race, and as the Lamb slain from the foundation of the world, Thou didst die as our substitute. May multitudes more come to know that salvation can only be found in the water and the blood which flowed from Thy riven side. Bought at such a price, may we be found living as unto Thee, for Thy name's sake. Amen!

Eighth Period: 2:20 p.m. – 2:40 p.m.

Seventh Word from the Cross: Contentment

(Name of pastor leading)
Read: Luke 23:46
Hymn: "O for a Faith That Will Not Shrink"

Prayer:

Grant us, O Lord, the grace to treasure in our hearts those last words of Thine, and at the end of our days may we be consoled by them, and rest in Thy precious invitation to Thine own—"*Come ye blessed of my Father, inherit the kingdom prepared for you from the foundation of the world*" (Matthew 25:34). Both in life and in death may we be found commending ourselves into Thy hands. We ask, not for dying grace, but for grace to live as unto Thee, believing that if we live well, we shall die well, if it is Thy will that we should reach heaven by way of a grave. In Thy name, amen!

Read: Psalm 31:1–5, 11–17
Hymn: "Our Times Are in Thy Hand"
Meditation:

Some writers suggest that the words, "*Father, into thy hands I commend my spirit,*" should be blended with the shout of conquest, "*It is finished,*" and that after these last sentences Jesus bowed His head and gave up the ghost. The Father's business was finished, and He commits His spirit, as a sacred trust, into His Father's hands. Thus, at evening time there was light for Jesus as He knew His Father was waiting to receive His beloved Son. In Della Robbia's *Crucifixion*, the artist represented the Father's face above the cross, bending over His Son with an expression of deepest compassion.

(Points to further expound.)
1. Christ's use of Old Testament Scriptures.
2. The hands of God as mighty, comforting hands.
3. The glorious hope of immortality.

Closing Prayer:

We beseech Thee, O Lord, to grant us increasing faith in Thy fatherly care and provision. Teach us how to leave all that concerns our mortal life in those hands of Thine which are ever open to satisfy all living. May we fear the grave as little as our bed, knowing that if our life is lived in Thee, we shall die in Thee and find death to be the opening of a gate into a richer, fuller life in Thy presence above. Thou hast said, "*Precious in the sight of the* LORD *is the death of his saints*" (Psalm 116:15). Hear us, we pray Thee, through Jesus Christ, our Lord. Amen.

Ninth Period: 2:40 p.m. – 3:00 p.m.

The Word from Those around the Cross: Exaltation

(Name of pastor leading)
Read: Mark 15:39
Hymn: "There Is a Green Hill Far Away"
Prayer:

Almighty God and Heavenly Father, our hearts are filled with praise for the accomplishments of Thy beloved Son whom Thou didst send into the world to die for our redemption. In these final moments of our remembrance of His passion wilt Thou bring us to a fuller understanding of what it means to be crucified with Christ. Because Thy mercies are without number, purge our hearts, and grant us the touch of Thy Spirit as we linger in Thy presence. For the sake of Him who died and rose again, amen.

Read: Psalm 45:1–8
Hymn: "In the Cross of Christ I Glory"
Meditation:

Among the expressive and impressive testimonies to Christ in His last days, none is so striking as that of the centurion whose confession became the creed of Christendom: *"Truly this was the Son of God"* (Matthew 27:54). As this Roman soldier observed the manner of our Lord's suffering and listened to the words He uttered in His agony, he knew that the Man on the middle cross was totally different from the two men who were His companions in crucifixion. Had Christ been an ordinary man, His shed blood would have had no efficacy to emancipate sin-bound humanity; but there, at Calvary, it was the mighty Maker who died for the creature's sin. He was—and is—the Son of God. Of one substance with the Father and with the Holy Spirit, the Crucified One, now at the right hand of the majesty on high, will yet be seen as King of Kings and Lord of Lords. Our present obligation is to crown Him Lord of our life; to give Him His coronation in our hearts because of all He endured on our behalf on that old, rugged cross. May the hours we have spent together beneath the cross of Jesus result in a complete surrender to the Master's claims for "Love so amazing, so divine, demands our soul, our life, our all."[2]

Closing Prayer and Benediction:

Gracious Lord, now that our season of remembrance and worship is at an end, accept our thanks for the consciousness of Thy presence in our midst. May we carry with us the fragrance of our meditations upon Thy sufferings, so that those with whom we live and labor may take knowledge of us that we have been with Thy self and have learned more of Thy redeeming grace. May something of Calvary's passion and compassion possess our hearts as we part and go out into a world that sees no beauty in Thee that Thou shouldst be admired! Grant that Thy sacrificial love may inspire us to seek the lost around us and thereby crown Thy once thorn-crowned brow with fresh honor and glory.

Now, the God of peace, that brought again from the dead our Lord Jesus, that great shepherd of the sheep, through the blood of the everlasting covenant, make you perfect in every good work to do his will, working in you that which is well pleasing in his sight, through Jesus Christ; to whom be glory forever and ever, amen.

COMMUNION SERVICE DURING HOLY WEEK

Apart from the accustomed observance of the Lord's Supper in churches of all denominations, it is most fitting to gather around His Table at some time during Holy Week and remember His death on our behalf. For the guidance and help of the preacher, we herewith include an order of service and message for such an hour of loving remembrance.

Hymn: "'Till He Come"

Prayer:

Our gracious Heavenly Father, we thank Thee for the liberty of access we have into Thy most holy presence through the merits of Thy beloved Son, our Savior.

> There was no other good enough
> To pay the price of sin;

---

2. Isaac Watts, "When I Survey the Wondrous Cross," 1707.

He only could unlock the gate
Of heaven, and let us in.[3]

As we prepare to gather around His Table reminding us, as it does, of His dying love, we pray that our hearts may be strangely warmed as we survey the wondrous cross on which the Lord of Glory died. Grant that our worship and remembrance may be glorifying to Thee. In the Redeemer's name, amen.

Read: 1 Corinthians 11:23–29
Hymn: "According to Thy Gracious Word"
Message: "Married to His Remembrance"

The story is told of a brilliant young doctor who married an equally brilliant young woman, both of whom gave themselves to the relief of the diseased. Their love-bargain was that if one died, the other should continue the sacrificial task. After a year or so, the husband died from overstrain and his grief-stricken partner bravely continued the noble service of healing.

Sympathetic friends, feeling that the loneliness of her life and labors were telling upon the devoted doctor, urged her to seek a suitable companion. Although she received many offers of marriage, she never gave her hand. To one and all she had the same answer: "I am married to his remembrance."

There are two precious thoughts latent in this sweet story which we can apply to the memorial feast Jesus instituted with the words, *"This do in remembrance of me"* (Luke 22:19). First of all, there was the sacrificial lover. The doctor gave his life for others. He died through seeking to bring alleviation to smitten ones. Did not the lover of our souls die that the sin-diseased might live? Is it not by His stripes that we can be healed? (See Isaiah 53.) In the second place, there was the devoted partner. The gifted widow remained wedded by remembrance to her dead husband. Paul speaks of us as being married to Christ. By faith we are united to Him, and before long we are to sit down at the marriage of the Lamb. Presently, He is our absent lover, but according to His command, we perpetuate His mission. Part of the love-bargain is that we preach the Gospel to every creature.

When we gather in His name around His Table we indicate thereby that we are married to His remembrance. Was not such a feast intended to keep Christ ever fresh in our forgetful memories?

---

3. Cecil F. Alexander, "There Is a Green Hill Far Away," 1847.

It Is a Feast of Remembrance

The bread and the wine constitute our "In Memoriam." Above all else it is a "sweet memorial till He come."

It Is a Feast of Faith

His Supper bids us realize that well-nigh 2,000 years ago He died for our sins—that His body was broken for us; and that by a definite act of faith on our part, He secured for us all the benefits of His cross.

It Is a Feast of Love

The Methodists recognize it as "The Love-Feast." The table is the believer's love-feast. It calls us to look up with true, grateful, loving hearts and worship our Lord, the Advocate on high.

It Is a Feast of Hope

Participation is only *"till He come."* The Lord's Table is a finger pointing back to Calvary and forward to His glorious appearing for His own, with its eternal union of the Redeemer and the redeemed. When the world seeks to court us, crave for our hand and heart, let us think of Him to whom we are betrothed and remain true to Him. He has lovingly requested us to remember Him, and complying with His dying wish, we remain married to His remembrance until we see Him face to face.

Hymn: "When I Survey the Wondrous Cross"

Service of the Table

Hymn: "Here, O My Lord, I See Thee Face to Face"
Prayer:

Accept our praise, O Lord, for the sense of Thy presence in this hour of meditation upon all that Thou didst accomplish at Calvary for our salvation. Although the sacred feast is over, may its spiritual influence abide, and by Thy grace enable us to live in eager anticipation of "the great bridal-feast of bliss and love," when we gather for the marriage supper above. The grace of our Lord Jesus Christ, the love of God our Father, and the fellowship of the Holy Spirit be the portion of all. Amen.

We include a few meditations on The Lord's Supper. Pastors might like to have these on hand for further use.

Shadow and Substance

The ancient annual Jewish feast known as *Passover* was a figure of the true, a shadow of good things to come (see Hebrews 9:9; 10:1); and the student of Scripture will find it most profitable to note comparisons and contrasts between this Old Testament celebration and the New Testament Lord's Supper.

On that memorable night of the Passover 1900 years ago, on the evening of the 14th day of the month of Nisan, Jesus was the bridge, so to speak, leading from the one Covenant to the other. On that night of the betrayal at the family feast, gathered around the Paschal Lamb, Jesus brought to an end the old order observed by the faithful, for He came as the end of the Law. Thus it was meant to be the "last" supper, for the new Supper He introduced was to remain as a memorial of a far greater emancipation. Shadow was to give way to substance.

Although the disciples may have gathered in a formal way at the customary yearly celebration in which they had participated since they were children, there was One present to keep the feast with more intense feelings. He knew that He was there to transform it into a feast of deeper significance. Thus, He said, *"With desire I have desired to eat this passover with you before I suffer"* (Luke 22:15). This is the only instance in the New Testament where the word "suffer" is used in the absolute sense; and who can fathom the depth of its meaning as it was uttered by our blessed Lord that night? He alone knew its full significance.

Furthermore, as one feast was merged into the other, there was the promise of a kingdom. *"I will not any more eat thereof, until it be fulfilled in the kingdom of God...I will not drink of the fruit of the vine, until the kingdom of God shall come"* (Luke 22:16, 18). What a glorious future was thus envisioned by the disciples as their rejected Messiah was sitting with them at the table. Surely such a promise anticipates the day of Israel's full restoration. (See Matthew 19:28.)

All the acts in connection with the Passover have a symbolic and typical significance. The sacrifice of the lamb betokened the natural guilt of the one who offered it, which needed an expiation of the shedding of blood; and the sprinkling of the blood on the doorpost was an acknowledgment that by the application of such blood, there punishment would be remitted. (See Exodus 12.)

The parallel is evident. The Paschal Lamb prefigured *"Christ our Passover* [or paschal Victim] *is sacrificed for us"* (1 Corinthians 5:7). His blood atones for sin, and our presence at His Table indicates that we have been washed, and that the punishment our sin deserved is forever banished.

The lamb had to be a male "without blemish," of the first year, and taken from the flock four days before being killed by the effusion of blood. Here our Lord's spotless purity is typified, for He came as the Lamb of perfect purity (see 1 Peter 1:19) and at Calvary poured out His soul unto death.

The lamb had to be "roasted with fire," suggesting the fires of testing the Savior experienced in Gethsemane and at Calvary. We will never know how dark the night was that the Lord passed through to find the sheep that were lost.

The lamb's bones had to be kept whole. "Neither shall ye break a bone thereof" (Exodus 12:46). It may seem to be a casual circumstance that not a bone of Christ was broken at the cross, although the bones of the two thieves crucified with Him were broken. (See John 19:32–36). But such a particular was a fulfillment of prophecy. (See Psalm 34:20.) The integrity of the victim is proved in the way it was prepared for consumption.

The lamb had to be eaten with "bitter herbs," betokening the sense of sin which truly embitters the world. This demands the bitter remedy of repentance. As we eat the bread and drink the wine, a sense of shame possesses us, for it was our sin that nailed the Lamb to the cross. The custom of dipping the bitter herbs seems to accord with Christ's words: *"He that dippeth with me in the dish"* (Matthew 26:33); *"He to whom I shall give a sop, when I have dipped it"* (John 13:26).

At the last Passover, there was strife among the disciples as to who should be accounted the greatest. Even amid the solemnities of the Last Supper, we witness the unchanged evil of man's heart. Ambition and pride appeared on the scene even as the disciples were receiving the memorials of His broken body and shed blood. Those envious disciples forgot the *"bitter herbs,"* and Christ had to lead their thoughts from self to service. Had He not come to minister and give His life as a ransom for many? And this true greatness could be found only in lowly, sacrificial service.

The lamb had to be eaten with unleavened bread. It was because of this command that the Passover was called *"the days of unleavened bread,"* because it was unlawful to eat any other bread during the seven days of the feast. (See Exodus 23:15; Mark 14:1; Acts 12:3.) This removal of leaven suggests the necessity of purity, leaven being from its putrefying nature an apt emblem of impurity. Did not Christ warn His disciples against the leaven of the Pharisees and Sadducees? (See Matthew 16:6.)

Such a necessity is no less binding on those who have participated in the benefits of Christ's sacrifice. This is why we must examine ourselves as we seek to remember His agony and shame. If anything is countenanced, prejudicial to the soul's purity, there can be no true remembrance at the Table. We must keep the Feast *"not with old leaven, neither with the leaven of malice and wickedness; but with the unleavened bread of sincerity and truth"* (1 Corinthians 5:8).

The lamb had to be eaten by all. It was a feast for *"the whole assembly of the congregation of Israel"* (Exodus 12:3–11). It was a family feast, partaken when all were together in place. One lamb had to be offered for each family, and if its members were too few to eat a whole lamb, then two families would join together. Josephus reminds us that a paschal society consisted of at least twelve persons to one lamb.

The Passover was a communion of blood, that is, of the life of the lamb, for the Israelites owed their common life to the death of the Lamb. Its blood symbolized salvation from death, and its roasted flesh eaten provided the participants with sustenance. The first group at the Table on the night of the betrayal consisted of Christ and His twelve disciples (see Matthew 26:20); and when He said, *"Take eat…take drink,"* Jesus indicated the communal aspect of the Supper. *"Drink ye all of it"* (Matthew 26:27). The perversity of the Mass is that only the priest participates. The Church of England's *Homily Concerning the Sacrament* reads, "Every one of us must be guests, not gazers, eaters and not lookers, feeding ourselves, and not hiring others to feed for us." Furthermore, mutual fellowship in the Lord's Supper is not after a spiritual manner without material elements. Christ gave us the symbols of bread and wine as tokens of participation in all that He accomplished on our behalf; and the Supper is not only for once a year at one prescribed place, as in the case of the Passover, but at any time and in any place. *"As often as ye eat."*

Cups were used at the Passover Feast. The first cup was taken by the master of the house, at the beginning of the feast, and a blessing pronounced—a blessing referring to the coming Messiah's reign. The second cup came after the bitter herbs had been eaten. Psalms 113 and 114 were then sung after this cup, which is called Elijah's cup, in the belief that Elijah will announce the Messiah's coming. The third cup, called *"the cup of blessing,"* was used after the lamb had been eaten, and was followed by the use of Psalms 115–118. The fourth cup came at the conclusion of the feast and was handed by the host to all assembled.

When our Lord instituted the sacrament of His body and blood, two of these cups were used. *"He took the cup, and gave thanks, and said, 'Take this, and divide among yourselves.'"* After the supper He said, *"This cup is the New Testament in my blood, which is shed for you"* (Luke 22:17, 20). Then, we have the concluding hymn (see Matthew 26:30) made up of Psalms 115–118. Thus in what seemed an almost casual, simple, and unpremeditated way, Christ effected a transformation—the force of which has been powerfully realized through the centuries. As He broke the bread and took the cup and ministered the elements, the Jewish Feast passed into the Christian Sacrament.

The lamb had to be eaten with *"loins girded, your shoes on your feet, and your staff in your hand; and ye shall eat it in haste"* (Exodus 12:11). These acts suggested urgency and impressed on the delivered Israelites that they had to leave their settled yet suffering life in Egypt and become pilgrims. And what a long pilgrimage was theirs before they reached Canaan! Among old and devout Jews, it is still customary for the master of the household to sit in exactly the manner prescribed in Exodus, with his loins girt, his staff in hand and shoes on his feet, just as if he had gone out of Egypt yesterday.

When we meet to remember our deliverance from Satan's dominion, it must be as those whose loins are girt about with truth, whose feet are shod with the shoes of peace, and in whose hands rests the staff of the Shepherd. (See Psalm 23:4; Isaiah 3:1; Ephesians 6:14.) Remembering that we are pilgrims and strangers in the wilderness of this world, we haste to eat and drink, knowing that our heavenly Canaan is not far away.

The Passover was established to celebrate the loving-kindness of Jehovah, and for the people to rejoice in Him as the God of their salvation. When death fell upon every Egyptian home, the destroying angel passed over every Israelite home (see Exodus 12:26–27), and the "Passover" was God's appointed ordinance at which the Jews expressed their gratitude for all the past and prophetic future. Through the three days of Egyptian darkness, God had been His people's Sun (see Exodus 10: 23), and had proved Himself to be the people's shield in the hour of Egyptian persecution. There was the wail of sorrow in every Egyptian home, but there is a melody of joy in every Jewish home every Jewish home, for they were *"blood covered"* (Exodus 12:13). In obedience to the divine command, the Jews sprinkled the door post and lintels, and by faith the Passover was kept. (See Hebrews 11:28.)

The Christian parallel is obvious. The Lord's Supper has both a backward and forward glance. When we meet to remember Him in His appointed way our minds are taken back to Calvary where the Savior tasted death for every man and made possible a perfect deliverance from sin's tyranny and bondage. As the Israelites knew that they were safe from death because of their blood-sprinkled homes, and by an act of implicit obedience in God's promise, so, as His blood-washed ones, we know that we are saved and safe. And as we remember Christ our Passover, slain for us (see 1 Corinthians 5:7) we eagerly anticipate His return to end earth's pilgrimage and to bless us with the final installment of our redemption, namely the redemption of the body. (See Romans 8:23.)

"Lamb of God! Whose Bleeding Love"[4]

Lamb of God! Whose bleeding love
We now recall to mind,
Send the answer from above,
And let us mercy find.
Think on us, who think on Thee,
Every struggling soul release;
O! remember Calvary,
And bid us go in peace.

By Thine agonizing pain,
And bloody sweat, we pray,
By Thy dying love to man,
Take all our sins away.
Burst our bonds, and set us free,
From iniquity release;
O! remember Calvary,
And bid us go in peace.

Let Thy blood, by faith applied,
The sinners' pardon seal,
Speak us freely justified,
And all our sickness heal:
By Thy passion on the tree,
Let our griefs and troubles cease;
O! remember Calvary,
And bid us go in peace

---

4. Charles Wesley, 1884.

"According to Thy Gracious Word"[5]

According to Thy gracious word,
In meek humility,
This will I do, my dying Lord,
I will remember Thee.

Thy body, broken for my sake,
My bread from heav'n shall be;
Thy cup of blessing I will take,
And thus remember Thee.

Gethsemane can I forget,
Or there Thy conflict see,
Thy agony and bloody sweat,
And not remember Thee?

When to the cross I turn mine eyes,
And rest on Calvary,
O Lamb of God, my sacrifice!
I must remember Thee;

Remember Thee, and all Thy pains,
And all Thy love to me:
Yea, while a breath, a pulse remains,
Will I remember Thee.

And when, O Lord, Thou com'st again,
And I Thy glory see,
For ever, as the Lamb once slain,
Shall I remember Thee!

The Sacramental Symbols

There is no fear of our gathering at the Lord's Table becoming mechanical or formal if we constantly keep before us the true spiritual significance of the elements we handle. It is beneficial to pause occasionally and ask our hearts the question, "What do we mean by this service?"

The acts of Jesus are as significant as His life. Thus, His handling of the bread and the cup in the upper room convey deep truths to our adoring hearts.

---

5. James Montgomery, 1825.

The Bread and His Body

That night when Jesus took the bread and blessed and broke it, He associated the bread with His body *"This is my body"* (Mark 14:22). As a symbol it was most apt, well-chosen and beautiful.

Bread is indispensable—so are the sufferings Christ endured in His body on the tree.

Bread is common—and the finished work of Christ provides us with a *"common salvation"* (Jude 3), that is, a salvation for all.

Bread is cheap—so redemption was procured for mankind without money and without price. (See Isaiah 55:1.)

Our Lord used four little phrases which are so suggestive of the nature and completion of His redemptive work.

He took it. This was a voluntary act suggesting His willingness to take upon Himself the likeness of our sinful flesh in order to save us. He took a visible body at His incarnation so that through it, He might secure life for a sinning race. That long road from His glory to the manger and then on to Calvary—He took it.

He blessed it. Christ was ever grateful. Here He gives thanks for the privilege of coming and dying for you and me. Because of the greatness of our redemption, He was the only One fit and able to accomplish, so He came. But our Lord's action also signifies the act of sanctifying a thing and making it holy. His body was *"that holy thing"* (Luke 1:35), and therefore fit for sacrifice. His body was blessed by the Spirit's indwelling, and made the medium of blessing to others. What rivers of living water flowed from His body!

He broke it. This act suggests His voluntary death. His life, although taken by wicked men, was given. Christ asserted His power to lay down His life. (See John 10:18.) Thus the broken bread reminds us that He gave Himself for our sins. The sufferings on earth, the shame of the judgment hall, the agony and darkness of Calvary were all self-imposed. Wonderful virtue springs from His sacrifice because of its voluntariness.

He gave it. By this act, Christ indicated His desire to bestow the saving virtue of His broken body on others. His own hands supplied what His sacrifice secured. Salvation is His gift: *"I lay down my life for the sheep"* (John 10:15).

Then, there are two words describing our response to what Christ offers—

We must *take.* This is appropriation. His hand offers all; our hand takes all. He gives; we take. He supplies; we appropriate by faith. "I take—He undertakes."[6]

6. Albert Simpson, "I Clasp the Hand of Love Divine."

We must *eat*. This is assimilation. *"Except ye eat the flesh of the Son of man, and drink his blood, ye have no life in you"* (John 6:53). What Christ provided becomes part and parcel of ourselves. And such assimilation results in transformation. As bread is eaten, it changes into bone, brain, and body. But as we assimilate to Christ, He does not lose His identity as bread does. We lose our identity. He changes us into His likeness. *"Not I, but Christ"* (Galatians 2:20). May we know more of this holy appropriation and assimilation resulting in likeness to Him!

The Cup and His Blood

When our Lord instituted the memorial feast, He took what was on the table at that time, namely, the common food and drink of those days. Although wine is not actually mentioned in connection with the Lord's Supper, He must have took the cup and said, *"This is my blood"* (Mark 14:24), referring to the contents of the cup.

The fruit of the vine—*"the blood of the grape"* (Deuteronomy 32:14)— being red like blood, fitly symbolizes, "His blood, so red, for us was shed." Moses reminds us that *"the life of all flesh is the blood thereof"* (Leviticus 17:14); thus, when Jesus shed His blood, He poured out His soul unto death. (See Isaiah 53:12.) The broken bread speaks of all He suffered bodily; the out poured blood indicates the surrender of the life within His body on our behalf. Here, again, are precious phrases to be distinguished.

He took it. His cup of suffering and bitter anguish were voluntarily endured. Knowing full well the contents of the cup, He drained it to its dregs. Because *"there was no other good enough to pay the price of sin,"*[7] He willingly took the cup from the Father's hand and drank its contents.

He gave thanks. We cannot possibly fathom the depths of His grace inferred by these pregnant words. He not only took the symbol of His awful death, but gave thanks for it. Christ delighted to do the will of God, even though He knew that it meant death on the cross.

Our Savior could thank the Father for the privilege of dying as our substitute. Have we reached this stage in spiritual experience? Can we give thanks for our distasteful cup? Are we not guilty of murmuring and complaining over our sorrows and trials? Do we not drink the cup grudgingly, unwillingly? Yet when grace is ours to give thanks in everything (see 1 Thessalonians 5:18), we know how to turn our Marahs into Elims.

---

7. Cecil F. Alexander, "There Is a Green Hill Far Away," 1847.

He gave it to them. Is there not a sweet thought here for our adoring hearts to feed on? There is that continuance of the Supper. *"This do ye"* (1 Corinthians 11:25)—and we take the bread and the cup in obedience to His command. As those redeemed by His blood, we lovingly obey. Then is there not a suggestion here as to partnership in His sufferings? Giving thanks for the cup, then handing it to His disciples, did He not express the desire for them to enter into fellowship with His sufferings? Had He not asked them, *"Are ye able to drink of the cup that I shall drink of"* (Matthew 20:22)? The mystic truth is that Jesus did not bear the cross alone—for we were crucified with Him. (See Galatians 2:20.)

They all drank of it. Jesus had previously said, *"Ye shall indeed drink of the cup that I drink of"* (Mark 10:39). By becoming martyrs for His sake, those first disciples drank of their Master's cup. Toil, anguish, shame, and death were in the cup of that little band. As we partake of the cup, may ours be the determination to drink of all that it symbolizes. Let there be the experience of bearing about in our body the dying of the Lord Jesus. (See Galatians 6:17.) If we are partakers of His sufferings, then we shall be partakers of His glory. (See 1 Peter 4:13.)

They all drank of it! Thus there is a part of that cup for each of us. Your phase of the cup may not be mine. Suffering for Christ may differ for you and me. But suffering for His sake is the lot of all who are His. *"Take this, and divide it among yourselves"* (Luke 22:17). Taking from His pierced hand our cup, may we trust Him for grace to drink of its bitter contents.

"Lord Jesus, In Thy Name"

Lord Jesus, in Thy name
We round Thy table now
Remember thus Thy death of shame,
Thy thorn-crowned brow.

Master! from Thy blest hand
This broken bread we take,
Responsive to Thine own command,
For Thy name's sake.

We in this wine would see
The measure of Thy love,
That love which bids us joy in Thee
Enthroned above.

Here would we rest, O Lord,
Here banish doubt and fear,
Here feast on Thee, Thou Living Word,
And know Thee near.

Keep us Thine own, we pray,
Our Savior! So may we
In thought, in word, in deed, always
Remember Thee.

"By Christ Redeemed"[8]

By Christ redeemed, in Christ restored,
We keep the memory adored,
And show the death of our dear Lord,
Until He come.

His body broken in our stead
Is seen in this memorial bread,
And thus our feeble love is fed,
Until He come.

The drops of His dread agony,
His life-blood shed for us, we see—
The wine doth tell the mystery,
Until He come.

Until the trump of God be heard,
Until the ancient graves stirred,
And with His great commanding word,
The Lord shall come.

Oh, blessed hope with this elate,
Let not our hearts be desolate,
But, strong in faith, in patience wait
Until He come.

A Blessed and Beneficial Meditation

Theologians are divided on the question of the author of Hebrews, which has been assigned to various writers. Perhaps Jerome was nearest the truth

---

8. George Rawson, 1857.

when he said of the epistle—"God alone knows who wrote it." There are strong reasons for believing that Paul wrote it seeing that the person of our Lord dominates the epistle. How the apostle loved to exalt the Lord he dearly loved!

Divine pronouns like *He*, *Him*, and *Himself* are scattered over its pages and we are exhorted to *"consider him"* (Hebrews 12:3); and to *"look unto him"* (verse 2). The teaching of the whole epistle can be expressed in the language of the chorus, "Turn your eyes upon Jesus," and no other meditation could be more pleasant and profitable as David and Paul join in affirming. *"My meditation shall be sweet unto him"* (Psalm 104:34). *"Consider him"* (Hebrews 12:3).

The Nature of Meditation

Consider

This word is an important one to note as we study this Leviticus of the New Testament. *Consider* is used in a variety of ways, owing to the flexibility of its Hebrew and Greek meanings. In Hebrews the word is employed in five different ways.

1. We are to consider Christ as "the Apostle and High Priest" (Hebrews 3:1).

Here the word "consider" means to clearly perceive or understand, to examine closely as though the observer had to bend down for the purpose. This is the significance when we *"consider the lilies"* (Luke 12:27). The writer is commanding us to bend down, even on our knees, to examine closely the two great offices of our Lord, the one past—the other present.

The Apostle

During the period of His earthly life, Christ was God's sent One, but His apostleship ended at the cross when He cried, *"It is finished."* It may be that Paul does not mention his name and office in Hebrews because he felt himself unworthy to be called an "apostle." There was only One worthy of the title— Christ Jesus, God's Apostle or "sent One."

Jesus Himself chose twelve apostles, but God needed only One. Why? There is a great difference between the Apostle and apostles. God's chosen, sent One perfectly represented Him. He was the image of His person (see Hebrews 1:3), and fully revealed the Father in every way. Christ, however, could not get one apostle to completely manifest Him, so He chose twelve men with different temperaments, outlooks, and gifts to express His image. Each apostle saw Christ in a different way, and in the sum of their united testimony they present a perfect Christ. Thus, the twelve apostles around Christ were as twelve mirrors turned in to receive and then reflect His image.

The High Priest

Furthermore, we are to reverently consider His present work, the office He assumed when He entered heaven and which He continues to exercise on behalf of those for whom He was sent and saved. *"He ever liveth to make intercession for us"* (Hebrews 7:25). And whenever we gather around His Table, our minds should be exercised with what Christ has done and is doing for us.

2.   We are to consider how great Melchisedec was. (See Hebrews 7:4.)

In this case, the word "consider" means to be a spectator of, or looking at an object with admiration and wonder—which is what we do as we think of this mystic person. He is *"King of righteousness and peace"* (Hebrews 7:2), who typifies our Lord. Are not our hearts filled with adoring wonder as we consider Melchisedec as a forerunner of Christ's coming kingdom and glory?

3.   We are to consider one another. (See Hebrews 10:24.)

The meaning here is the same as in Hebrews 3:1, but with a different and daring significance. In the context, we have life within the veil and actions outside the veil, and the one aspect influences the other. We too often criticize instead of considering one another. But the more we observe closely in order to help one another, the less criticism we will have. The more we strive to help, the less we will hinder. The more we consider Jesus at His Table, the more will we lovingly consider the welfare of those around our own table, and around us in a world of need.

4.   We are to consider Jesus lest we be weary and faint in our minds. (See Hebrews 12:3.)

This is the only time the particular word for "consider" is used in Hebrews. Here it means to count up or weigh in the balances. The direct application of the word is that we are to count up our sufferings and see how they tally with the Lord's. We are to put our trials and adversities on the one side and His sorrows on the other to see how the scales turn.

5.   We are to consider the influence of the conduct of saints. (See Hebrews 13:7.)

In this instance, "consider" carries the idea of looking up toward a reverential regard as in Acts 17:23, *"Behold your devotions."* We are enjoined to remember the true teaching we have received and imitate the faith of our teachers, aspiring to their reward. We can only do this profitably as we consider Him first. Sometimes when we consider others first, we meet disappointment.

The Object of Meditation

Him

The poet has reminded us that we are part of all that we have seen. We are so constituted that we are influenced by what we gaze on. An object influences character. They that make gods will become like unto them. (See Psalm 135:18.) As there is no more beautiful, holy, loving object than Christ, we are changed into His likeness when we behold Him. (See 2 Corinthians 3:18.) The more we meditate on Him, the more we reflect Him.

We are to consider not Moses who, although admirable in so many ways, was guilty of murder; nor Abraham who, although he was the father of the faithful, denied his wife; nor Elijah who, although so fearless in his witness, yielded to despondency; nor David who, although a man after God's own heart, became an adulterer. We are to consider Jesus, with all His oceans of wonder and glory, and the One before whom the best of earth are as nothing. When we gather in His name at His Table, He, and He alone, must dominate our thoughts. If ours is a complete reliance upon the Spirit, then He will occupy our minds with the grace, goodness, and glory of our adorable Lord.

The Value of Meditation

Lest ye be wearied and faint in your minds. (Hebrews 12:3)

Weymouth translates it, "*If you would escape becoming weary and faint-hearted compare your own sufferings with those of Him.*" Our greatest peril is that of growing faint, weary, and giving up. We often come to His Table in a defeated, despondent frame of mind. The load of the past week is heavy on us.

The only effective antidote for our weariness is the constant contemplation of Him who was never discouraged. (See Isaiah 42:4.) The Christ, whose death we remember, fits life at every joint. He knew all about temptation, misunderstanding, sorrow, and the mysteries of providence, and is therefore the brother born for adversity. We grumble less when we think of Him as our helper in any kind of trouble. When we meet around His Table, He seems to say to our fearful hearts, "Because I conquered death and hell I am your sufficiency in any crisis that may arise." And as we consider Him our hearts are cheered and our faces become radiant. (See Psalm 34:5 ESV.)

"How Sweet and Sacred"[9]

How sweet and sacred is the place
With Christ within the doors;
While everlasting love displays
The choicest of her stores!

While all our hearts and all our songs
Praise Him who makes the feast;
We can but cry, with thankful tongues,
"Lord, why am I a guest?"

'Twas the same love that spread the feast
That sweetly forced us in;
Else we had still refused to taste,
And perished in our sin.

"Jesus, Lord, We Know Thee Present"[10]

Jesus, Lord, we know Thee present
At Thy table freshly spread,
Seated at Thy priceless banquet,
With Thy banner overhead;
Precious moments at Thy table,
From all fear and doubt set free;
Here to rest we now are able,
Occupied alone with Thee.

Here, rejoicing in Thy nearness,
Gladly by the Spirit led,
Calmly in the blest remembrance
Of Thy precious blood once shed.
Lord, we take each simple token
In fond memory of Thee;
Muse upon Thy body broken,
And Thy blood which made us free.

---

9. Isaac Watts, "How Sweet and Sacred,"
10. Mrs. Bishop Thompson

Oh, what joy it is to see Thee,
In these chosen emblems here;
In the bread and wine of blessing—
Bread to strengthen, wine to cheer!
Lord, behold us met together,
One in Thee, our risen head,
Thus we take the cup of blessing,
Thus we share the broken bread.

Lord, we know how true Thy promise
To be with us where we meet,
When in Thy loved name we gather
To enjoy communion sweet;
Dearer still that looked-for promise,
To each waiting, yearning heart,
That with Thee we soon shall be, Lord,
Yea, "forever" where Thou art.

Sacramental Recognition

The Emmaus walk is one all believers should often take, for on that road the Lord is found giving His blessed company to companions. As Cleopas and his friend travel out to the country and talk as they walk, a Stranger joins them, courteous as a friend. As the three journey on together, He leads them into a long, continued, detailed Bible study about Himself.

There are at least six deft touches in the wonderful story, self-evidencing in its matchless simplicity, which Luke—the beloved physician gives us—in Luke 24:

The Sad and Mournful Conversation (verses 14–17)

The Drawing Near of Christ (verse 15)

The Partial Vision of the Two (verse 16)

The Wonderful Bible Exposition (verse 27)

The Stranger Entertained (verse 29)

The Sacramental Recognition (verse 35)

The question demanding an answer is, How did Christ become known to the two disciples as Jesus broke the bread? What peculiar feature in such an act suggested Him to His hosts?

Perhaps it was the position He occupied. He immediately assumed the central position at the table and dispensed the bread. Sitting between His two friends would at once suggest the Supper He presided over. Although invited as a guest, He took the head of the table and turned an ordinary meal into a sacramental feast.

Perhaps it was the act of blessing. Jesus was ever grateful, and the upward look of gratitude as He gave thanks may have caused them to recognize the stranger as the Savior. At once they remembered the loaves and fish and the institution of the Supper in the upper room.

Perhaps it was the act of breaking the bread. In a certain, characteristic way, Jesus may have taken the loaf and reverently broken it and distributed it to the others, making Him immediately recognizable.

Perhaps it was the vision of the scars. With eyes fixed on Jesus' holy hands as He took the bread, the fresh scars became visible, revealing Him to adoring hearts. He may have used His hands in such a way as to make those ugly wounds conspicuous, and thus display Himself as the crucified, risen Lord.

Thomas came to know those pierced hands as the means of identification, for when he saw them he confessed, *"My Lord and my God"* (John 20:28). And when we see Him face to face, we shall know Him by His nail-pierced hands. Now, as we gather for the breaking of the bread, He makes Himself known to our worshiping hearts.

We Recognize Him

On His day, we do not meet around a table merely, but around the Lord Himself. "His presence makes the feast." We think of Him not only as One who died, rose again, and ascended into heaven, but also as One who is blessedly near and real. At the festal meal of the church, Jesus is not on the table, as Romanism wrongly teaches, but at the table. His spiritual presence with His people is a blessed reality.

We Recognize His Love

As we drink the wine and break the bread, He not only makes Himself known to us, but also His love. Thus, the table becomes a love-feast, and our love for Him is intensified. Because of His love, He left the Father's abode, and taking upon Himself our flesh and sins, provided a perfect salvation for a sinning race. Love not only drew salvation's plan in a past eternity—it also executed that plan in agony and shame on the cruel cross. Loving us, Christ gave Himself for us. (See Galatians 2:20.)

We Recognize His Claims

When our forgetful minds are brought back to the cross and all He endured on our behalf is afresh revealed unto us, we see Him not only as our Savior, but as the Sovereign of our lives. Because of Calvary, He has every claim upon all that we are and have. With His thorn-pierced head, He bought my head with all its powers. By His pierced heart, He purchased my heart with all its love. Those pierced hands declare that He must have my hands. His torn feet redeemed my feet to walk with Him. That deep grave reminds me that I must seek to remain dead to the old life and walk with Him in the newness of life.

We Recognize His Power

It was the resurrected Christ whom the Emmaus travelers saw. How different was their vision of Him now to that of the upper room. Then He was going out to die (see Luke 22:17); now, He is going up into glory. So we have the note of triumph, *"The Lord is risen indeed and hath appeared unto Simon"* (Luke 24:34).

When next we gather at His Table, may He appear unto us. May we catch a fresh vision of Him as the risen, yet ever-present One! As we partake of and pass the bread and wine, may this silent prayer ascend, "Lord, make Thyself known to my heart in this Sacramental Feast." Unseen, yet so near, the adoring heart can hear Him say, *"Eat, O friends; drink, yea, drink abundantly, O beloved"* (Song of Solomon 5:1).

"Blessed Feast! Most Gracious Token"[11]

Blessed feast! Most gracious token
Of Thy dying love, O Lord!
Symbols of Thy body broken,
And Thy precious blood outpoured.

In this holy rite partaking,
Help us on our pilgrim way;
Sin in every shape forsaking,
Be our heart's resolve today.

Sacred pledge that naught can sever,
Blessed Savior, from Thy love;

---

11. John Ross McDuff.

Sealed to be Thy guests forever,
At the ceaseless feast above.

There, in sweet communion blending,
With the vast, ingathered throng,
Ours shall be a bliss unending,
An eternal, festal song

The King at His Table

Devout hearts of every age have accepted the rich, deep, spiritual application of the Song of Solomon. The expressed intimacy between the peasant girl and her shepherd lover is sweetly illustrative of the union and communion existing between Christ and His church.

In the "beloved" of the Song, so devoted and beautiful, we have a picture of the Savior as the lover of the soul.

In the Shulamite, so black and comely, we see ourselves as sinners, now washed and fit for His presence.

In the king, who tried to steal the girl from her lover, we detect the seductive forces of the world.

Among so many aspects of the bridegroom and the bride scattered throughout the book is the appealing one of the king and his subjects seated together in joyful communion. *"While the king sitteth at his table, my spikenard sendeth forth the smell thereof"* (Song of Solomon 1:12). Here are two precious thoughts for us to ponder as we meet to remember Him:

The Royalty of the Table

First of all, royal company gathers around the festive board. The king sits with members of his household at the table. Mephibosheth sat and ate at the king's table as one of the king's sons. (See 2 Samuel 9:11.) Through grace we are children of the King. As saints, we are members of the household of faith. Unless it is not possible for us to be present, let not our place be empty at the table. (See 1 Samuel 20:25.)

The "king's" table suggests *"the Lord's Table"* (1 Corinthians 10:21). It is a table of His own providing, and one in which we find Him. While it is for our remembrance of Him, it is yet for Him as well as for us. As we remember all His pains, so does He! His Table is a mutual feast of love and fellowship. He sups with us, as we with Him. He is both the host and guest. (See Revelation 3:20.)

He sits at the table as King. The elements of the supper declare that He defeated sin, death, and the powers of darkness. We worship Him with loving, obedient hearts. Alas, we do not always realize that the King in all His beauty is present at the table! Being at His Table is to be included in His circle. How privileged we are to form part of His inner circle of guests!

We also think not only of His kingly person, but likewise of His royal provision. It is no empty table at which we sit. Ours is a fuller provision that Solomon made for his Table. (See 1 Kings 4:22–24.) He who is coming as the King of kings spreads for us the best and choicest viands.

He spreads the gospel table with the richest provision for life both here and hereafter.

He spreads the fellowship table at which we can eat in peace amid the turbulence of an agitated world.

He spreads the memorial table on which the bread and wine speak of His body and blood freely sacrificed for us.

How blessed we are to have His person and provision to feast on!

There is no reason for any subject of His to live as if they were spiritually starved. May ours be the inner sustenance which unbroken fellowship produces.

The Redolence of the Table

Redolence means the diffusion of odor, fragrance. Solomon's word reminds us that we have not only favor but fragrance—"*My spikenard sendeth forth the smell thereof*" (Song of Solomon 1:12). Sitting as favored ones at His Table, we go out to emit something of His fragrance. Thus "redolence" implies the life and character which fellowship with the heavenly King makes possible.

The *"spikenard"* can represent the graces of the Spirit in lively service and affection called forth by the remembrance of the box of ointment He broke at Calvary. The presence and thought of Christ as we assemble and tarry in His name should draw forth every grace in the believer and all grace to live as His. How base and ungrateful to sit in His royal presence and yet not have a heart filled with praise to Him! The spikenard which Mary poured on the Lord expressed her overflowing love for Him.

What unworthy companions of the King we would be if we had no strong feeling of love toward Him! It is useless coming to His Table if we have little desire for closer nearness and clearer likeness to the King. Going back to the

supper at Bethany which Jesus attended (see John 12:1–4)—a supper of gratitude for the miracle He performed in raising the dead—we note that Lazarus
was there and that he represents those who have fellowship with Christ in
resurrected life. Martha was also present and she typifies those engaged in
active service for the Master. Then Mary was another guest and she represents
those whose hearts' affections are drawn out toward the Lord. As saints, we
are a combination of all three of them as we sit with the King. We have been
raised—we serve and we worship.

We should take notice of the word *while*. It is only while we are in unbroken fellowship with Him that the sweetness of worship can be ours. He is with
us according to His promise to be present when we gather together in His
name. Is ours the consciousness of his nearness? If we have no deep realization of His presence, then my—note the personal pronoun here—spikenard
will send forth no smell. If our spikenard of gratitude and worship and love is
sealed, its odor will never fill the house. The box must be broken—our loving
gratitude and heartfelt worship must be expressed. Our inner souls must only
be ravished. Our lips and life must be fragrant with praise and witness.

Lord Jesus Thou who only art
The endless source of purest joy;
Oh, come and fill this longing heart,
May nought but Thou my thoughts employ;
Teach me on Thee to fix my eye,
For none but Thou canst satisfy.

Amidst Us Our Beloved Stands[12]

Amidst us our beloved stands,
And bids us view His pierced hands,
Points to His wounded feet and side—
Blest emblems of the Crucified.

What food luxurious loads the board,
When at His Table sits the Lord
The wine how rich, the bread how sweet,
When Jesus deigns the guests to meet!

If now, with eyes defiled and dim,
We see the signs but see not Him,

---

12. C.H. Spurgeon

Oh, may His love the scales displace,
And bid us see Him face to face!

Thou glorious Bridegroom of our hearts,
Thy present smile a heaven imparts;
Oh, lift the veil, if veil there be,
Let every saint Thy beauties see

Till He Come[13]

"'Till He come!" Oh, let the words
Linger on the trembling chords;
Let the "little while" between
In their golden light be seen;
Let us think how heaven and home
Lie beyond that "'Till He come."

When the weary ones we love
Enter on their rest above,
When their words of love and cheer
Fall no longer on our ear,
Hush! be every murmur dumb;
It is only "'Till He come."

Clouds and darkness round us press:
Would we have one sorrow less?
All the sharpness of the cross,
All that tells the world is loss,
Death, and darkness, and the tomb,
Pain us only "'Till He come."

See, the feast of love is spread;
Drink the wine and eat the bread
Sweet memorials, 'till the Lord
Call us 'round His heavenly board,
Some from earth, from glory some,
Severed only "Till He come!"

---

13. Edward Bickersteth

4

LENTEN PREACHING

SERMON THEMES FOR LENTEN PREACHING

Literature on the events and experiences related to our Lord from Palm Sunday to Passion Sunday is as vast as it is varied. Both in religious and secular literature, more has been written on Christ's rejection, betrayal, trial, death, and resurrection than any other aspect of biblical truth. From sources, ancient and modern, we have gathered the following themes and outlines for the benefit of those who have opportunities of ministering the Word during Holy Week. A superb work, the *Passiontide Sermons* by Canon H. P. Liddon, published in 1892. These remarkable sermons were preached by the Canon when he was Chancellor of St. Paul's Cathedral in London. One wishes these homiletical treasures could be republished. As can be seen from the "Contents," the coverage offers preachers a wide range of themes which the Canon himself developed at various Easter services.

+ The Sinlessness of Jesus Christ (See John 8:46)
+ The Humiliation of the Eternal Son (See Philippians 2:5–8)
+ The Person of the Crucified (See 1 Corinthians 1:13)
+ The Accepted Offering (See Hebrews 10:5–7)
+ The Cleansing Blood (See Hebrews 9:13, 14)
+ The Conqueror of Satan (See Hebrews 2:14)
+ The Corn of Wheat (See John 12:24)
+ The Appeal of the Crucified Jesus (See Romans 10:21)
+ The Solitudes of the Passion (See Psalm 22:11)
+ The Silence of Jesus (See John 19:9)
+ The Ass and the Foal (See Matthew 21:3)
+ Popular Religious Enthusiasm (See John 12:12, 13)
+ Religious Emotion (See Matthew 21:9)
+ The Traitor-Apostle (See Matthew 26: 24)

+ The Economy of Religious Art (See Matthew 26:8–10)
+ The Living Water (See John 4:13–15)
+ The True Life of Man (See Luke 12:15)
+ The Death of the Soul (See Psalm 6:5)
+ Guidance of the Penitent (See Psalm 32:9)
+ Disapproval of Friends (See Psalm 38: 11)
+ The Idea of Sin (See Psalm 51:4)

Dr. A. G. Mortimer, Rector of St. Mark's in Philadelphia, Pennsylvania, published *Meditations on the Passion*, in which he not only dealt with the three hours' agony of Christ on the cross with special reference to the seven words, but also on the following aspects—

+ The Scourging of Our Blessed Lord
+ The Mockery of Our Blessed Lord
+ The Presentation of Our Blessed Lord to the People
+ The Cross-Bearing of Our Blessed Lord
+ The Piercing of Our Lord and Savior, Jesus Christ
+ The Uplifting of the Cross of Our Lord

A later work, *Verbum Crucis*, by Dr. William Alexander, archbishop of Armagh, Ireland, is a most remarkable volume for its insight into the ministry and message of the cross. In the "Preface," the author says in preaching these sermons and then putting them in book form was "to deliver his soul; to preach the gospel as he has received it; and speak peace to the children of God; and to hold up Christ crucified and risen; living in His church, and working through His Word and sacraments to reflective people, who in an age of perplexity, desire to reconcile that in them which feels and prays with that which thinks." What a compendium of Calvary theology this precious volume contains! We urge preachers to ransack well-known secondhand religious bookstores for a copy. Here are the "Contents"—

+ The Incarnation and the Mystery of the Cross (See Matthew 1:18)
+ The Self-Oblation of the Cross (See Isaiah 53:12)
+ The Forgiveness of the Cross (See Luke 23:34)
+ The Absolution of the Cross (See Luke 23:42–43)
+ The Legacy of the Cross (See John 19: 26–27)
+ The Dereliction of the Cross (See Mark 15:33–34)
+ The Bodily Pain of the Cross (See John 19:28)
+ The Completeness of the Cross (See John 19:30)
+ The Peace of the Cross (See Luke 23:46)
+ The Witness of Human Language upon the Cross (See John 19:19–20)

- Prophecy and the Gospels (See Acts 10:38–43)
- The Church's Structure, Life and Gifts (See Acts 2:42; 1 Corinthians 10:11; 12:11)
- Benediction of the Bishop and of the Saint (See Numbers 6:23–27)
- Fidelity—Development—Peace (See Colossians 3:15)

A most suggestive study of the passion is that by Pastor S. J. Reid entitled *Do Not Sin Against the Cross*, published by Wm. B. Eerdmans Co. in 1940. The author convincingly proves that, "The Cross may suffer eclipse, but when the shadows have passed, it will be seen with its power and splendor undiminished. The greatest need of the church today is the preaching with fervor and conviction, continuous and loyally, Christ crucified." What a wealth of material preachers will find in the chapters bearing these captions—

- The Cross of Calvary (See Luke 23:33)
- The Cross and Christ (See 1 Corinthians 1:23)
- How Did Christ Regard His Cross? (See John 12:32)
- The Cross and God (See Revelation 13:8)
- The Cross and the Church (See Ephesians 5:25)
- The Cross and the Christian (See Galatians 6:17)
- The Cross and the World (See Galatians 5:11)
- The Cross and Power (See 1 Corinthians 1:18)
- The Cross and Service (See Matthew 16:24)
- The Cross and Sin (See 1 John 1:7)
- The Cross and Redemption (See Galatians 3:13)
- The Cross and Paul (See Galatians 2:20
- The Cross and Human Failure (See Galatians 3:7)
- The Cross and the Victorious Resurrection (See Luke 24:26)

Attention must also be drawn to the incomparable Easter messages to be found in Professor W. M. Clow's two remarkable volumes, *The Day of the Cross* and *The Cross in Christian Experience*. They are a must read for preachers with a desire to enrich their gospel phraseology.

PROPHECIES OF THE PASSION

For one of his messages during Holy Week, the preacher could prove that "the golden casket" of the Bible is "the Heaven-drawn picture of Christ, the Living Word." A summary like the following by A. T. Darch, which appeared in *The Witness* in London several years ago could be enlarged on.

When our Lord undertook to fulfill the law and the prophets (see Matthew 5:17), He not only undertook to obey the Ten Commandments perfectly, and to be the anti type of the Old Testament types, but he also undertook the great task of fulfilling all the Old Testament prophecies relating to His first advent. To do this He needed to know all the Scriptures that would relate to His first coming as distinct from those relating to His second coming. He would fulfill Zechariah 9:9, but not Zechariah 14:4. As the result of this, thirty-one prophecies about His sufferings, written one thousand to five hundred years before, were fulfilled in Him during the twenty-four hours leading up to and during His crucifixion. They were—

1. He was forsaken by God. (See Psalm 22:1; Matthew 27:46.)
2. He was to be betrayed by a friend. (See Psalm 41:9; 55:12–14; Matthew 26:47–50; John 13:18.)
3. He would be sold for thirty pieces of silver. (See Zechariah 11:12; Matthew 26:14–15.)
4. The money obtained was to be cast to the potter: (a) silver; (b) thirty pieces; (c) thrown down; (d) in the house of the Lord; (e) used to purchase a field. (See Zechariah 11:13; Matthew 27:3–10.)
5. His disciples would forsake Him. (See Zechariah 13:7; Mark 14:27.)
6. He was to be accused by false witnesses. (See Psalm 35:11; 109: 2; Matthew 26:59–60.)
7. He would suffer indignities: (a) smitten; (b) on the back; (c) spit upon; (d) on the face. (See Isaiah 50:4–6; Matthew 26: 67–68; Luke 22:17.)
8. He would be dumb before His accusers. (See Isaiah 53:7; Matthew 27:12–14; 1 Peter 2:23.)
9. He was to be wounded and bruised. (See Isaiah 53:5; Matthew 27:26–30.)
10. His hands and feet would be pierced. (See Psalm 22:16; Luke 23:33; John 20:25–27.)
11. He would be crucified with thieves. (See Isaiah 53:12; Mark 15:27–28.)
12. He would pray for His persecutors. (See Isaiah 53:12; Luke 23:34.)
13. They would shake their heads at Him. (Psalm 22:7; Matthew 27:39.)
14. The people would ridicule Him. (See Psalm 22:8; Matthew 27:41–43.)
15. They would part His garments and cast lots for His vesture. (See Psalm 22:18; John 19:23–24.)

16. They would give Him gall and vinegar to drink. (See Psalm 69:21; Matthew 27:34.)

17. His friends would stand afar off. (See Psalm 38:11; Luke 23:49.)

18. His bones were not to be broken. (See Psalm 34:20; John 19:33.)

19. His side would be pierced. (See Zechariah 12:10; John 19:34, 37.)

20. Darkness would cover the land at noon. (See Amos 8:9; Mark 15:33.)

21. The kings of the earth, and the rulers would take counsel against the Lord and against His Anointed. (See Psalm 2:1–2; Acts 4:25–28.)

22. There would be none to help Him. (See Psalm 22:11; Matthew 26:56.)

23. They gaped upon Him. (See Psalm 22:13; Matthew 27:36.)

24. He was wounded for our transgressions; He was bruised for our iniquities. (See Isaiah 53:5; 1 Peter 2:24.)

25. He was a Man of Sorrows. (See Isaiah 53:3; Matthew 26:37–38.)

26. He was brought as a lamb to the slaughter. (See Isaiah 53:7; Matthew 26:57.)

27. He would be smitten with a rod on the head. (See Micah 5:1; Matthew 27:30.)

28. The assembly of the wicked would enclose Him. (See Psalm 22:16; Mark 14:43; Luke 23:1.)

29. He would commit Himself to God. (See Psalm 31:5; Luke 23:46.)

30. He would be buried in a rich man's tomb. (See Isaiah 53:9; Matthew 27:57–60.)

31. He would rise again from the grave. (See Psalm 16:9–11.)

It is beyond belief that it was by chance that so many diverse experiences should meet in one person in so short a period of time as twenty-four hours. Only God could foresee, foretell, and fulfill this. It is Him who calls, or rather commands, us to put our undivided trust on Him in whom all these things came to pass. We must trust Him as our personal Lord and Savior, submitting entirely to His authority. *"To him give all the prophets witness, that through his name, whosoever believeth in him shall receive remission of sins"* (Acts 10:43).

Here are further outlines for the preacher to develop as he deals with the "Seven Words from the Cross." It is more than likely that those last words were uttered in the following order—

1. Before the Darkness

"Father forgive them" (Luke 23:34).

"Verily I say unto you" (Luke 23:43).

"Woman, behold thy son" (John 19:26).

 2. During the Darkness

"My God, My God" (Matthew 27:46; Mark 15:34).

 3. After the Darkness

"I thirst" (John 19:28, fulfilling Psalm 69:21).

"It is finished" (John 19:36).

"Father, into Thy hands" (Luke 24:46; see Psalm 31:5).

The same Seven Words have been described in this way—

1. Propitiatory—*"Father, forgive."*
2. Promissory—*"Today shalt thou be with me."*
3. Provisionary—*"Woman, behold thy son."*
4. Protestatory—*"My God, My God"* (See Matthew 27:46 ASV).
5. Peremptory—*"I thirst."*
6. Proclamatory—*"It is finished."*
7. Pacificatory—*"Father into thy hands."*

In this order Christ's last words express theologically—

1. Divine Forgiveness
2. Assurance of Immortality
3. Good Works
4. The Awfulness of Death
5. The True Humanity of Christ
6. The Perfection of Christ's Atonement
7. The Divine Complacency

As we look at the scenes taking place we must realize that we are seeing...

STEPS TO THE CROSS

1. Jesus is condemned to death.
2. Jesus is made to bear His cross.
3. Jesus falls the first time under the weight of His cross.
4. Jesus meets His afflicted mother.
5. Simon the Cyrenean helps Jesus to carry His cross.
6. Veronica wipes the face of Jesus.
7. Jesus falls the second time.
8. Jesus speaks to the daughters of Jerusalem.
9. Jesus falls the third time.
10. Jesus is stripped of His garments.
11. Jesus is nailed to the cross.

12. Jesus dies on the cross.

13. Jesus is taken down from the cross.

14. Jesus is placed in the sepulcher.

If, during Holy Week services, the preacher decides to emphasize the significance of some of the above events, the following suggestions may help to prove that the meditation of the last stages of our Lord's passion can be of great potential spiritual value whether used publicly or privately. It is in the province of the Holy Spirit to reveal these truths to us.

Jesus Condemned to Death (Matthew 27:24–26)

Hymn: "Man of Sorrows, What a Name!"

Prayer:

> Gracious Savior, who by Thy cross didst redeem the world, we humbly bow before Thee beseeching mercy for ourselves and for all sinners. Give us to see that our sins were the cause of Thy passion, and by Thy grace bring us into a fuller understanding of our fellowship with Thy sufferings. Grant us Thy patience to endure the humiliations and crosses of this life. For Thy dear name's sake. Amen.

Narrative: After Christ was betrayed by Judas, and after He endured blasphemy in the presence of Caiaphas and mockery in the presence of Herod, He was bound and led by the chief priests and elders to Pilate, whose conscience told him that the august prisoner was innocent. Jesus was then scourged, crowned with thorns, and condemned to a criminal's death. Weak Pilate delivered Him up to be crucified.

Meditation: What contrasts are suggested by the phrase *"And Jesus stood before the governor"* (Matthew 27:11)? Of the tribe of Judah Jesus came as the governor to rule His people Israel (see Matthew 2:6), but in Pilate's judgment hall, the heavenly governor of whose government there is to be no end (see Isaiah 9:7) stood shackled before a Roman governor who failed to righteously govern. All judgment was committed into Christ's hands. Although He will yet judge the world, He submits to the unjust sentence of an earthly judge. As Man, Christ stands at the judgment seat of one of His own creatures. The marvel of marvels is that the one perfect Man who was *"the express image of the Father"* (Hebrews 1:3) suffered Himself to be branded as a criminal. Having no sin, He was yet made sin for us.

The first Adam was created innocent, but he sinned and defaced the image of God, and took the whole human race down with him. *"By one man sin entered into the world*" (Romans 5:12). None who followed Adam was capable of repairing the damage he caused. Because thereafter all born of man were born in sin, there was no mediator sinless and capable of bridging the man-created gulf between sinners and God.

When the Second Adam appeared and took our human nature on Himself, He was exposed to the temptations under which the first Adam fell, but emerged from the conflict with Satan victorious. None could convict Him of sin. When Jesus stood before Pilate, He was conscious of His complete innocence and of the cynical miscarriage of justice perpetrated by the religious leaders and climaxed by Pilate's pronouncement of death. But before His judge, He was silent and delivered Himself up rather than be delivered up by others. His life was not taken but given, submitted to the Father. Consequently, although all men died in the first Adam, they can be made alive in the Second Adam. Pilate's condemnation of Jesus was unjust, for He was completely innocent. But at the great white throne, when the world judges the wicked, the Savior's judgment will be just and righteous. He cannot act contrary to His own nature or character.

Questions to Ask and Apply: Christ's obedience unto death and willing submission to a human and unjust condemnation can be applied in many ways, as Francis L. Wheeler suggests…

1. Do I see, or try to see, obedience to legitimate authority as part of the Christian virtue of humility?
2. Is my obedience to the commands of God and His church grudging and ungenerous? Do I interpret them laxly, seeking to do only the minimum?
3. Is my obedience to those set over me prompt, complete, and uncomplaining?
4. Do I, through human respect or fear of adverse human judgments, in any way neglect my duty to God?
5. Do I ever try to accept uncomplainingly, in union with the humility of Christ before Pilate, criticism and misjudgment?

Suggestions for Intercession:

Let us pray:

+ for those under the condemnation of eternal death because of their rejection of the Savior's grace and love.
+ for all those who like Jesus are unjustly condemned and suffer for righteousness sake.

+ for all prisoners of war, and captives, and for all the condemned in prison cells that they might repent of their sin and turn to the judge of all earth who ever does that which is right.
+ for ourselves that we may have grace to forgive those who have injured us, and love our enemies for Christ's sake, who never rendered to any man evil for evil.

Closing Prayer:

Blessed Savior, who was condemned to die for our sins, grant that we may hate and forsake all sin, and continually delight to do Thy will. Through the merits of Thy passion cleanse us anew, and make our lives an offering meet for Thy honor. Inspired by Thine ineffable compassion, may we be the means of delivering those from the condemnation justly due to them for their guilt. Renew us more perfectly in Thy image, so that reflecting Thee, others will be drawn to Thee. For Thy name's sake, amen.

Jesus Receives the Cross (John 19:16–17)

Hymn: "Jesus, I My Cross Have Taken"
Prayer:

Gracious Lord, we adore and bless Thee for all Thou didst accomplish on our behalf when Thou didst shoulder that heavy cross and then die upon it. Give us to understand that, afflicted by our sins, we can only be cleansed and delivered through Thy cross-bearing. Thou who didst willingly accept the cross of ignominy and shame, grant us true contrition of heart, and prepare our minds for the further and fuller revelation of Thy wondrous cross, through thy most holy name. Amen.

Narrative: The heavy, rugged cross was laid upon the wounded and weary shoulders of Jesus, and He carried it without complaint. He knew it would be the only instrument whereby He could redeem lost sinners, and so with joy He endured it. Having told His own to take up the cross and follow Him, He leads the way in cross-bearing.

Meditation: We will never be able to fathom all the anguish implied by the phrase *"And he, bearing his cross, went forth."* He—His cross! The spotless, sinless Son of God had done nothing to deserve that cross which represents God's condemnation of sin—the only avenue of escape from sin's thralldom. Thus it was not His cross, but ours. Yet because of His love He made it His cross. His obedience to the will of God is seen in that act of taking the instrument of an ignominious and horrifying death. The cross He bore, bore Him as He died accursed for our salvation.

Bearing the cross symbolized Christ's willingness to bear our grief, carry our sorrow, and be bruised for our iniquities. On that cross laid upon His shoulders was the iniquity of us all. What a gory spectacle it must have been as Jesus trudged alone, weighted down, not only by the wooden cross itself, but also by increasing pain and exhaustion which His last hours had produced. It was a staggering load He bore; not only was there physical agony, but also an inner anguish He hinted at when He cried, *"Now is my soul troubled"* (John 12:27). Bless His name! He could have refused to take up that cross, but, obedient to God's will, He shouldered it for our sake.

> Make me to feel it was my sin,
> As though no other sins there were,
> That was to Him who bears the world
> A load He could scarcely bear.[14]

Questions to Ask and Apply: As true discipleship involves taking up the cross and following Christ, how do we react to the following questions as we follow Him to His death?

1. Do we sincerely accept His command about cross-bearing and by His grace carry it into affect?
2. Do we find ourselves resentful under the cross of physical pain and disability?
3. Do we take our suffering and try to offer it in reparation for our sins in union with the sufferings of Christ?
4. Do we further fail by allowing our sorrow or bereavement to turn us away from Him who bore our cross, and consequently become estranged from Him?
5. Do we refuse the cross because of its offense, and the mockery or hostility our identification with it would expose us to?

Suggestions for Intercession:

Let us pray:

+ that we might accept our cross-bearing uncomplainingly, believing that the hardship and adversities of life can ennoble our life.
+ that we can be saved only through the cross of the only begotten Son of God, so others around are blessed when we are willing to lay in the dust life's glory dead.

---

14. Frederick W. Faber, "My God! My God! And Can it Be?", 1849.

✦ that we must pray for all those who bear the cross of temptation, cruel and unjust treatment, misrepresentation and mockery, cruelty and neglect, and sickness and suffering.

Closing Prayer:

O Lord, when the waters come in even to our soul, haste Thou to our help. Thou who didst bear the cross for us, deliver us from the burden of our sin. Uphold and sustain those who bear the cross of any adversity, and carry on Thy shoulders the desolate and oppressed. Through Thy merits and mediation pardon our iniquity, and in Thy wrath remember mercy, Thou who art full of compassion. For Thy name's sake. Amen.

Jesus Falls Beneath the Cross (Luke 23:26)

Hymn: "O Christ What Burdens Bowed Thy Head"
Prayer:

Heavenly Father, as we approach Thee through the finished work of Thy beloved Son, the Redeemer of the world, enable us by Thy beloved Son, the Redeemer of the world, enable us by Thy Holy Spirit, who witnessed the sufferings of Christ, to fully understand the humanity of Him who fell beneath the dreadful load of His cross. Stricken for our sins, we would prostrate ourselves before Thee, beseeching Thee to cleanse our hearts anew from all that is alien to Thy holy mind and will. Because Thou art unfailingly patient with Thy erring children and with sinful men who know Thee not, prepare our minds to receive in a new way the message of the cross through Jesus Christ our Lord. Amen.

Narrative: Proceeding slowly through the streets of Jerusalem on His way to Calvary, mocked and insulted by watching crowds, Jesus fell beneath the load of His cross. The sufferings of the previous night, the agony and bloody sweat of Gethsemane, the loss of blood from the scourging of His foes exhausted the human body of the Man of Sorrows. In taking on the limitations of our humanity, Jesus likewise experienced the weariness, pain, and suffering to which the flesh is heir. The paradox of His incarnation is that although He came as very God of very God, He became physically exhausted and fell under the burden placed on Him by His creatures.

O Savior Christ, Thou too art Man:

Thou hast been troubled, tempted, tried;
Thy kind but searching glance can scan
The very wounds that shame would hide.[15]

Meditation: Although Jesus stumbled under the weight of the cross which Simon shouldered for Him, He never had a moral or spiritual fall. His body was drained of its strength and resistance by man's brutal treatment of Him, but He kept the inner citadel of His soul inviolate. As Francis L. Wheeler put it, "He fell, physically, because He bore the consequences of our sins. The physical weight of the cross is the outward sign of the inner burden He bears of the accumulated malice and evil of mankind."

The hope of the sinner is in that sinless, drained, battered and helpless body of Christ's. Through His humiliation, He gained the power to raise a fallen world unable to save itself. Having fallen from grace, man can only be raised from the dunghill and made to sit among princes, as he repents of his sin and reposes his faith in Him who was willing to lie prostrate to the dust of those Jerusalem streets, and then rise and painfully continue His journey outside the city wall and die upon its green hill. He fell that we might rise from our dead selves to a higher, better life. He died that we might live forever.

Questions to Ask and Apply: At this time we have need to pause and ask our hearts if we have fallen into any grievous sin and are in danger of becoming a backslider.

1. Do we understand the difference between shame for sin and true repentance?
2. Do we immediately pray for divine restoration, as the Spirit convicts us of a fallen condition?
3. Do we regularly and prayerfully examine our conscience to discover where we have strayed from Christ, and when made conscious of our failure immediately repent and then go forward determined by God's grace and power never to fall and fail in such a way again?

Suggestions for Intercession:

Let us pray:

+ that you may be kept straight in the way of truth and obedience.
+ that you may ever be watchful of thoughts, words, and deeds and thereby preserved from falling into sin.
+ that sustained by Christ you may carry your cross without stumbling.

---

15. Henry Twells, "At Even, Ere the Sun Was Set," 1868.

 ✦ that in full dependence upon divine mercy and pardon you will believe that God will not exact vengeance for your past sins, nor reward you as your iniquity deserved.

Closing Prayer:

O Savior Christ, who didst fall under the weight of the shameful cross, empower us by Thy passion to stand victorious in the arena of this mortal life so that when the warfare against Satan and sin ceases, we may share Thy throne on high. Thou who didst fall under the cross, forgive us when we fall into sin. Thou who didst become prostrate beneath the cross, bear us up and cause us to be triumphant in the hour of temptation. We ask these mercies in Thy own matchless name. Amen.

Jesus Meets His Mother (Luke 23:27)

Hymn: "Once in Royal David's City"
Prayer:

O Lord, because Thou wast born of a woman and experienced all the lights and shadows of human relationships, we thank Thee for the woman Thou didst choose to be Thy mother and for the mutual care and solicitation exhibited until Thou didst commit the one who bore Thee to the care of Thy well-loved disciple. Truly, Mary is honored above all women for she magnified Thee as the One who would bring down the enemies of Thy people. Before the sword of judgment awoke against Thee as the Shepherd of Israel, the sword of sorrow pierced the heart of Thy mother, and she entered into the fellowship of Thy sufferings. With Thy death and resurrection, O Lord, Thou didst sever human relationship, and it is only through Thee that we now have redemption and access to the Father. Thou alone art our Intercessor in heaven for which we praise Thee. Amen.

Narrative: Because Mary was our Lord's mother, she had to be associated with Him in suffering, and doubtless followed Him with the other daughters of Jerusalem as He, her first-born Son, was led out to be crucified. If the shadow of the cross was ever darkening the life of Jesus, that shadow commenced to cross Mary's early days of motherhood when in her heart she knew that *"the holy thing"* born of her was to be the Savior of the world. Now as she accompanies her illustrious Son to His death, her spirit more than ever rejoiced in Him who was to die as her Savior as well as the Savior of the world.

Meditation: While our Lord had a human mother, He did not have a human father. He was the only babe the world had ever known who did not have a father according to the flesh. Although born of a virgin, Jesus was conceived by the Holy Spirit, and during the first thirty years of His life was surrounded by those who were bound to Him by human ties. After His birth, we have only one glimpse of Him in His humble Nazareth home before He left it at the age of thirty for His brief ministry of some three years. Because He came as the personification of love and honor, He must have acted most graciously toward His mother at all times.

The gospels reveal, however, that Jesus never allowed earthly relationship to interfere with heavenly obligations, a fact borne out when Mary discovered her Son in the temple and received His mild rebuke, *"Wist ye not that I must be about my Father's business?"* (Luke 2:49). Mary knew that the Father's business would be fulfilled in sacrifice and death, and that she must not merely stand helplessly aside but drink of her Son's bitter cup which she did as she followed Him to Calvary and stood by His cross until the end of His bitter passion. No preferential treatment was to be hers, and on the way to the cross her presence and sympathy comforted the Son of her womb. "Amid the hostile crowd is the faithful handmaid of His Heavenly Father. Amid the sea of hatred and mockery the full force of her unspoken love and compassion is poured out on Him." As Mary followed that execution-procession, she was one with her Son in His desire to accomplish the will of His Father in heaven. No wonder all generations call her blessed!

Questions to Ask and Apply: Because Jesus was born of Mary to die for the sins of the world, the sword of sorrow pierced her heart ere it slew the Savior. Peace and reconciliation are now ours because of all both Mary and her Son endured. As we examine ourselves in the light of Christ's association with His holy mother, can we give a satisfactory answer to these questions?

1. Do we fully respect our human relationship, loving and caring for those nearest to us?
2. Do we ever strive to give God first place in our lives and endeavor to place the heavenly obligations before earthly ones?
3. Do we give the Father's business the precedence in our lives? Do we recognize that He has the first claim upon our love?

Suggestions for Intercession:

Let us pray:

+ that we may share the compassion Jesus manifested toward His mother.
+ that we may not be negligent of our duty in respect to our parents.

+ that we may be as fully surrendered to the purpose of God as Mary was when she prayed *"Be it unto me according to thy word"* (Luke 1:38).
+ that we may emulate the courage in suffering and sorrow, as Mary did in her Son's passion week.
+ for all mothers bereaved of their children.
+ for the salvation of all selfish,cruel and neglectful mothers.
+ for all who have the care of children in homes and institutions.
+ for all widows and fatherless children.

Closing Prayer:

Almighty and everlasting God, we thank Thee anew for Thy beloved Son who, in the virgin's womb, fused together deity and humanity and appeared as God manifest in flesh. Open blind eyes to see that as Mary's Son He knows all about our human needs, and, as Thy well-beloved Son is able to meet all our needs. May our faithfulness to Thee as our Heavenly Father find an echo in our love and loyalty to those who are bound to us by human ties, in our Redeemer's prevailing name. Amen.

Simon of Cyrene Carries the Cross
(Matthew 27:32; Mark 15:21; Luke 23:26)

Hymn: "Must Jesus Bear the Cross Alone?"
Prayer:

O Lord, Thou who didst become the Man of Sorrows for our redemption, hear our prayer as we seek Thy forgiving grace for all that our sin meant to Thee. Enable us to understand what it means to share Thy cross, and to fill up that which is behind of Thy affliction for the sake of Thy church! As Thy followers, lead us into the secret of living in union with Thy passion. May we be found worthy to suffer for Thy sake! We would not resent and reject the suffering true discipleship often brings with it but ever sing with grateful heart—

> Jesus, I my cross have taken,
> All to leave and follow Thee;
> Destitute, despised, forsaken,
> Thou, from hence, my all shalt be.[16]

---

16. Henry Lyte, "Jesus, I My Cross Have Taken."

Narrative: Because of all the Master had endured during the hours ending in His condemnation, He was at low ebb physically. As He proceeds wearily to the place of crucifixion, His strength is drained away, and He cannot carry the heavy cross any further by Himself. His guards, seeing His exhaustion, arrested from the watching crowd a strong-looking bystander named Simon, from Cyrene, and compelled him to shoulder the weightier part of the cross. How Jesus must have been grateful for Simon's relief, and we wonder how Simon must have felt to have been Christ's first cross-bearer! What an honorable ignominy was his! Wonderful, was it not, that Jesus, in His extremity, was helped by one far removed from the inner circle of His intimates, even by a colored man from Africa!

Meditation: God decreed that an African rather than an apostle, a foreigner rather than a follower, should come to the aid of His beloved Son in His hour of dire need. Doubtless when the Cyrenean was pulled from the crowd to carry the heavy cross, he reluctantly obeyed, not knowing what a privilege it was to assist the Savior of the world. It can be assumed that this grim event and the sight of Jesus dying on the cross led this benighted soul to become a disciple. He was the father of Alexander and Rufus, and if the Rufus mentioned affectionately by Paul (see Romans 16:13) was the son of Simon, it would seem that Simon or his widow became a Christian—hence Paul's reference about the mother of Rufus surrounding him with motherly care during his apostolic labors.

The cross was laid on Simon, just as every follower of the Lamb is laid the obligation and privilege of sharing in the sufferings of Christ. Too many professing Christians reject this indispensable condition of true discipleship. The contemplation of Christ's passion as something to be shared in is somewhat morbid to them and to be avoided. Yet we only *"come after"* Christ if in obedience to His call, we take up the cross and follow Him.

> Must Jesus bear the cross alone
> And all the world go free?
> No, there's a cross for everyone,
> And there's a cross for me.[17]

While Jesus died for the sins of the world, and His sufficient redemption requires no addition of man, yet all who form His mystical body are required

---

17. Thomas Shepherd, "Must Jesus Bear the Cross Alone?" 1693.

to *"fill up that which is behind of the afflictions of Christ for His body's sake, which is the church"* (Colossians 1:24).

What is the exact nature of the cross-bearing the Master calls us to? When a particular trial comes our way we are apt to say, "Ah, well, this is my cross and I suppose I must bear it. "If we live with someone who is hard to get along with, we treat such a lack of harmony as a daily cross. But as one has reminded us, "Cross-bearing is not merely the stoical endurance of trials and tribulations inseparable from life in this world, but the deliberate, creative, supernatural acceptance of suffering of any and all kinds for Christ's sake, in union with His passion...Jesus, in the form of sorrows, sufferings, disappointments, and the like, detaches and lays upon us fragments from His cross. We are to accept them as our share of expiation and try to unite our sufferings with His."

We have no knowledge of Simon's attitude to the cross-bearing thrust upon him, whether he chafed under the task or was full of compassion for the suffering One. We do know that he was not allowed to stand in the crowd watching the barbarity of Christ's foes. Simon was removed from the role of spectator to that of a participant in cross-bearing. Jesus, for the joy set before Him endured the cross and despised the shame. For His disciples, Calvary is not a place or experience to be avoided, but entered into if we would know, experimentally, what it is to be crucified with Christ.

Questions to Ask and Apply: As Jesus was helped by Simon to bear His cross, and He willingly accepted the relief of a stranger, do we understand what it means to fill up what is behind of Christ's afflictions? Do I ask my heart these pertinent questions?

1. Do I accept my cross grudgingly or gladly?
2. Do I recognize my Christian obligation to help those in trouble or need?
3. Do I not only take advantage of the opportunity of doing good, but constantly seek avenues of service?
4. Do I endeavor, according to my means, to assist those societies caring for the needy?
5. Do I pray unceasingly for those weighted down in distress of mind or body?

Suggestions for Intercession:

Let us pray:

+ that grace may be ours to be active in good works.
+ that we may be used for the oppression and injustice inflicted upon the colored peoples of the earth by other races.

+ that those of the African continent may come to know the Savior who died for all men.
+ that justice and freedom becomes the possession of those whose skin happens to be darker than our own.

Closing Prayer:

Most merciful Father, who hast created and redeemed men of every race and color to be Thine own possession, and didst use colored Simon to assist Jesus bear His cross, enable us to share Thy love and compassion for all men. May we see in our trials and tribulations for Thy sake a bearing of Thy cross! Crucified unto the world and the world dead unto us, may we not resent nor reject the call to cross-bearing but count it a privilege to be thus associated with Thee. For Thy sake. Amen.

Wiping the Face of Jesus

Hymn: "When I Survey the Wondrous Cross"
Prayer:

O Lord, who didst die for the redemption of lost men and women, may our contemplation of Thy sufferings move us to loathe our sins that sent Thee to Thy cross, and inspire within us a deeper love of Thee. As we continue our pilgrimage with Thee to Calvary, may the Holy Spirit cause Thy image to be graven on our minds. Because Thou didst not hide Thy face in the time of trouble, we know and believe that Thou wilt incline Thine ear unto our prayer. In Thine own name. Amen.

Narrative: As Jesus walks with heavy step through the streets of Jerusalem, His face is blood-bespattered as the result of His sweat of agony, and the oozing blood from His thorn-crowned brow. Legend has it that among the daughters of Jerusalem who were moved with compassion as they looked upon Christ's crimson-stained countenance was one, Veronica by name, who pushed her way through the crowd and wiped His face with a handkerchief. Accepting it with gratitude, He gave it back to Veronica who found that the suffering One had performed a miracle, for on her linen cloth was the image of His marred face.

Meditation: How true is the word of the prophet that Christ's visage was marred more than any man's! Truly there was no beauty in such a bloody spectacle that men should desire Him! Despised and rejected, how could He be desired? The pitiable creature Veronica saw had every shred of majesty and dignity torn from Him. The face of God manifest in flesh was bruised and gashed from the soldiers' blows and was heavily lined from all agonies He had undergone. To those who watched Him as He stumbled pitifully along, looking like many a criminal who had passed that way, He was without form or comeliness. But while that wounded face aroused no pity in those who hounded Him to His cross, Veronica saw beauty in the blood, and by her act of reparation sought to alleviate something of the injury inflicted upon Him who came as the express image of His Father. Veronica may have wiped the blood from His face, but on the cross, He shed His blood to wipe away sin with all its disfigurements and restore God's image in us.

Questions to Ask and Apply: Consoling the weeping women of Jerusalem, Jesus told them not to weep over His agony but to weep for themselves and for their children and the trials awaiting them. What questions are there for our hearts to answer as we think of the sympathetic action of the women?

+ Are we too self-centered, thinking only of our own trials and sorrows?
+ Are we moved to compassion by the needs of others?
+ Are we sacrificial in our prayers and help of the needy? It has been said that, "The most fruitful prayer is the prayer with the drop of blood on it."
+ Are we conscious that sin obscures God's image in our life?

Suggestions for Intercession:

Let us pray:

+ that God will defend your cause against ungodly people
+ that He would give you strength to suffer in union with Christ
+ that He would cause reparation to be made for the oppression and injustice inflicted upon the colored peoples of the world
+ that He would heal wounds, and not to exact vengeance

Closing Prayer:

O blessed Redeemer, capture our hearts anew with that ineffable compassion of Thine. By Thy blood, free us from the guilt of our sins and from the punishment they justly deserve. Blot out our transgressions and renew in us Thy image. In all our sorrows, be Thou our help and strength; and enable us to glorify Thee in all our ways. These things we ask in Thy blessed name. Amen.

The Savior Falls Again Beneath His Cross

Hymn: "Drawn to the Cross Which Thou Hast Blest"

Prayer:

Gracious Savior, who didst fall beneath the load of Thy cross, and on the cross permit Thyself to be crushed by the load of our sin, have mercy upon us, and forgive us for our repeated stumbling into sin. Enable us by Thy grace to be more determined in our fight against sin. Having redeemed us, bear and carry us as Thou hast promised and keep our feet from stumbling and support us by Thy grace. We lift our hearts to Thee beseeching Thee to grant us a fuller understanding of the cross. In Thy name we pray. Amen.

Narrative: As Jesus slowly proceeds to the place of crucifixion, pain, and blood loss, and despite the forced help of Simon of Cyrene, the Savior falls the second time. There were no strong arms upon which He could lean. Was there ever sorrow like unto His sorrow? As we follow Jesus to Calvary, we must not be emotionally stirred by outward events merely, but dwell on the causes of which His pangs and pains were the effects.

Meditation: Contemplation of the passion of our Lord will be useless if it does not inflame our affections and move our wills to resist more effectively the sin for which He died.

> Drops of grief can ne'er repay
> The debt of love we owe.[18]

Jesus no longer bears a heavy wooden cross, the outward sign of our iniquity, and now the instrument of our salvation. Once and for all He bore our sins, and the weight crushed Him. But always we have to be on guard lest we fall by the way and forget that without Him we can do nothing. Because "spiritual vitality drains out of us with each sin, on account of things left undone as well as those done amiss," we have constant need of every scrap of grace the God of our salvation offers us. Did not Paul mean that we can walk without stumbling when he said, *"I can do all things through Christ who strengtheneth me"* (Philippians 4:13)?

Questions to Ask and Apply: As we pray that the evil one may have no advantage over us, and that we may be kept upright and victorious, let us ask ourselves as we close each day:

+ Have I resolutely avoided persons and places and circumstances which might have caused me to err from the way?
+ Have I taken pains to discover the sin easily besetting me?

---

18. Isaac Watts, "Alas! And Did My Savior Bleed?" 1707.

+ Have I been sincere in my desire for the destruction of all that is antagonistic in my life to the divine will?

Suggestions for Intercession:

Supplicate the throne:

+ that grace may be ours never to falter no matter the nature of our cross, and enter thereby into the fellowship of His sufferings.
+ that we may be ever ready to relieve the burdened saints we may meet on the rugged pilgrimage of life.

Closing Prayer:

By Thy cross and passion, O Lord, may I be continually empowered to overcome sin, and to do Thy will. Because Thou wast prostrate beneath Thy cross, raise me from the death of sin unto newness of life. Cleanse me from grievous sins and faults, and subdue any rebellion of will of which I may have been guilty. In adversity save me from failing by reason of weakness and make me more than a conqueror, for the Redeemer's sake. Amen.

Christ Consoles the Weeping Women (Luke 23:28–31)

Hymn: "At Even, Ere the Sun Was Set"

Prayer:

O Savior, Thou who art so considerate and compassionate, as we continue to follow Thy way to Calvary, we would mourn over Thy sufferings and over the way sin had defaced Thy image within our lives. Enable us so to weep over our failures, and then be comforted by Thy merciful pardon. Vouchsafe unto us the fruits of Thy passion and compassion. Deliver us from grieving the Holy Spirit by our sins, negligence, and ignorance, and enable us to live for Thy pleasure. Hear us, we beseech Thee, and hearing forgive and bless, through Thy name alone. Amen.

Narrative: At this place in Christ's suffering, we think again of the sisters of mercy in the great company of people walking with Jesus to the place of a skull, those who bewailed and lamented Him. Unashamed of the feelings toward the heavenly sufferer, they openly expressed their concern and compassion. Their tears revealed the love of their hearts for the One, born of a woman, who was about to die. Suffering as He was, Jesus paused to console the women of Jerusalem. Foreseeing all the horrors awaitingthem with the fall of the city, He bade them weep, not for His woe, but for the sufferings awaiting them.

Meditation: Our Lord was not harsh in His rejection of the tears of those Jerusalem women. One wonders whether He detected a shallow emotionalism in their weeping. Were their sobs those of intuitive women who knew that Christ was suffering unjustly or were they the result of a purely natural revulsion at the sight of physical anguish? Had it been Barabbas falling beneath the cross, as it should have been, would they have wept just the same?

What Christ did was to redirect and deepen their sorrow. Weep the women must, not only for His temporary suffering, but also for the sin of man in rejecting Him, and crucifying Him outside the city wall. With our smitten hearts we weep over His wounds and the stain of His blood on the stones on the way to Golgotha, but do we weep enough over our sin that took Him to the cross and nailed Him thereon?

> For sin I mourn, the sin that gave Thee pain;
> Thine was the burden, mine alone the stain;
> Lord, I repent; accept my tears and grief:
> Christ is my Joy; and out of all distress
> He doth deliver with His righteousness:
> Lord, I believe; help Thou mine unbelief.[19]

Questions to Ask and Apply: As we think of the compassionate women and the compassionate Savior, do we know what it is to weep with those who weep?

1. Does suffering merely move us or are we deeply stirred to help as well as weep?
2. When moved with compassion, is there the urge to bind up the wounds of the sufferer?
3. Is ours the fellow-feeling that makes us wondrous kind?
4. Do we weep enough over human wrongs as to redress them at any cost?

Suggestions for Intercession:
We must pray:

+ for Calvary hearts
+ for strength to suffer in unison with Christ
+ for insight into our needs, as well as of those around us
+ for grace and courage to stand firm and true when the dark days come

19. John S. B. Monsell, "My Sins Has Taken Such a Hold on Me," 1866.

✦ for the blessed moment when God shall wipe away all tears
Closing Prayer:

Our Heavenly Father, as we approach Thee in and through the merits of Thy beloved Son, our Savior, we beseech Thee to grant us compassionate hearts—bowels of mercy! Thou who didst acknowledge the tears of those who wept at Thy sufferings look down in mercy upon all those whose tear-stained faces look up to Thee, and give them to know that as the Man of Sorrows, and fully acquainted with their guilt and grief, Thou doest wait to give them the oil of joy for mourning. In Thy name do we ask these favors. Amen.

The Third Fall Beneath the Cross

Hymn: "There Is a Green Hill Far Away"
Prayer:

O Lord, while we may never know or be able to tell what pains Thou didst bear in our room and stead, impress the vision of Thy sufferings indelibly on our hearts and minds that we may truly hate sin. Spare us from imperfect penitence and any unreal acts of contrition. May ours be a genuine sorrow for all that is unworthy of Thee! Thou who didst allow Thyself to be led as a Lamb to the slaughter and opened not Thy mouth in protest, enable us to manifest the same resignation to the will of the Father. Strengthen us, for apart from Thy grace we are so frail and easily fall. According to Thy mercies, O Lord. Amen.

Narrative: Our finite minds cannot understand all that is meant by the phrase, "He endured the cross." Almost at Calvary, Jesus again reveals His humanity in His failing strength and stumbling steps. Early in His ministry, when weary with His journey, He could rest at the well and be refreshed by its cool and refreshing water. Now, so exhausted and pain-stricken, there is no respite. Falling, He is dragged to His feet by the heathen soldiers, and cruelly goaded the last few yards of His blood-marked way. None of the ransomed will ever know how dark the night was that the Lord passed through for their redemption. The way to the cross was strewn with much anguish, but for the joy beyond the cross, He endured all its agonies.

Meditation: How the weak and stumbling Christ reveals what Paul calls *"the weakness of God"* (1 Corinthians 1:25). Not for one moment were the painful shoulders relieved of the harsh touch of the tree, which He, as the

Creator, had fashioned. Had He not said, *"He that endureth to the end shall be saved"* (Matthew 10:22)? Here He practiced what He preached! Although very God of very God, He did not exert His omnipotence to save Himself further anguish. He permitted the brutal insistence of the crowd and the injustice of His executioners to force Him to drain the dregs of His cup of suffering as they forced Him on to the summit of Calvary. Ignominy and indignity were heaped upon Him, but He *"despised the shame."* He paid to the uttermost farthing for our salvation.

It is not difficult to apply this thought to our hearts. Jesus might have despaired, but He struggled on until His weary, blood-covered body was nailed to the cross. Despair led Judas to take his own life, and despair can damage the nerve of our spiritual life. Distressed by our failures, we tend to lose confidence and remain crushed and helpless under our repeated lapses. Despair robs us of hope and we doubt God's willingness and ability to stretch out His hand and lift us up out of our sin and misery. But it does not matter how far down we may be. He is able to lift us up out of the pit, and set our feet upon a rock, and, thereafter, keep us from falling.

Questions to Ask and Apply: As Jesus seemed to have no power of His own to release the crushing weight He bore, do we realize that we have no might against the enemies of our souls?

1. When we fall in sin, do we despair and remain fallen? Or do we turn at once to the Savior in penitence and faith, seeking His merciful forgiveness?

2. When cast down, do we despair of victory? Or do we seek out the causes of our failure and remedy them?

3. When we stumble and fall, do we feel that our sin or backsliding is too grave for God to forgive? Or do we truly repent and trust Him to restore our soul?

Suggestions for Intercession:

Let us pray:

+   that we may be ever conscious that we have no power of ourselves to save or keep ourselves.

+   that we may be prevented from frequent relapses into sin.

+   that ever conscious of our frailty, we may constantly hang upon the skirt of God.

+   that grace may be ours to persevere.

+   that in our last hour, pains of death will not dim our glorious hope.

Closing Prayer:

Gracious Savior, grant us the gift of perseverance. If we have fallen, raise us up and crush Satan under our feet. We beseech Thee to comfort and assist the weak-hearted, to give repentance to the sick and dying whose hearts have been destitute of Thy grace. Constantly deliver us from all evil hateful to Thee and hurtful to our hearts. Through Thy supporting grace, make us more than conquerors. Stand with us, and enable us to stand until we rest in peace. Hear us, we beseech Thee, for Thy mercy's sake. Amen.

Jesus Stripped of His Garments (Matthew 27:35)

Hymn: "In the Cross of Christ I Glory"
Prayer:

O Lord, Thou who didst lay aside the garments of eternal glory and majesty and wrap Thyself around with the robe of our humanity, and became obedient unto death, even the death of the cross, enable us to fully understand all that Thou didst suffer when Thou didst make Thyself of no reputation for our sakes. Because of the indignities endured when coarse and brutal men stripped Thee of Thy garments, help us to voluntarily humble ourselves before Thee. Strip us of all false shame, conceit, and pride, and clothe us with Thy holiness. In ourselves, we are naked in Thy sight, but we look to Thee for dress. Clothe us with Thy own humility, for Thy name's sake. Amen.

Narrative: Reaching Calvary, Jesus is prepared by the soldiers for crucifixion, which involved divesting the victim of all his clothing. Thus the prophetic word was fulfilled in this act of indignity which the Savior suffered, *"They parted my garments among them and upon my vesture did they cast lots"* (Psalm 22:18; Matthew 27:35; John 19:24). As He stood there, God-made Man, before the gaze of the mocking crowd, all who saw Him laughed Him to scorn.

> Bearing shame and scoffing rude,
> In my place condemned He stood.[20]

Because of His holiness and most sensitive nature, this divesture of His garments must have been hard to bear. He willingly laid aside the robe of His past glory. Now the linen clothes covering His human form are torn from

---

20. Phillip P. Bliss, "Hallelujah! What a Savior," 1875.

Him by loveless hands. How those who loved Him must have hidden their faces as the soldiers stripped Him and gambled for His seamless robe!

Meditation: Jesus entered the world in abject poverty. Rich before He left heaven, He became poor for our sakes, and for thirty years His life was one of obscurity and poverty. He carried His poverty with Him through His public ministry, and from the earthly point of view had no home, possessions, or security. When He urged the rich young ruler to sell all he had to follow Him, He was only asking him to follow His example. Now, in the moment of death, His lifelong poverty reaches its climax, for He died in the nakedness of utter want, and was buried in a borrowed grave. He had brought nothing into the world and at the end carried nothing out. He died as naked as when He was born of Mary. But blessed be His name, through His poverty we are made rich. Through His willingness to be humiliated, grace can be ours to renounce all attachments alien to His will and through such remuneration, attain full spiritual worth.

Questions to Ask and Apply: How are we affected by Christ's reduction to the nakedness of abject poverty? Are our consciences stirred so that we ask our hearts...

1. If we are poor, does poverty make us envious, bitter, and resentful of rich evildoers?
2. If we regard the luxuries of life as necessities, are we tempted to exercise undue desire for material possessions?
3. If we are tempted to indulge in excessive eating and clothing, are we tempted to turn a deaf ear to the voice of the Bible, as to fasting and abstinence?
4. If we have more than enough, do we strip ourselves of superfluous food and clothing that multitudes of starving souls might be fed, and more sufficiently clothed?

Suggestions for Intercession:

We must pray:

+ that all the filthy rags of greed, gluttony, fornication, all the deceits of the world, the flesh, and the devil, as well as our own self-righteousness be torn from us.
+ that a greater measure of self-denial may be ours to help the multitudes who are in need, both spiritually and materially.
+ that because Christ endured the shame of being stripped on account of our most shameful deeds, we might be found humbling ourselves in His sight.

◆   that when we find ourselves destitute of friends or material possessions, we may be consoled by the fact that God will not hide His face from us, but hasten to our aid.

Closing Prayer:

Thou Man of Sorrows, who sounded the depths of poverty, shame and suffering for our sakes, and who has invested us with the garments of righteousness and grace, enable us to be more closely identified with Thee in Thy renunciation of the flesh. Mercifully hear us as we confess our indulgences, and by the Spirit's power enable us to crucify the flesh with its affections and lusts. Prepare us to adorn our wedding garments at the marriage of the Lamb for Thy sake. Amen.

Jesus Is Nailed to the Cross (Matthew 27:35)

Hymn: "Beneath the Cross of Jesus"

Prayer:

As we draw near to Thy cross, Thou crucified, risen and now glorified Savior, help us to understand what it meant for Thee, the holy One, to take away our sin. Our sins were the nails that fastened Thee to the tree, and by Thy death Thou, didst blot out the handwriting that was against us. May unfailing, constant grace be ours to crucify the old man in us, and to die daily to the approach and appeal of our corrupt Adamic nature. As we survey the wondrous cross on which Thou, as the young "Prince of glory," didst die, may ours be a lively sense of faith that condemnation is no longer ours, because of Thy pierced hands and feet. May all who are still in the bondage of sin come to experience the loosing of their sins through the blood of Thy cross! May all who are Thine live as those who have been bought with a price! In Thy name do we pray. Amen.

Narrative: Reaching the place called Calvary, the heavy cross Jesus had struggled to carry was laid on the ground. Then His crucifiers stretched His crimson-stained body upon it, and drove the nails through His hands and feet. The cross, with its grim burden, was then raised, its foot being forced into an earth socket. Christ had two companions in His brutal death, for with Him were crucified two malefactors, one on the right hand, and the other on the left. Thus three crosses stood on that "hill ascending" with one man dying in sin, another dying to sin, and the Man Christ Jesus dying for sin.

Meditation: On the cross Jesus was numbered among His transgressors, and hanging upon a tree was accursed—cursed of God according to Jewish belief and tradition. *"Cursed is everyone that hangeth on a tree"* (Deuteronomy 21:23; Galatians 3:13). That old, rugged cross was proof enough for any orthodox Jew that the man nailed to it could not possibly be the Messiah. To Jewry of that time Jesus was an impostor, and they would not recognize His claim to reign over them. But, for the disciples, the One dying on that tree was their Lord. He had proclaimed Himself as *"the truth"* (John 14:6), but the spiritually blind fail to recognize and reward integrity when they see it personified. Thus the body prepared for Christ, and the perfect instrument of the divine will, is now tortured and humiliated. The hands that blessed and healed, and the feet ever swift and tireless on errands of mercy are now made fast by Roman nails to a cross, and the voice of truth is almost silenced. The heart so full of love for God and man is about to be pierced with a cruel spear. Cruel treatment could not injure the inner citadel of trust in God; all it could do was to destroy the outer physical form—kill the body, but not the soul.

The wonder of His cross is that Christ's life was not taken, but given. He gave Himself to save the lost. Having power to lay down His life and take it up again, His death and resurrection were both voluntary.

> Thirty years among us dwelling,
> His appointed time fulfilled,
> Born for this, He meets His Passion
> For that this He freely willed.
> On the Cross the Lamb is lifted,
> Where His life-blood shall be spilled.[21]

Questions to Ask and Apply: Contemplating how Jesus gave His back to the smiters and hid not His face from shame, are we brought to the spiritual significance of cross-bearing?

1. Are our lives as those emancipated from the guilt and government of sin marked by a cross, or are we somewhat indulgent and lazy?
2. Are we subject to the Spirit's prompting to voluntarily submit to discipline? Is our cross endured?
3. Are the hardships and trials coming to us because of our Christian profession and witness received as coming to us with God's permission?

---

21. Venantius Fortunatus, "Thirty Years Among Us Dwelling," 569.

    4.   Are we willing to become reasonable, holy, living sacrifices, acceptable unto God?

Suggestions for Intercession: As the Holy Spirit was a witness of the sufferings of Christ who, through the eternal Spirit offered Himself up to God:

+ let us ask Him to take of the mystery and meaning of the cross and reveal them to our hearts.
+ let us pray that we may be more closely identified with Jesus in His death, and accept shame and suffering for His name's sake, and bear in our body the marks of His dying.
+ let us pray that we may be kept from being cross Christians, living only as Christians of the cross.

Closing Prayer:

O Lord, who in Thy bitter passion didst taste death for every man, accept our thanks for deliverance from the condemnation our manifold sins deserved. When we fail Thee, grant us truly contrite hearts as we seek the shelter of Thy blood. Constantly preserve us from those sins which would prevent our tongues from proclaiming Thy truth, our hands from serving Thee, and our feet from following Thee. Help us to lay in dust life's glory dead, and in all our works, words and ways so to live as to cause Thee to see of the travail of Thy soul and be satisfied. Because Thou didst die for us, by Thy grace and power may we ever live for Thee, through Thy name. Amen.

Jesus Died Upon the Cross
(Matthew 27:50; Mark 15:37; Luke 23:46; John 19:30)

Hymn: "And Can It Be That I Should Gain?"
Prayer:

Blessed Redeemer, Son of the living God, who didst die for the salvation of a lost world, and upon the gibbet of the cross suffer and die for the forgiveness and removal of our sins, strengthen us in our endeavor to die daily unto sin, and to live as unto Thee. Obedient unto death, O Lord, may we be obedient unto Thee in all things. May daily grace be ours to fight under the banner of Thy cross against all evil! Make Thy victory over Satan and sin to be our victory. Help us to follow Thee in the train of Thy triumph, for Thy name's sake. Amen.

Narrative: For three long hours Jesus hung upon His cross, and what notable hours they were. In spite of His mounting agony, shame, and thirst, think of what He accomplished. He forgave His murderers—gave the penitent thief the promise of paradise—fulfilled prophecies of His death, committed His dear mother and His beloved disciple, John, to each other's care, bowed His head and, as He died in triumph, surrendered His spirit to His eternal Father. When He cried with a loud voice, *"It is finished,"* He knew that He slew death and made it possible for us to live evermore with Him. By His one offering He consummated a full, perfect, and sufficient sacrifice for a world of sinners lost and ruined by the fall.

Meditation: We are born to live; Christ was born to die. In a past eternity, love drew salvation's plan, and at Calvary that perfect plan was executed, for Christ was manifested and crucified to destroy the works of the devil. Because the life of the flesh is in the blood, when Jesus spilled His blood, He gave His life in order to deliver us from eternal death. The immensity of God's love is revealed in the completeness of that sacrifice upon the cross which, although was instrument of torture and death, was made the channel of salvation, life, and hope. For the crucified Savior, a crown of glory substitutes the crown of thorns. By His out poured blood, broken body, and agonizing death, He has every right to exhort us to crucify the old man and its lusts.

> Were the whole realm of nature mine,
> That were a present far too small;
> Love so amazing, so divine,
> Demands my soul, my life, my all.[22]

Questions to Ask and Apply: We are told that Christ did not save Himself when He was taunted to do so. What message does His self-renunciation and sacrifice have for your heart and mine?

1. Do we believe that the life of self is death, but that the death of self is life?

2. Do we accept it as one of the essentials of Christian living that we must die to self-love, self-will, self-honor, and self-aggrandizement?

3. Do we recognize that selfishness is sin and that we must resist it unto blood, striving at all times to exhibit in daily life that God is first?

4. Do we constantly pray—

---

22. Isaac Watts, "When I Survey the Wondrous Cross," 1707.

> Teach me, O Lord, to serve Thee as Thou deservest:
> To fight and not to heed the wounds,
> To toil and not to seek for rest,
> To labor and not to seek for any reward,
> Save that of knowing that I do Thy will, O Lord?

Suggestions for Intercession:
As we think of the dying Savior, let us pray...

+ for all those entering upon their last agony who may be dying in fear, neglected by friends, and alone that they might die in faith and in the fear of the Lord.
+ for ourselves that when we come to journey through the valley of the shadow of evil we may be conscious of the embrace of the arms of Him who died to deliver us from the fear of death.
+ for grace to live so that in our last hour grace will be ours to die in triumph.
+ that we may manifest the forgiveness of the cross, proclaim its message of hope for the repentant, and emulate its care for the welfare of our own.

Closing Prayer:

O Thou crucified, risen, and glorified Savior, victor of sin, death, and hell, grant that we may ever remember that we are crucified with Thee, and that because we died in that death of Thine, we now live in Thee, and like Thee are alive evermore. Sustain us by Thy grace as we seek the sinful, succor the sick, the suffering, and the sorrowful, and comfort the bereaved. When we come to die later may ours be the death of the righteous and a joyful entrance into the heavenly abode where Thou livest and reignest for ever and ever. This we ask in Thy name. Amen.

Jesus Is Taken From the Cross
(Matthew 27:59; Mark 15:46; Luke 23:53; John 19:40)

Hymn: "One Day"
Prayer:

Truly, O Lord, there was no sorrow like unto Thy sorrow! Godforsaken and rejected of men what anguish was Thine, yet Thou didst die in triumph, committing Thyself to Thy Father's care. Through Thy cross may we learn love's endless gift of love, and ever be found abiding 'neath the shadow of the cross. Loving hands removed Thy marred body from the tree, and clothing and perfuming it prepared it for the grave, but it was not suffered to see corruption, for death could not keep its prey. As loyal hearts cared for that lifeless body of Thine, may grace be ours to be kind, sympathetic, considerate and helpful toward those experiencing the ravages of death, ever remembering the end of our own journey. For Thy name's sake. Amen.

Narrative: The soldiers, having meted out the death decreed by the Roman government for criminals, leave the sordid scene as do the curious crowd who could witness such a brutal spectacle without emotion. *"Sitting down they watched him there"* (Matthew 27:36). But there on Calvary's summit was His mother, Mary Magdalene, Nicodemus, and Joseph of Arimathea who, taking the body from the cross, reverently paid it their last respect and tenderly bore it to a borrowed grave. Joseph wrapped that sacred body in a clean linen cloth and laid it in his own, new tomb. He rolled a large stone to the door of the sepulcher and went home. Thus, in His death and burial, Jesus was one with the human race doomed to die in sin. He was made like unto us except without sin. *"The soul that sinneth, it shall die"* (Ezekiel 18:4). Jesus was sinless, yet He died. He tasted death for every man. Made sin for us, He suffered the dire consequences of sin. Thus, low in the grave He laid, Jesus our Lord.

Meditation: The most conspicuous mourner at the cross and at the grave in the garden was the mother. Mary stood by the cross until her Son expired, and her presence must have consoled Him in His last hours. It is not without reason that she has been spoken of as the "Queen of Martyrs." Who is able to plumb the depth of sorrow she experienced as she gazed on her dead Son and assisted in His burial? When she brought her first-born Son into the world, it was prophesied that a sword would pierce her heart. Calvary must have been the deepest thrust of the sword of anguish. Yet at this tragic moment of her grief, she was still *"the handmaid of the Lord"* and lovingly gave back to God the Son whom He had given her. Our Lord did not suffer that His own might be exempt from suffering, but that they may be sanctified and ennobled through suffering. Mary, following the dead body of her Son to the tomb, exemplifies this. Thus, "through our tears and the pain of our infinitely lesser Calvaries, we should fix our eyes on those two figures, praying to learn from them the true Christian acceptance of suffering."

Questions to Ask and Apply: Are we conscious of those renunciations we must make when we examine our own hearts?

1. Have we asked forgiveness of those we have injured in any way by our sin and selfishness?

2. Have we sought by practical help and sympathy to help others bear this trial, sorrow and adversity?

3. Have we, according to our ability and opportunities been active in works of mercy?

4. Have we endeavored to give those we love bouquets of lovely flowers while they are alive to appreciate them?

5. Have we always been calm, submissive and trustful in the dark and difficult hours of life?

Suggestions for Intercession:

Let us pray...

+ that all who mourn may be divinely comforted.
+ that all who cry to God out of sorrow may be consoled by the remembrance that He is ever present in affliction.
+ that we may be made aware of the brevity and uncertainty of life, as well as number our days and apply our hearts to wisdom.
+ that in the hour of our departure we shall not be forsaken of friends.
+ that while we live, we may be found standing faithfully by the cross.

Closing Prayer:

Our blessed Redeemer, may all the glorious effects of Thy passion be experienced by us. Mercifully grant that, as those redeemed by Thy shed blood, we may never forget the sword that pierced Thy holy heart, and also the heart of the loving mother whose womb bore Thee. May we be fully prepared against the hour of death so that if we come to Thee by the way of a grave, our closing breath will praise Thee! By Thy grace, enable us to be obedient unto death. We present our petition in Thy merits and name, O Savior. Amen.

Jesus in the Tomb
(Matthew 27:60; Mark 15:46; Luke 23:53; John 19:41–42)

Hymn: "Low in the Grave He Lay"

Prayer:

Our Father who art in heaven, as we venture nigh through the merits of Thy Son who told His own that none can approach Thee save through His mediation, prepare our hearts for a further meditation upon all that Thou didst accomplish for unworthy sinners through

Thy death, burial, and resurrection. Thou who didst destroy death and defeat the devil, cause us to experience more deeply what it means to be buried with Thee in baptism unto death. Grant us a fresh and fuller cleansing from sin, and lift us from all dead things to the risen, higher life in Thyself. We praise Thee that Thou didst rise from the grave with an uncorrupted body, and ascend on high as our forerunner and advocate. In Thy name. Amen.

Narrative: Once the washed, clothed, and anointed body of Jesus was placed in the new tomb, the entrance was closed and sealed by the edict of the Roman government because of the rumor circulating that the crucified Nazarene would rise again. But only His precious lifeless form was in the grave awaiting the hour of prophesied resurrection. Jesus Himself was not in the place of death but was sharing the paradise He had promised the repentant thief. His soul had departed and was resting in peace with the faithful in Abraham's bosom. His passion ended in paradise, just as when we die we depart to be with Christ in heaven.

Meditation: Buried with Christ implies our death to sin and the newness of life He calls us to. The Anglican Baptismal Service reminds us that "Baptism doth represent unto us our Christian profession; which is to follow the example of our Savior Christ and to be made like unto Him; that as He died and rose again for us, so should we who are baptized die from sin and rise again unto righteousness." The gospel hymn says it well—

> Dying He saved me,
> Buried He carried my sins far away.[23]

Identified with Christ in His death, burial, and resurrection, we appropriate by faith making actual, thereby, in life all He made possible by His passion. Ours is a daily death when we bury in a tomb by confession and penitence the sins that would easily beset us. It is only in the power of the resurrection that we can live in conformity with the will of Him who is the risen head of His church.

Questions to Ask and Apply: We now come to a deep need to examine ourselves to discover how real and vital our union with Christ is.

1. Is our separation from the dead and beggarly elements of the world as marked as it ought to be?
2. Is the old life as deeply buried in Christ's grave as it ought to be? Is the old man completely dead?
3. Is freedom from the corruption of sin ours? Are we being saved daily from the government and power of sin by His risen, glorified,

---

23. L. Wilbur Chapman, "Living, He Loved Me; Dying, He Saved Me."

throne life? Did not Paul affirm that being saved from the guilt of past sin, by the blood of Christ, we can know what it is to be saved day by day from the dominion by Christ's risen life?

4.   Is ours the glorious hope of the resurrection at the coming of the Lord when all in Christ are to be raised to meet Him in the air?

Suggestions for Intercession:

Let us pray:

+ that if we come down to a grave and our sinful bodies return to the dust from whence they came, that the blessed assurance of life forever more will enable us to confess, "*O death, where is thy sting; O grave, where is thy victory*"?

+ that as we contact the dying and bereaved, our ministry will be one of consolation and hope.

+ that if we find ourselves in the presence of the dying who are not prepared to meet God, faithfulness will be ours to persuade them to seek the shelter of the precious blood of Jesus and thereby die in peace. Precious in His sight is the death of His saints.

Closing Prayer:

O Lord, because apart from the shedding of blood there is no remission of sins, we plead anew the merits of Thy passion. Purge our hearts anew and make us Thy profitable servants. Grant us a contrite heart for our conscious sins, and help us share Thy hatred for evil. We offer Thee not only our unworthiness, but also our love and obedience, and trust Thee for grace to walk in the light as Thou are in the light. In all sincerity we pray...

> Grant me a clean heart to see Thee,
> Detachment of spirit to serve Thee,
> True recollection to know Thee.
> Conform my spirit to Thy blessed human nature.
> Conform my soul to Thy holy soul,
> Conform my body to Thy most pure body.
> Free me from all that prevents my union with Thee. Amen.

Other hymns the preacher can use are those arranged around the cardinal points of the passion by Charles Wesley, whose hundreds of hymns are part of our spiritual heritage. Truly poetical, staunchly orthodox, and deeply devotional, all of them can be used as prayers—

- "God of Unexampled Grace"
- "The Sacred Heart"
- "Now I Have the Ground Wherein"
- "Two Bleeding Wounds He Bears"
- "Arise, My Soul Arise, Shake Off Thy Guilty Fear"
- "O Let Me Kiss Thy Bleeding Feet"
- "Neither Passion nor Pride, Thy Cross Can Abide"
- "Then Let Me Sit Beneath His Cross"
- "Arise, My Soul Arise, Thy Savior's Sacrifice"
- "Would Jesus Have the Sinner Die?"
- "Never Love nor Sorrow Was"
- "All Ye that Pass by, to Jesus Draw Nigh"
- "Lamb of God, Whose Dying Love"
- "O Thou Eternal Victim Slain"
- "Entered the Holy Place Above"
- "O God of Our Forefathers, Hear"
- "Let All Who Truly Bear, the Bleeding Savior's Name"
- "Why Did My Dying Lord Ordain"
- "We Need Not Now Go up to Heaven"
- "Lo! He Comes with Clouds Descending"

John W. Peterson, noted American gospel songwriter, has also written many Easter or Lenten cantatas. Among them are:

- "Behold Your King"
- "Hail, Glorious King"
- "The Glory of Easter"
- "Love Transcending"
- "No Greater Love"

And still other favorite American gospel Lenten hymns are:

- "'Tis Midnight—and on Olive's Brow"
- "Hallelujah, What a Savior"
- "Go to Dark Gethsemane"
- "Immortal Love, Forever Full"
- "Fairest Lord Jesus"
- "Jesus Paid It All"
- "Blessed Calvary"
- "My Redeemer"
- "Wounded for Me"
- "He Was Wounded for Our Transgressions"

+ "My Savior's Love"
+ "Bleeding Hands"
+ "He Carried the Cross for Me"
+ "His Wonderful Look of Love"
+ "Behold the Lamb of God"
+ "That Day at Calvary"
+ "Throned Upon the Awful Tree"
+ "Sweet the Moments, Rich in Blessing"
+ "Come to Calvary's Holy Mountain"

In his adaptation of sermon suggestions we have indicated under *Programs* and *Preaching*, the Pastor will find illustrative and poetical material to enlighten and enforce the Holy Week messages under Chapters 5 and 6 of this Sourcebook. For prayers to guide him in the devotional part of a service, attention is drawn to Chapter 6.

THE DAYS OF PASSION WEEK

In a companion volume to this sourcebook, bearing the title, *The Week That Changed the World*, I endeavored to produce a harmony from the four gospels as to the happenings on each day of our Lord's last week, from Palm Sunday to Easter Day. At this point, we briefly sketch how the Holy Week can be divided up, if services are held each day of the period.

Palm Sunday (Matthew 21:1–11; Luke 19:28–38)
The Day of Triumph

Although Jesus enacted in detail the prophecy about *"a King coming to you, gentle and mounted on an ass"* (Zechariah 9:9), the crowds did not actually recognize Him, for they shouted, *"Who is this?"* Approaching Jerusalem, He wept over the city's ignorance of the conditions necessary for peace—namely, justice, righteousness, and the recognition of God's laws.

Monday (Matthew 21:12–14; Mark 11:15–17)
The Day of Authority

While this period of eight days has been referred to as the "still week," it was certainly not still for Jesus whose days were crowded with incidents. Reaching Jerusalem, He entered the temple which He cleansed and declared His messianic authority, only to have it challenged by His foes. He sought to free the religious life of the city from abuses which had come to be accepted.

Tuesday (Matthew 23:37–38; Mark 12:28–34)
The Day of Controversy

What a day of questioning and of action this was! The answer to questions Jesus gave in the temple, were so clear and compelling as to bring an end to the interrogation. Then there came the parables of the two sons; the wicked husbandman, the ten virgins; the talents; the marriage of the king's son; the tribute to Caesar; the resurrection; the Greatest Commandment; the discourse against the scribes and Pharisees; the two mites;buried seed; the coming judgment; all combined to make this day of word and action one of the most outstanding of the week.

Wednesday (Matthew 21:17; Mark 14:3–9)
The Day of Retirement

After His appearance before the nation and the temple, Jesus sought the solitude of the home of His friends at Bethany. While there, a woman surprises and shocks those gathered within the home by anointing Him with a box of expensive perfume. Judas' calculation suggests that it was a wasteful act, but love does not stop to calculate. Therefore, Jesus commended the woman's generosity in anointing Him for burial. Mary's act was symbolic of His cross. She kept nothing back. Nothing was too costly for Him who was about to offer up Himself for man's redemption.

Thursday (John 13:1–17, 35; Luke 22:7–39)
The Day of Fellowship

The preparation for the Passover, the feet-washing, the Lord's Supper, the farewell conversations, and the high priest prayer were not fully understood by the disciples until the events of Easter were over. It was only after Christ's ascension and the coming of the Holy Spirit that they truly understood the character of God revealed by Christ. At the conclusion of this day He said, "Arise! Let us go hence" (John 14:31), which meant going out into the midnight ending at Calvary.

Friday (Matthew 26:36–27:61; Luke 23:32–43; Colossians 1:19–22)
The Day of His Cup

It would be interesting to know how this dark day came to be called Good Friday. It certainly was not "good" for Jesus who died in agony and shame. Good for us? Yes! Had He not died the just for the unjust, we would not have had hope of eternal life. He was crucified between two thieves, and in spite of His extreme suffering, Jesus guided one of the criminals into the presence of God. Those who are branded as "criminals" and cast outside of society are never outside the love of God, and, by the token of the dying, repentant thief on Calvary, ought to be our particular concern.

Saturday (Matthew 27:62–66; John 20:3–8)
The Day of the Grave

Elaborate precautions were taken to insure that Jesus would remain in the sepulcher. The forces of organized religion, the authority of the State, and the power of the military conspired to prevent Jesus from fulfilling His repeated prophecy about rising from the dead. The disciples were so distraught and demoralized by the events of the Friday, that the foes of the One who was reposed in the new tomb had no occasion to fear any action on their part to rob the grave of its treasure. But death and the plotters could not keep their prey for Jesus arose a victor o'er the dark domain.

Easter Sunday (Matthew 28:1–20; John 20:1–20)
The Day of Resurrection

Our Lord's declaration as to what happened on that Friday, Saturday, and Sunday should ever be remembered: *"I am he that liveth, and was dead; and, behold, I am alive for evermore, Amen; and have the keys of hell and of death"* (Revelation 1:18). The startling facts of Easter became the basis and the driving force of the witness of the early church. Her central message was: *"God hath made that same Jesus, whom ye have crucified, both Lord and Christ"* (Acts 2:36).

The Spirit-empowered disciples knew that they had been summoned as heralds to proclaim a Savior who had died, but whom God raised from the dead. And out they went to proclaim forgiveness of sin, power to live as sons of God, the assurance of eternal bliss, and the abiding presence of God. No wonder their radiant faith in a risen, glorified Lord turned the world upside down.

EASTER MESSAGE FOR WOMEN'S GROUP

During Passion Week, women of a church usually plan an Easter service of their own, and if the pastor is asked to give the message on such an occasion, the following exposition might help him. If a fitting poem is required, there is none better than that by Christina Rossetti, sister of the famed poet and painter, Dante Gabriel Rossetti. A poet in her own right, Christina Rossetti expressed some of her finest talent in religious verse, as found in her poem entitled *Good Friday*:

Am I a stone, and not a sheep
That I can stand, O Christ, beneath Thy cross,
To number, drop by drop Thy blood's slow loss,
And yet not weep?

Not so those women loved
Who with exceeding grief lamented Thee;
Not so fallen Peter weeping bitterly;
Not so the thief was moved;

Not so the sun and moon
Which hid their faces in a starless sky,
A horror of great darkness at broad noon—
I, only I.

Yet give not o'er
But seek Thy sheep, true Shepherd of the flock;
Greater than Moses, turn and look once more
And smite a rock.

The Women at the Cross

Now there stood by the cross of Jesus his mother, and his mother's sister, Mary the wife of Cloephas, and Mary Magdalene. When Jesus therefore saw his mother, and the disciple standing by, whom he loved, he saith unto his mother, Woman, behold thy son! Then saith he to the disciple, Behold thy mother! And from that hour that disciple took her unto his own home.

(John 19:25–27)

In his work, *Suffering Savior*, Dr. Krummacher wrote:

...a society had been formed in Paris, the sittings of which the most celebrated infidels of the time used weekly to attend, in order, as they phrased it, to "discover the absurdities of the Bible," and make them the object of their ridicule. But one evening when the members were busy at their work, and for their devilish purpose had read some portions of the Gospel, the well-known philosopher, Diderot, who had hitherto been the last and least voluble of the blasphemers, suddenly began to say with a gravity which was customary with him, "However it may be with this book, gentlemen, I freely confess, on behalf of the truth, that I know no one, either in France, or in the whole world, who is able to speak and write with more tact and talent than the fishermen and publicans who have written these narratives; and I venture to assert, that not one of us is capable of writing even, approximately, a tale which is so simple, and at the same time so sublime, so lovely and affecting; and having such powerful influence on the mind, and possessing such unwearied and pervading effect after the lapse of centuries, as each individual account of the sufferings and death of Jesus Christ, in the book before us." He ceased, and all at once, instead of the laughter which shortly before had run through the hall, a general and profound silence ensued. The truth of the speech was felt, and perhaps even something more. The company solemnly broke up, and it was not long before the entire society of scoffers was dissolved.

The biographers of Christ are inimitable writers. What an effort there would be for one of the celebrated correspondents of what is called the "Leading Journal" to describe the events of this chapter for effect! What artistic talent! What struggling inventions of genius there would be to produce an effect! But after all, the impression would be nothing to that of the simple narrative before us.

It is observed by some that these words in the original seem to be broken and jerky, indicating the physical torture of the speaker. Parched with thirst and convulsed with agony, Jesus could only speak abruptly and at intervals. The words are few but full of meaning.

There are four things worthy of devout attention here:

1. *Heroic Love.* This is seen in the presence of the "mother of Jesus," the other women, and John, who was now at the cross. In a temporal sense, they could not have taken a more perilous position. Who was there?

> Priest, beggar, soldier, Pharisee—
> The old, the young, the bond, the free;
> The nation's furious multitude,
> All maddened with the cry for blood.

Yet they stood by the cross, and expressed their sympathy with Him whom *"the nation abhorred,"* against whom it was now launching its fiercest thunders of indignation. The other disciples had fled; even bold and defiant Peter, panic struck, had rushed away. The calm, tender, unpretentious love of John and these women raised them above fear, enabling them to stand. Love is the soul of courage. There is no power on this earth either for endurance or brave deeds equal to that of calm, tender, womanly, affection. You can trust such love. The thing that is called love, which comes out in florid utterances and spasmodic effort, you cannot trust; it is all sound and show. It is the quiet love, like that of contemplative John and those unassuming women that you can rely on. Such love clings to its object as the ivy to the old castle. Green and fresh it will remain amidst the scorching of summer and the blasts of winter. It will survive the ruin of the object it embraces, conceal the ravages which time or fortune may make on it, and spread a beauty over its grave. They say that a woman has more nerve than a man. It is love that steels her nerves and makes her heroic in trial. The man with a giant frame, if he has not love, will be a moral coward.

2. *Parental affliction.* What must Mary have felt when she witnessed the agonies of her wonderful son! Now was fulfilled the prophecy of old Simeon, who took Him in his arms as an infant and said, *"This child is set for the fall and rising of many in Israel…Yea, a sword shall pierce through thy own soul also"* (Luke 2:34–35). Few trials are equal to that of the affectionate mother in the death of her child. Rachaelsin the world over weep for their children and refuse to be comforted. But there are circumstances which tend wonderfully to mitigate the agony of grief in such a case: (a) should the child die in unconscious infancy, or, (b) should he reach maturity and gradually die amongst his friends, or, (c) should he be one of a large number. But Mary had none of these mitigating circumstances. Her son was in the prime of life. He was dying a violent death amongst enemies. It is said of Socrates, that he spent his last hours in quiet amongst his friends. His consoling friends and disciples were about him; and even his executioner was touched with sympathy when he gave the fatal cup of hemlock into his hand. But Mary saw nothing of this kindness toward her son. Then, too, Joseph, her husband, was in his grave. Here is parental affliction! Weeping parents think of Mary.

3. *Filial sympathy.* "*Behold thy son.*" It is as if He had said, "I am leaving the world, but John will be a son to thee." These words must have been as a gleam of unearthly sunshine to Mary, claiming the fury of the tempest.

From this incident I infer…

First: *That no sufferings, however great, can quench love.* The sufferings of Christ at this moment, in intensity and aggravation, surpass all conception. Every nerve of His frame is in torture, a mysterious load of sorrow on His heart—yet, notwithstanding this, He did not forget His mother. Her uplifted, tearful, loving eye met His glance and touched His heart. Christ seems to have forgotten His own sufferings for the moment in His loving concern for His mother. Children, learn a lesson from this! Use no personal inconvenience as a reason for neglecting your parents. This love in death prophecies a reunion.

Second: *That no engagements, however vast, can justify the neglect of domestic duties.* Men much engaged in public life—statesmen, reformers, ministers of the Gospel, and others—are sometimes heard to plead the large number of their engagements as an excuse for inattention to home duties. Let this example of Christ annihilate the sentiment. How vast were His engagements! He was fighting the moral battles of the universe. Earth, heaven, and hell were interested in His position. It was "the hour." It was a crisis in the history of the moral creation. Notwithstanding this, He was alive to His private duties. He tended to his mother.

Third: *That no legacy, however precious, is equal to the legacy of love.* Christ could have made His mother the mistress of an empire. But He did not do so. He left her love. He bequeathed to her the affection of a noble and a loving soul. What is to equal this? Give me cities, empires, continents. What are they in value to one loving soul, the friend of God? Let heaven give me friends, like the sainted John, and the gift will be greater than that of empires.

Fourth: *That no argument, however plausible, can justify us in regarding Mary as an object of worship.* I will bow to no one in profound sympathy for Mary. The mother of Paul, Luther, Milton, or of any great man, I hold in high veneration, but much more so the mother of the Son of God. Albeit I cannot believe that this poor, disconsolate, destitute woman whom Jesus now commended to the charity of John is "The Queen of Heaven."

4. *Obedient Discipleship.* *"From that hour that disciple took her unto his own home"* (John 19:27). "A tradition," says Tholuck, "relates that John would never forsake the dear trust which his dying Savior had committed to him, and that he never went beyond the borders of Palestine until the mother of his Lord had breathed her last in his arms."

    His obedience was prompt and full. "From that hour." He felt the sanctity of the dying request. There are only three admissible reasons supposable for not attending *at once* and *fully* to Christ's commands as John did. (1) If the command is found to be inconsistent with the eternal principles of right. Or, (2) if there are difficulties in the way of obedience which procrastination is likely to remove. Or, (3) if there be good ground to expect an amount of help in the future which is not obtainable now. Such reasons, though supposable, do not exist, and therefore, should be dismissed. From "that very hour" in which the command is first given, begin obeying. *"Whatsoever thy hand findeth to do, do it with thy might"* (Ecclesiastes 9:10).

SERMONIC AIDS

In the development of church life and work in our modern age, pastors find themselves faced with demands encroaching upon their time; so much so, that they do not have the opportunity for the prolonged personal prayer and study periods which their predecessors enjoyed a half a century ago. Today, pastors are called on to serve too many tables (see Acts 6:1–7), and are consequently robbed of the time that is necessary to feast on the Word. Hence, the ever-increasing amount of sermonic literature designed to help hard-pressed pastors is sought to shape in their own way for a pulpit preparation. It is for this end that we give some of our own gathered spoil with the hope that such fuel will assist preachers to kindle their own fire.

Crucified Afresh

Our Savior is sometimes pierced from pulpits—His Golgotha is among the gowns; His Calvary is in a church. It is in many so-called holy places—where least expected—that He hears the old-time cry: *"We will not have this Man to reign over us"* (Luke 19:14).

The dark tragedy of Calvary is being reenacted in these apostate days within the precincts of the church. Jesus receives His deepest wounds where He expects the deepest sympathy. And, let us remember that our homes and businesses are privileged places if we profess to love and serve the Lord. Therefore, let us try as redeemed servants not to wound our anew in these places as well.

It is perfectly true that both Jew and Gentile had a hand in the dark crime of the cross, thus bringing the guilt of Christ's death upon the whole world. It was Pilate, a Gentile ruler, who gave the verdict and committed Jesus to the tree. It was a Gentile's death He died. It was Gentile soldiers who carried out the grim work of killing the spotless Lamb of God.

But let it not be forgotten that these Gentiles were only tools. Pilate, a heathen ruler, tried his best to save Christ from His cruel kinsman.

Listen to Peter on the day of Pentecost: *"Ye men of Israel...Jesus of Nazareth... ye have taken and by wicked hands have crucified and slain"* (Acts 2:22–23). No wonder these Pharisees, scribes, and rulers were pricked to the heart!

Truly we are in the presence of a great mystery here, for it was these devout religious leaders of a professedly holy nation who were guilty of Christ's shameful death. Those who were so exact and particular about the law and temple worship, who even rebuked Christ for His seeming Sabbath desecration, were the men who crucified Christ. He was not surrounded by a furious mob or a horde of wild uncivilized men, thirsting for His blood. Our divine Lord was rejected, wounded to death—beaten and bruised and broken by so-called "holy" men.

Can we realize that the people among whom He came, whose national-ity He took, were the very men who gloated over His cruel death! And yet, strange as it sounds, we are living in days when such a dark crime is being repeated, for Jesus is being wounded in the house of His friends. His foes are still within His household—base, coarse, brutal men, who are sunken in sin.

Many in these days admire Jesus when brought face to face with His claims. Under the preaching of His cross they often fall at His pierced feet in love and submission, rising to live transformed lives, becoming beautiful by His grace.

It is not the wayward and godless who crucify Him afresh, but those in the household of the church. Those who are professedly religious despise Christ's claims and hurry Him out to Calvary. Ministers and laymen who are modern rationalists must be included among His murderers. They may deny it, but the declaration is true. When leaders of religious thought treat Jesus as they do, relegating Him to the place of ordinary humanity, denying His miraculous birth, His sinlessness, His powers of deity, they repeat the crime and cry of the Pharisees, "*Crucify Him!*"

Let us come nearer as we look at our own hearts. Do we realize that it is sadly possible to add to the wounds of Jesus? Whenever we slight Him, disobey His voice, and act contrary to His wishes, we pierce our precious Lord anew. Whenever we spurn the entreaty of the Holy Spirit within and thereby grieve Him, we hurt Jesus as well. We can fasten Him to the cross with the nails of self-love, self-glory, self-pride, and self-righteousness—those most bitter of all nails! Oh, let us add to His pleasure, not His pain!

Crucified! Ah, He is still crucified, or as God's Word puts it, "*crucified afresh.*" Every time we turn away from Jesus, despise His mercy, resist His Spirit, we hurry Him to the cross of rejection. Every time we yield to the devil, we crown the beautiful brow of Jesus with more cruel thorns.

Will not one such terrible death suffice? Is one Calvary not enough? Has Jesus not borne plenty without the addition of more grief and pain? Then why add to it?

When you drown the voice of conscience and silence the inner call of God, you are really slaying the Son of God afresh. When He presents Himself for your choice, all passions and desires rise, crying, "*Crucify Him.*" And the tragedy is that all too often, you are on the side of those forces, insisting upon the expulsion of Christ from your life. The voices of the chief priests prevailed. And thus is it with many a sinner; the siren voices of the world, flesh, and the devil prevail on the inner voice of the Holy Spirit, as He urges your will to release Jesus, giving Him the throne of your life.

God Forsaken

Jesus spoke seven times from the cross, and the poignant question before us constituted His fourth cry. What the utterance means is too deep and mysterious to explain. We can only think of the words with hushed hearts. They must be approached with reverence, for the place where we stand is holy ground.

There we behold the Savior in the depth of His sorrows, for the cry indicates the black midnight of His terror. At this moment, physical weakness was united with acute torture arising from the shame and ignominy through which He passed. The world, of course, had been prepared for such a cry, seeing that it commences the Calvary Psalm where His agonies were foretold with such clarity. (See Psalm 22.) This fourth saying from the cross indicates the bitterest drop in His cup.

My God! My God!

Throughout the Passion Week, Jesus had born His inexpressible agony in sublime silence of soul. Now that this climax was reached, He gave vent to such a heart-rending cry. Martin Luther says that the verse suggests "God forsaken of God!" And the repetition speaks of the depth of anguish Jesus must have felt.

Truly the cross presents strange contrasts. Hands once stretched forth in blessing for man are now stretched out upon a cross, mangled and torn by those whom they had blessed. Feet that had trodden no forbidden pathway but which were ever active on errands of mercy are now so cruelly pierced. The brow upon which the dove of peace had rested is now encircled with thorns, the symbol of sin. Lips into which grace had been poured, and out of which gracious words had flowed are now the parched lips of a lonely sufferer, crying, *"My God, my God, why hast thou forsaken me?"* (Matthew 27:46).

It should be noted that Jesus did not say "Father" as in His first cry, and also in His last, but *"My God."* He usually addressed God as "Father" but here it is "God," for He appeals to divine righteousness. In spite of the mystery of the moment, He knew that God as God must be doing right.

It is also blessed to realize how faith can cling in the dark. Although God's face could not be seen, Jesus could still call Him *"My God."* There was extreme trust in extreme trial! And it is somewhat remarkable that He used the Syrian word for God, *Eloi*, meaning "My Strength." Crucified in weakness, He needed the strength of the mighty One. Hence His cry.

If somehow we lose sight of His countenance, may this be our attitude. In the hour of darkness, may we lay hold of His strength. As we pass through inexplicable experiences, when it seems as though the Father's smile has been eclipsed by the clouds, may we learn to sing with a desperate faith...

> Thou knowest my soul dost dearly love
> The place of Thine abode;
> No music drops so sweet a sound
> As these two words—My God.

Why?

This is the only time wonder filled the heart of Christ concerning anything His Father had allowed. And perhaps an answer to His "why" can be found in Psalm 22:3, *"But thou art holy."* Jesus was on the cross as the representative of sinful humanity. As one writer expressed it,

He gazed across the awful gulf through which He must wade, He looked down into the horrible pit in whose depths He must struggle and up whose insurmountable sides He must painfully climb with bleeding hands and feet. He saw sins, sins, sins, pressing in upon His holy body from this side and that, from behind, before, and above, and knew that as the sin-bearer He must bear them all and so He was left alone—alone with human sin, with your sin and mine.

The face of the Father, then, has turned not so much away from Christ as from what He was bearing, namely, the load of the world's sin, which load ultimately broke His loving, compassionate heart. He was there on the plane of sinners with mountains and mountains of guilt encircling Him, thus the Father hid His face from such a horrible load, seeing that He was of purer eyes than to behold evil.

We dishonor Christ if we think that some of His cries in Gethsemane and on Calvary were only moans of anguish stimulated by a natural fear of death. Thousands of His followers have faced a death equally as cruel with quietness of resignation and a spirit of victory, with no cry whatsoever escaping from their lips. But at that moment Jesus was not dying as a martyr; He was tasting the bitter cup of every life and facing the mystery of bearing all our sins.

And such a cry makes Him our brother in mystery. There is a "why" in every life. Some have stood at the side of an empty cradle and asked "Why?" Others with blasted hopes, blighted friendships, and broken vows have said, "Why?" The Sunday after Dr. Joseph Parker of the City Temple had buried his beautiful wife, the congregation wondered what text he would preach upon. He chose the one before us and said, "I thank God there was a 'why' in the Savior's life." Yes, and such a fact brings comfort amid our loneliness and desolation.

Have you reached a Calvary? Do you feel as if the Lord has left you? O thou poor, distressed and seemingly God-forsaken one. If you are in darkness, remember that the Father is still with you! Cling to Him! Trust Him even though you cannot trace Him.

We live in a world of "whys" and "wherefores." What God permits we know not now, but we shall know hereafter. If presently you see through a glass darkly, you must be patient, for the paradise of revelation is ahead. If, like your Lord, you are being made to suffer although innocent of what is being laid at your door, if your heart is torn by a sorrow of some kind, for which an unkind hand is responsible, you must realize you are not alone; Jesus is your brother in adversity! Although the innocent One, and nearer to God's heart than any other has ever been, He yet cried, "Why?"

> The scourge, the thorns, the deep disgrace
> These Thou couldst bear nor once repine;
> But when Jehovah veiled His face,
> Unutterable pangs were Thine.[24]

Forsaken

What a tragic word! We seem to hear the moan of a broken heart within it. To forsake means to leave behind in any state or place. And the word leaving the lips of Jesus, as it did, conveys the idea of desertion. What a term to come from One who was bathed in the sunshine of His loving Father's presence! The nails in His flesh, the insult of His enemies, the shame of the cross, the cruelty of men, did not cause anything like the grief Christ experienced when, for the time being, He seemed to lose the sense of His Father's presence. As He walked among men, in spite of their hostility, He could say, "*I am not alone, because the Father is with me*" (John 16:32). But here He is apparently abandoned by God.

The darkness of earth, then, was in keeping with the darkness which hung over the Redeemer's spirit as He was God-forsaken. There was darkness around and darkness within. But worst of all, there was darkness above, seeing that God's face was hidden. The crowning crime of man was the crime of killing the Prince of life, casting out thereby the Lord of nature from His own world. And such a crime may not be allowed to pass without some protest from nature herself, hence midday was turned into midnight. Denser darkness, however, came with God's withdrawal.

Is darkness abounding in your life at this moment? Do you wonder whether God is near, or whether He hears your cry? Have you been forsaken, deserted, betrayed? If close, creep closer to your Lord and listen to His voice echoing down the corridor of your being—"*I will never leave thee, nor forsake thee*" (Hebrews 13:5). Jesus was forsaken in His lone hour that He might have grace to tell you that He will be with you always, even unto the end of the road.

Me

What poignant grief this personal pronoun carries! Me! Yes, Me above all others—Me, Thy well-beloved Son! I always did the things pleasing to Thee;

---

24. John W. Cunningham, "From Calvary a Cry Was Heard," 1824.

I ever glorified Thee on earth. I was the One in whom Thou delightest. Why? Why hast Thou left Me to bear this bitter load alone? Surely there was never such a cry from earth as the long, lonely cry from the cross. *"Why hast thou forsaken Me?"* It was a cry of surprise and consternation, the irrepressible cry of a life tried to its utmost limit of possibility. What a mystery! We cannot fathom it. We only know that for one brief moment it seemed as if Jesus were forsaken by His Father, that He was left to die—alone!

This pronoun is possibly an echo of your heart's experience. You find yourself saying, "Why has God treated mein this way? I have always strived to live a holy, separated life. I have loved His Word, His house, His people. My life and substance have always been at His disposal. Then why does He treat me thus? Lord, what have I done? I can understand a sinner suffering for he is but reaping the harvest of his evil deeds, but Lord, why hast Thou allowed this heavy cross to fall upon my shoulders?" Sorrowing, perplexed heart, the Master has not left you alone, for He has promised never to forsake you. Never mistake feelings for actualities. If indwelt by His Spirit, then you can never be deserted, for the God above will never forsake the God within you. The Holy Spirit is your "perpetual Comforter and eternal Inhabitant," as Saint Augustine calls Him.

> Yea, once Immanuel's orphaned cry
> His universe hath shaken,
> It went up single,
> My God, I am forsaken.
> It went up from holy lips
> Amid His lost creation;
> That of the lost, no son should use
> These words of desolation.[25]

The Indelible Record

It was the custom in the days when crucifixion was the form of capital punishment to inscribe the crime and name of the criminal on the board and affix it to the cross so that the passer-bys might know who was dying and for what.

So was it with Jesus, the supposed felon, as He died upon His cross. Pilate wrote the title and put it on the cross, *"Jesus of Nazareth, the King of the Jew,"* outlining His name and crime. This inscription was written in the chief

---

25. Elizabeth Barrett Browning, "Cowper's Grave."

languages of the earth, so that all the spectators could read it. Hebrew was the language of the Jews, Greek the current language of the Gentiles, and Latin the official language.

The Jews urged Pilate to alter the title as to express, not Christ's real dignity, but His false claims to it. Jewish ecclesiastics wanted to make His crime more specific. *"Write not, the King of the Jews, but that He said, 'I am the King of the Jews'"* (John 19:21). In Pilate's reply we have his contempt of the Jews, for his answer carries the sting of impatience as well as the assumption of authority, *"What I have written, I have written."* Having yielded frequently to the Jews, and having intended to spite and insult them by the title because they got him to act against his own sense of justice, he flatly refused them.

As the words *"What I have written, I have written"* left Pilate's lips, it was obvious that they came from an ill-tempered man on bad terms with himself and those about him. Pilate had forfeited the self-respect of his fellow men. His jurisdiction of Judea had made him hated by the Jews. In turn, Pilate hated them and was ready to quarrel with them. It was thus that, in the spirit of spiteful triumph, he caused the superscription, so offensive to the Jews, to remain. Pilate had surrendered Christ to the angry mob against his better judgment, but was unwilling to concede a mere detail, when no principle was involved.

Pilate's declaration was prophetic of a sad end. What he had written, he had written. His own life story had been written with the pen of expediency and the ink of cowardice, and such a shameful story could not be rewritten. His writing remains against him, for the world points a finger of scorn at this weak-minded man who should have written over the middle cross, "Barabbas, the Murderer." And if legend be true, Pilate reaped what he had sown, for, seeing that he was disgraced, he committed suicide.

Let us note the various applications of Pilate's harsh and authoritative reply, *"What I have written, I have written."*

True Description of the Past

"What I have written, I have written!" There is a fatefully significant ring about those words as we apply them to a faded year with its story to which all of us have contributed. A deeper and more solemn truth than we can imagine is resident in Pilate's declaration, for the past is beyond recall. All of us think of what we would do if only we could live our lives over again. We think of kind words we should have spoken, for which it is too late—those people are no longer living. If only they could return for five minutes, we might try to

make amends. We think of kind deeds we might have performed, but the opportunity has gone. We think of the holy life we might have lived, but the door is closed upon the past with its heaps of broken vows and blighted resolutions.

We cannot undo what we have done, or erase what we have written. It may be possible to unravel a sock one is knitting to fix a mistake, but we cannot do this with our past faults. Our past has turned its back upon us forever, and departed into eternity. We may cry, *"O return, and let me make amends!"* but there will be no response to our appeal. When David heard of the death of his child he said, *"I shall go to him, but he shall not return to me"* (2 Samuel 12:23). And this is true of our past. It will not return to us, but we must go out to meet our past. God grant that it will not rise up in condemnation against us!

The Unalterable Character of God

"What I have written, I have written." There is a sense in which we can apply these words to God and His Word. In the Bible, the fixed, unchanging, immutable, eternal character of God is extolled. He is never sorry for anything He does, never retrieves any step, never takes anything back. His constancy runs like a golden thread through the Scriptures. *"God is not a man, that he should lie; neither the son of man, that he should repent: hath he said, and shall he not do it? or hath he Token, and shall he not make it good?"* (Numbers 23:19); *"I know that, whatsoever God doeth, it shall be forever: nothing can be put to it, nor any thing taken from it: and God doeth it, that men should fear before him"* (Ecclesiastes 3:14); *"For I am the Lord, I change not; therefore ye sons of Jacob are not consumed"* (Malachi 3:6); *"And being fully persuaded that, what he had promised, he was able also to perform"* (Romans 4:21); *"Every good gift and every perfect gift is from above, and cometh down from the Father of lights, with whom is no variableness, neither shadow of turning"* (James 1:17).

Returning to Pilate's inscription, we realize that the finger of God was behind it. In effect, the title on the cross was the execution of a divine command, seeing that it was the title decreed by God, written by Pilate's hand. "Tell it out among the nations, that the Lord is King!"[26] The curious irony is that Pilate was marked out to declare Christ's kingship. As one expositor said, "Amidst the conflicting passions of men, was proclaimed in the chief tongues of mankind, from the cross itself and in circumstances which threw upon it a lurid yet grand light, the truth which drew the Magi to His manger, and will yet be owned by all the world!"

---

26. Frances R. Havergal, "Tell It Out," 1872.

The finger of God is likewise behind all which the Bible holds. Modernists may deny this part of the Word, but the whole is His revelation. What He has written, He has written! He wrote the Ten Commandments, and they still hold good. *"Ye shall not add unto the word which I command you, neither shall ye diminish aught from it, that ye may keep the commandments of the LORD your God which I command you"* (Deuteronomy 4:2).

Let us see how we can apply the God's willingness to fulfill any declaration of His, to specific promises of Scripture. For example, there is the promise of security. *"And I give unto them eternal life; and they shall never perish, neither shall any man pluck them out of my hand"* (John 10:28). Our name will never be erased from the Lamb's Book of Life. His gifts are without repentance. *"For the gifts and calling of God are without repentance"* (Romans 11:29). For our support and succor, we have: *"Blessed be the LORD, that hath given rest unto his people Israel, according to all that he promised: there hath not failed one word of all his good promise, which he promised by the hand of Moses his servant"* (1 Kings 8:56). *"...for he hath said, I will never leave thee, nor forsake thee"* (Hebrews 13:5). Yes, what He has written, He has written! As to our final redemption, the Lord will keep rendezvous with His own, and return according to His Word. *"Let not your heart be troubled: ye believe in God, believe also in me. In my Father's house are many mansions: if it were not so, I would have told you. I go to prepare a place for you. And if I go and prepare a place for you, I will come again, and receive you unto myself; that where I am, there ye may be also"* (John 14:1–3). The night is dark! Daybreak is at hand. Christ's promise to deliver us from a groaning creation will not be broken.

The Determined Allegiance of the Saint

"What I have written, I have written!" Applying Pilate's answer to the Jewish request to alter the title he had placed over the cross to ourselves, we realize that it is imperative to write well and then abide by what is written. Our common fault is that we are too movable, oscillating, weak, shifty, and undependable. We are not men and women of our word. We do not have Jephthah's determination, who said *"I have opened my mouth unto the LORD, and I cannot go back"* (Judges 11:35). A similar integrity is brought before us in Numbers 30:2; Esther 1:19; 8:8; and Ecclesiastes 5:4–5.

How we need more conscience about fulfilling of our vows and covenants! Luther, facing a hostile world cried, "Here I stand. I can do no other. God help me!" If you recently trusted Christ, writing your name on a "decision card" may God preserve you from going back on your decision. Or if you have taken upon yourself solemn baptismal vows, do not keep back part of the price. Go out to live the baptized life! Surrender to no one but God. Endeavor so to live that you will not be ashamed of your record when it hails you in eternity. May grace be yours to write well, to be more reliable and dependable! The Lord would have us known and beloved by all, a living epistle.

The Sad Confession of a Sinner

"*What I have written, I have written!*" Life is full of tragic illustrations of this inscription. There we have many sad confessions of the heart! We reap what we sow. "*Be not deceived God is not mocked: for whatsoever a man soweth, that shall he also reap, for he that soweth to his flesh shat of the flesh reap corruption; but he that soweth to the Spirit shall of the Spirit reap life everlasting*" (Galatians 6:7–8). David was graciously forgiven and not until then could he write Psalm 32, but the fruit of his sin dogged his footsteps to the grave. Salvation does not always remove the effects of sin, along with its guilt and penalty. Prodigal ways of parents in early life have their fruit in the godlessness of their offspring.

Here and now we reap what we sow. Sinners should not be elated if they are not presently suffering for their sin. God's accounting day is coming! Lost innocence can never be regained. The bloom rudely brushed from the flower can never be restored. Therefore, it is imperative to see how we live our days, seeing that the stains of the soul are retained. That foul impressions abide, even the saved can testify with shame.

It is also true that hereafter we reap what we sow. There may be those who appear to lightly forget what they have said and done wrong in the past, but while they may try to forget it, it is not forgotten elsewhere. Every trace remains with all the force and power of written evidence, which is the most damning of all. If a thing is in black and white, it cannot be gainsaid. And so, whether saint or sinner, let us never forget that a copy of the story is written by God's recording angel above.

If we go on, heedless of our ways, the time is coming when we shall be horrified and distressed as we reread the story of our lives at the judgment bar of God. Our sin, like Judah's, is written with the pen of iron and the point of a diamond. Yes, the day is coming when men must read the writing of a useless life and a Christ-less character that they are penning today. "*Out of thine own mouth will I judge thee*" (Luke 19:22).

Our only hope of deliverance from condemnation is to confess and repent of our sins. Only then is the handwriting against us blotted out. Christ's nail-pierced hands can erase the past. "*I have blotted out, as a thick cloud, thy transgressions, and, as a cloud, thy sins: return unto me; for I have redeemed thee"* (Isaiah 44:22).

Cleansing us from the guilt of sin, and daily delivering us from the power of sin, Christ will overrule the effect of sin. Let us turn anew to the Savior, then, that under the inspiration of the Holy Spirit, we may write in the pages of life with the pen of faith and ink of love, a life story of which we shall never be ashamed to say, *"What I have written, I have written!"*

The Calvary Tableaux

What a haunting refrain that Negro spiritual has—"Were you there when they crucified my Lord?" As He died over nineteen hundred years ago, of course, we were not actually present at the cross, but many others were and reacted to that grim scene in different ways for the cross is the test of character.

Strange though it may seem, the cross distinguishes man from man and is the acid test of one's attitude toward truth. The world has its way of dividing men into classes: rich or poor, high or low, learned or ignorant, fortunate or unfortunate. God, however, has His way of separating men. He judges them by His Son's cross, and not as the world judges.

Calvary is the judgment of this world. (See John 12:31.) Thus, as every man comes into the sight of the cross, he finds himself judged there and the way it affects him and what it makes of him, proving it to be the testing point of character.

As we think of those gathered around the cross, we cannot but be impressed with its varying effect upon those who gazed on the Savior's agony. And the witnesses of that terrible spectacle are representatives of men today, for around the cross the whole human family is gathered—any race of any man are judged 'neath its shadow. The cross reveals the best and the worst in human nature.

> I see the crowd in Pilate's hall,
> I mark their wrathful mien.
> Their shouts of "Crucify" appall,
> With blasphemy between.
> But of that shouting multitude,
> I know that I am one.

With the gospels open before us, let us try this Easter season to identify those who went to make up the Calvary tableaux. How opposite in appreciation were those who were there when they crucified our Lord! Their varied attitudes prove that the cross is, for all time, *"the savour of life unto life or of death unto death"* (2 Corinthians 2:16).

Simon of Cyrene Was There

Would you not like to know more of this Simon who was pressed into carrying our Lord's cross? Reaching Calvary with this heavy load, he must have stayed to see the bitter end. What happened to this cross-bearer and what effect did this privileged service have on him? Tradition has it that he became a Christian. His two sons, Alexander and Rufus, were well-known individuals in the church during the time Mark wrote his gospel. (See Mark 15:21.)

Do you not wonder why, out of the whole crowd streaming to the place of crucifixion, the centurion fixed on this man from Cyrene to shoulder the cross that had become too heavy for the Man so badly beaten up, whose flesh on His back and shoulders was so raw and lacerated? (See Luke 23:26.)

Was this colored man from North Africa chosen to take up the cross because he possessed a pair of good, broad shoulders? Was this Cyrenean suspected of being a secret disciple and made sharer of his Master's humiliation? Who also has the right to bear His cross, but His own?

"On him they laid the cross." How striking! What pride Simon must have felt when, in later days, he recounted the story of the Via Dolorosa. Has the cross been laid on our hearts? Does it cast its shadow over our entire life?

"Bear it after Jesus." How sweetly put, and how true! Because He bore it first, it is lighter for you and me. Artists represent Jesus carrying the heaviest end with the lightest end on Simon's shoulder. Christ always takes the heavy end. Are we sharers of His cross? Have we entered into the fellowship of His sufferings?

Does Jesus not command us to take up the cross and follow Him? (See Matthew 16:24.) Such a cross is not any adversity, trial, or sorrow. The Christian has only one cross—it is His! This cross means self-denial. *"Let him deny himself."* At Calvary Christ died, not only for sin, but to self. *"Himself he cannot save"* (Mark 15:31). He willingly gave Himself. (See Galatians 2:20.) If our life is ruled by the principles of self, then we are not on the blood-red road, sharing the cross of Christ.

The life of self is death
The death of self is life.

The Daughters of Jerusalem Were There

Among those swelling the crowd as Jesus painfully walked the Calvary road were the daughters of mercy from Jerusalem. (See Luke 23:27.) How overcome with pity they must have been as they watched the sufferer sinking beneath His load! As women are more accustomed to pain and suffering than men, they felt for this mother's Son. Although their tears for Christ were sincere and commendable, these women lamented and bewailed each victim passing that way to such a cruel death. They were not animated by any sentiment beyond mere pity evoked by the plight of the Man of Sorrows.

If theirs had not been mere emotion, Jesus would not have answered their lamentation with the sad severity that He did when He said, *"Weep not for me, but weep for yourselves, and for your children"* (Luke 23:28). They were enjoined to keep their tears, for they would have need them for their own future sorrows.

Are there not many all around us who, like these emotional women, are animated by sentiments of genuine pity and compassion for the Savior? Struggling under their crosses was a daily occurrence for these compassionate women. Owing to their soft nature, they accompanied sufferers to the place of crucifixion. But beyond their sentimental pity and perhaps wonder and admiration for Christ's amazing patience under affliction, their hearts did not travel.

As the coarse soldiers drove the nails into His hands and feet, they had no glimpse of the divine glory of Christ as the Son of God. Their rejection of Christ, while not as blatant and hateful as the Pharisees, was nevertheless as fatal as theirs. And those weeping women are represented by those who are emotionally moved as they hear and read about the cross. Their hearts swell with sorrow at the sight of Calvary, but they fail to admit Christ's claims as Master and their own personal need of His saving grace.

They watch Him with sincere interest, but live lives of detachment from Christ. To these people, he says, "Keep your tears. I want your trust and submission rather than sobs. Weep for yourselves, for although you are good and easily moved, there is the danger of a fate as tragic as that awaiting the most rebellious." Jesus does not want our pity nor patronage, our sympathy nor sighs, but contrition of soul and the full surrender of all we are and have to be used in His royal service.

The Usual Crowd Was There

There are idlers who always crowd around an exciting scene, whether it is a marriage or a murder. Luke says that *"the people stood beholding"* (verse 23:35), a phrase that does not imply stolid indifference. The look of the crowd was more than a casual glance of indifference. The original denotes the look of fixed, intense, and special interest—an unfeeling stare or gaze at the Crucified One hanging there between heaven and earth.

Well might the crowd have stood there "beholding," for there hung the incarnate Son of God. However, they beheld without being transformed (see 2 Corinthians 3:18), just as crowds today hear and read the story of the cross. They admire such a supreme sacrifice, but the Christ who died does not claim their allegiance. It is to be hoped that you are not one of the crowd who merely observes Easter, but that you realize that the One who died demands the full surrender of your life.

Loving Friends Were There

Many of our Lord's closest relatives and friends followed Him to the cross and were silent witnesses that awful day (see Luke 23:49), their gaze altogether different from the rest around Calvary's hill. What agony they experienced as they watched Him there—the One who had become dearer to them than all else! We think particularly of the three Marys. (See John 19:25.)

1. There was Mary, His own mother, who now in unutterable agony understood Simeon's words about a sword piercing her heart. Now the mystery was solved as the Son of her womb hung on the middle cross.

   Seeing Jesus had no wife, who else should have been there standing by His cross, but His mother? Hers was the first face He saw following His birth—now it is the last. Christ's dying thought was of His mother's future welfare, and so He tenderly committed her to John's care.

2. There was the other Mary, the virgin's sister, and the brokenhearted aunt of our Lord. Relationship makes a great difference when it comes to sorrow. It was this Mary's nephew who was dying there. Thus, a common feeling united these two Marys together and kept them at the cross until the One bound to them by human ties was dead. What a binding influence sorrow has!

3. There was Mary Magdalene. Where else would this Mary be, as her wonderful emancipator died, but at His cross? Was it not the dying One who had delivered her from seven demons? She was there, not merely to support the other women in their grief, but because of her own love for Jesus, who had saved her from something worse

than death. The Man who was bearing the sins of many was the One who had given her back her reason and self-respect, so she too stood by the cross, that its image might be stamped upon her heart.

The action, common to all three women, is that they stood by the cross, thereby comforting Christ by their presence. This was an incident mentioned only by John, proving that he was also an eyewitness. These women were not prostrate on the ground with grief. They stood like sentinels. The word for "stood" means to stand fast or still, and is used in opposition to one falling. Others sat, but these women stood.

In these modern days, when many are forsaking the cross in theology and life, may we be found standing fast by it. Let us imitate John Bunyan's Mr. Steadfast, whose last words were "Me thinks I stand easy." Let us keep our post at the cross through scorn, ridicule, or shame. *"Having done all to stand"* (Ephesians 6:13).

Before we leave these beloved Marys, we might also make this observation. Woman had no hand in the death of Christ, although it was through the first woman's sin that He, the Son of a woman, came to His cruel death. Woman has paid the full penalty of Eve's transgression and has atoned for her disobedience. A woman gave the world its Redeemer. No woman spoke against or insulted Christ. A heathen woman, Pilate's wife, interceded for Him. Women bewailed Him, assisted at His burial, were the last at His grave and the first there on that resurrection morn. From cradle to the cross, Jesus was surrounded with the gracious ministry of devoted women.

Peter Was There

Doubtless he was on the fringe of the crowd listening to the jeers and jibes of the godless, and was shamefaced at seeing John and the women standing so courageously by the cross. We know Peter was there when his Lord was crucified, for he tells us that he was a witness to Christ being slain and hanged upon a tree. (See Acts 5:32.)

What tears of penitence he must have shed as he watched the One for whom he had vowed to go to death, die such a death. Yet Peter died the same kind of death as Christ. Legend says that he felt so unworthy to die in the same way as his Lord, that he begged his crucifiers to crucify him upside down.

John Was There

The disciple whom Jesus loved is the only other person mentioned by name, beside the women, at the cross. Spiritually, he was nearer to Christ than anyone else. Had he not leaned on that bosom—now bare and blood-covered—and learned His secrets? To whom else could Christ commit His dear mother but this disciple who lived so close to the heart of the Master?

In that dark hour when faith was severely tried, devoted friends like John and the Marys never swerved in their allegiance to Christ. They stayed with Him to what they thought was the end. True, there were many onlookers that dark Friday, but only a faithful few who kept a true-hearted vigil.

Calvary is a marvelous, prophetic tableau of the history of the Christian centuries. Today, countless numbers have diverse feelings as they think of the cross. Some cavil and scoff. Cultured and superior in learning, they despise the cross, as did the Greeks of old. Then there is the sentimentalism of those who talk well of Christ with one breath but think Him to be on a par with Buddha and Mohammed. But as faith is sorely-tried and iniquity appears to flourish, and truth and Christ are on the scaffold, may we be found among Christ's devoted friends who love and trust on, like the few of old who stood by the cross.

The Religious Leaders Were There

Matthew and Luke describe the members of the Sanhedrin as *"the priests, scribes and elders"* (Matthew 27:20; Luke 23:35). We read that these religious leaders derided Jesus as He hung on the cross. The word "deride" implies "the curled lip and distended nostril of scorn." How they gloated over the agonies of the One they had rejected and unjustly condemned! It was these men who cried, *"Away with Him, crucify Him!"*

The soldiers represented the rough, coarse, uneducated section of the crowd at Calvary; the Pharisees and Sadducees; the religious, educated section. Tragic, is it not, that these most eminent leaders in thought and religion joined with the soldiers in their cruel jeers and taunts hurled at the dying Man? It was these gray-bearded elders who mocked Christ saying, *"He saved others, himself he cannot save"* (Matthew 27:42). Their reviling attitude represents those who want religion but not a Redeemer—a Messiah without the cross.

A large mass in Christendom are greatly interested in religious matters. They go about to establish their own righteousness but reject the claims of the righteous God. They are confident about their own moral standing. Religious before men, they have yet no room for the cross, either in their religion or inner experience.

Some are like the Sadducees who want to see a proved miracle before they believe. *"Let him now come down from the cross, and we will believe him"*

(Matthew 27:42). They desire so convincing, overpowering proof in this twentieth century that Jesus is the Son of God. They parade their agnosticism, their intellectual difficulties with the virgin birth, atonement, and resurrection. Reason usurps revelation and faith. Perhaps those religious leaders were the most hopeless clan around the cross that terrible day. Paul, who was a Pharisee, confessed that he rejected Christ *"ignorantly in unbelief"* (1 Timothy 1:13).

Yet once the rage of those religious rulers had spent itself upon the One they hated, and they witnessed the solemn manifestation of divine power in the earthquake and resurrection of some of the dead, we read that they went home beating their breasts. Perhaps many of them were among *"the great company of priests"* who afterward believed. (See Acts 6:7.)

> The chief priests took counsel against Him,
> To put our Lord to death.
> "He is a blasphemer," cried they,
> "He is a King, He saith.
> We have no king but Caesar,
> To him is homage due!"
> Tradition meant more than Jesus—
> Are you a priest too?

The Soldiers Were There

These rough pagan vassals of the Roman army, to whom the task was assigned to drive the nails through the hands and feet of the condemned, had little sympathy for the sufferings of those whose flesh was being fastened to a cross of wood. They were too accustomed to their brutal task to turn a hair. Hammer and nails were used with brutal insensibility. The calloused hearts of the crucifiers remained untouched.

Having performed what they were ordered to do, the soldiers sat around the foot of the crosses watching the victims die. Part of their duty was to guard the crosses, lest any victims were stolen before they were actually dead. How could they sit and watch Christ bleeding and dying on that middle cross? (See Matthew 27:36.) How calloused men can become! While the highest love on the cross was praying, deepest hate was beneath it heartlessly rejecting.

It is to be hoped that ours is a different watch and that we know what it is to sit down in some quiet spot away from the rabble, maddening throng and watch Him there. A passing glance is not sufficient. We must learn to gaze on that old rugged cross until we are lost in wonder, gratitude, and worship.

Sitting at the foot of the cross, four of those soldiers were guilty of a sordid act. They gambled for the coat that Jesus wore. Surely this gamble should make men loathe gambling of any sort. We are not told what happened to His garment. Perhaps the soldier who had won it wore it as a memento. If he wrote it, then wearing Christ's coat did not make him a Christian, just as a mere association with a Christian church does not make the attendant a Christian.

One of the soldiers pierced the heart side of Jesus as He ended those hours of intolerable pain. How dead those soldiers were to the appeal of the suffering! What coarse, brutal natures they possessed! Yet in those rough, ignorant men we have a type of a large class who reject the Son of God through ignorance and spiritual stolidity.

Are there not thousands who, like those soldiers, not so much hate Christ, but are profoundly indifferent to the appeal of the Crucified One? They live in a Christian community and daily hear His name and see Him reflected in the witness of His sincere followers, yet they remain sunken in spiritual insensibility. They never stop to think that that the "passion drama" demands their all.

Like the official crucifiers of Christ, they are not concerned about Him; by their rejection of Him, they crucify Him anew. Their only concern is to get the most out of this world. They live only for personal gain and comfort. As the soldiers could sit at the cross, making something out of the occasion by dividing His garments, so there are those who use the secular advantages the influence of the cross has brought to advance their own earthly plans and worldly ends. How many there will be this Easter whose only interest in such a sacred season is commercial! Others in hardness of heart and vanity of earthly reject Christ with scarcely a thought.

The Two Thieves Were There

The two malefactors had something in common with the Man on the middle cross. All three were dying the same death, enduring the same terrible anguish. However, this marked the difference: the thieves were dying for their own sin; Jesus was dying for your sin and mine.

What opposite effects the cross had on these two companions of Christ in suffering! One thief saw himself as a lost sinner, and at the eleventh hour cried for mercy and was remembered by the dying Christ. Browning puts it, "The last kind word Christ spoke was to a thief."

The dying thief rejoiced to see
That fountain in his day.[27]

The thief that entered paradise was the first trophy of the efficacious Redeemer's blood. The other thief died without a word of penitence on his lips. He died, even as he had lived, without God and without hope. From one side of the cross, a thief goes to paradise; from the other side, a thief went to perdition. "One was saved that none might despair, but only one that none might presume."

The Centurion Was There

A centurion—the word is related to "century"—was an officer in the Roman army who commanded a company of one hundred soldiers. The centurion at Calvary was the one in charge of the soldiers detailed to carry out the brutal task of crucifying the three victims. Therefore, both Jews and Gentiles were associated in the dastardly action of killing the sinless Son of God.

There was one, however, who was deeply impressed by the demeanor of Christ as He suffered on the cross; the centurion saw the man to be much different than the others the centurion had to crucify, and those with him were smitten with fear as the earthquake rocked the city and cried, *"Truly this was the Son of God"* (Matthew 27:54). This Roman officer was not a Christian, yet he had an insight into the God-like character of Christ. Here was One exhibiting righteousness, holiness, and love.

The centurion had heard the taunt of the scribes and elders, *"He trusted in God; let him deliver him now...for he said, I am the Son of God"* (Matthew 27:43), and he felt that these words were true of the One whose death he had to carry out.

What is our conception of the Man on that middle cross? Whom do we see? Do we, by faith, see One who identified Himself with sinners; One who bore all our curse; Own who is now able to save all kinds of sinners? Surveying the wondrous cross on which the Prince of glory died, do we see a delighted God, a defeated Satan, a Savior mighty to save and deliver?

Barabbas Was There

While the gospels do not specifically state that this notable prisoner was present at the cross, it is logical to conclude that he was there as a token of his gratitude for the Man who had taken his place and was dying his death. This

---

27. William Cowper, "There Is a Fountain Filled with Blood," 1772.

robber, who had taken a prominent part in an insurrection, had committed murder, and awaited crucifixion with the other two thieves under the capital punishment of the Roman government. (See Matthew 27:16–17; Luke 23:19; Mark 15:7.)

Pilate, eager to shift the dreaded burden of responsibility from himself, gave the multitude a choice that was spurred on by the chief priests and elders. The clamor was for the release of Barabbas, and Pilate complied and surrendered Jesus in the place of the robber. Although Pilate washed his hands to relieve his conscience, the fearful guilt of blood remained. If legend has it, Pilate was haunted by his weak attitude and committed suicide.

Actually, all of us are in the position of Barabbas. He should have died, but Jesus died in his place; Christ was his substitute, even as He is ours. Our sins deserved eternal death, but Jesus bore our load and died our death. The cross was not endured for mankind as for a multitude indiscriminately, but for each individually. Christ died that every human being might truly say, *"He loved me, and gave himself for me"* (Galatians 2:20). Because Christ died for you and me, we were there, representatively, when He was crucified.

God Was There

The fourth cry escaping the parched lips of Christ as He died suggests that His own Father was not there as He bore the load of human sin. *"My God, my God, why hast thou forsaken me?"* (Matthew 27:46). God, as God, could not look upon the sin of the world which His Son was bearing. (See Psalm 22:1–3.)

Yet God was near in the darkness, and in His last conscious moment, Christ knew that His Father was at hand, hence His last cry: *"Father, into thy hands I commend my spirit"* (Luke 23:46). What a victorious way to die! May our end be as His, committing ourselves to the Father's care!

Nature Was There

How could the Creator die such an ignominious death, and the universe He brought into being not hasten to His aid? Was not the firmament His handiwork? (See Psalm 19:1.) Thus it was that nature hurried to turn midday into midnight in order to hide the shame heaped upon her Lord, covering His nakedness with a garment of black. (See Matthew 27:45.)

Godless eyes would look at Him and stare (see Psalm 22:17), and so darkness covered the earth so that His unrobed body could not be seen. (See

Luke 23:44–45.) He had no other garment to part with; His nakedness is typical of the sinner He was dying to save, who must come to Him for dress.

> Well might the sun in darkness hide,
> And shut His glories in,
> When Christ, the mighty Maker, died
> For man the creature's sin.[28]

The mysterious rending of the temple veil, the quaking earth, and the resurrection of some of the dead were further evidences of nature's interest in the happenings of that black Friday. (See Luke 23:45; Matthew 27:50–54.) These unusual happenings testified to the deity of the One whom men were crucifying as a felon on a wooden gibbet.

Joseph of Arimathaea Was There

Although the majority of the disciples tarried afar off, looking with tear stained eyes at their slowly dying Master, one or two came forward to pay their last respects to His sacred body. Joseph was one. Jesus was cared for by a Joseph at His birth and another Joseph at His death. The latter was *"an honorable counselor"* (Mark 15:43), that is a Sanhedrin member, and was looking for the kingdom of God. He was also *"a good man and a just"* (Luke 23:50), and *"a disciple but secretly for fear of the Jews"* (John19:38).

Legend has it that Joseph of Arimathaea came to Britain and founded the church of Glastonbury; some say that the staff he carried was stuck into the ground, took root, and brought forth flowers, thereby becoming the parent of all the Glastonbury thorns to this day. This we do know, however, that as soon as Jesus died, Joseph hastened to the palace and begged Pilate's permission to bury His body. Pilate, willing to help the friends but not the foes of Christ, willingly gave His permission. Reverently, Joseph clothed Jesus' body and buried it in his the new tomb prepared against his own death.

As disciples, not secret it is to be hoped, let us never withhold anything from our Lord which He may desire to use. What we surrender is always divinely blessed. Graves become the chambers of resurrection glory.

Nicodemus Was There

John mentions this highly educated and deeply religious Jewish teacher is mentioned three times (see John 3:1–2; 7:50; 19:39), and always as *"the one who came to Jesus by night."* It was this Nicodemus who prepared the Jesus'

---

28. Isaac Watts, "Alas! And Did My Savior Bleed?", 1707.

body for burial. Costly myrrh and aloes were used to perfume the body and linen clothes. These spices must have been secured by Nicodemus as soon as he knew the leading members of the council decided to kill Christ.

Nicodemus was apparently a man of the same class and type of character as Joseph whom he assisted in the reverential offices of Christ's burial. He respected Christ as a wonderful Man and a heaven-sent Teacher and half believed to be the Christ, but until now had shrunk from confessing Him before men. Mary gave her spices to Jesus while He was alive and could appreciate them—Nicodemus kept his spices until Christ's death. However, no corpse can appreciate rich perfumes. Why save all our flowers until our friends die? Why not let them enjoy their fragrance while they live!

Another Easter has rolled around and is another reminder of all that Jesus endured and provided for a lost world. We have been considering those spectators of the Calvary scene who felt that when Jesus gave up the ghost, that that was the end of their hopes. Truth, however, can never stay buried. So the glorious Gospel of Easter is that He said: *"I am the truth,"* rose again, and is alive for evermore.

John Masefield, the British poet laureate, has written a story called *The Trial of Jesus.* It is semi-historical, semi-imaginative, but withal a reverent treatment of the theme.

At one point in the story, Masefield relates a conversation between Pilate's wife and the centurion who was in charge of the crucifixion. Procula says to Longinus: "Do you think he is dead?"

Longinus replies, "No, lady, I don't."

"Then where is he?" asked Pilate's wife.

"Where is he?" exclaims the centurion, "Let loose in the world, lady, let loose in the world where neither Roman nor Jew can stop his truth."

Such is the victory of God that we witness in the resurrection of Jesus Christ; Jesus the Savior let loose in the world where none can stop Him! They crucified Him to silence Him, get rid of Him, and stop Him cold, but God raised Him from the dead so that nothing might silence or stop Him, world without end.

Only one Cross!
And to that Cross He leadeth all His own;
They gather round it, and its healing falls
Upon each sinful one.

OUTLINES

The Six Miracles of Calvary

1. The Supernatural Darkness (See Matthew 27:45)
2. The Rent Veil (See Matthew 27:51)
3. The Earthquake (See Matthew 27:51)
4. The Fulfillment of Prophecy at the Cross (See John 19:23–24)
5. The Miraculous Conversion of the Centurion (See Luke 23:46–47)
6. The Fact that He, the Prince of Life, Died (See John 10:17–18). This can be explained by the revelation that He voluntarily *"laid down his life"* to accomplish our redemption.

Six Miracles That Didn't Happen at the Cross

1. He Didn't Come Down From the Cross (Mark 15:30–32)
2. Elijah Didn't Come to Save Him (Mark 15:34–37)
3. He Didn't Call for the Twelve Legions of Angels He Could Have Called for (Matthew 26:53)
4. He Answered "Nothing" When Abused (Matthew 27:12; Mark 14:61–63)
5. He Didn't Resist Arrest When Judas Kissed Him (Mark 14:44–50)
6. He Didn't Turn Against God When He Suffered So, but Endured It All

The Six Miracles of the Resurrection

1. The Great Earthquake (Matthew 28:2)
2. The Angel Who Rolled Back the Stone and Sat on It (Matthew 28:2; Mark 16:4)
3. A Partial Resurrection of Old Testament Saints (Matthew 27: 52–53)
4. The Angels in the Tomb (Luke 24:4; John 20:12)
5. The Miraculous Arrangement of the Grave clothes (John 20:6–9)
6. The Resurrection—Fully Attested to—of a Bloodless, Pierced Body (John 20:19–28)

The Consolation Easter Brings

"Why weepest thou?" (John 20: 13, 15).

The resurrection of Jesus, rightly understood, prevents us from shedding life's bitter and common tears. Easter Day consoles those...

1. *Who sorrow because of the apparent defeat of goodness and truth.* Often the cause of freedom, purity, and prayer seems defeated. However, since the buried Christ rose from the dead, goodness and truth shall also rise. There shall be a time of restitution of all things.

2. *Who sorrow because of human death.* Oceans of tears have been shed over the death of others, and over the prospect of one's own death. Philosophy may speculate about death and its issue, and poetry may dream of the future, but it is only the Christian faith that can console. Jesus arose and became the first fruits of them that slept. The knowledge and belief that Jesus died and rose again inspires the confidence that if we are in Him, dying like Him, we shall also rise like Him.

> My knowledge of that life is small,
> The eye of faith is dim;
> But 'tis enough that Christ knows all,
> And I shall be with Him.[29]

Christ's Surrender of His Spirit to God

"Father, into thy hands I commend my spirit" (Luke 23:46). There are at least three truths to be gathered from Christ's last word at Calvary:

1. *That the human spirit survives the dissolution of the body.* True philosophy renders this highly probable; the Bible reveals it as an incontrovertible fact.

2. *That the glory of human nature consists in being with the Father.* "Into thy hands." They are the hands of love and wisdom to guide me in my endless course—to supply the wants of my imperishable being.

3. *That the attainment of glory involves the voluntary effort of man.* "I commend my spirit," or, I give it up to Thee, to be ruled by Thy law; to be employed in this service; to be blessed by Thy love.

---

29. Richard Baxter, "Lord, It Belongs Not to My Care," 1681.

4. *That this voluntary effort gives a moral grandeur to death.* This, in truth, makes death not a conquest, but a victory; not a calamity, but a boon; not destruction, but a salvation; not an end, but a beginning.

⟿

The Inscription on the Cross

"It was written in Hebrew, and Greek, and Latin" (John 19:20).

Pilate's inscription on the head of the cross of the blessed Savior, and the fact that the inscription was written in the three languages—Hebrew, Greek, and Latin—together illustrate…

1. *The Unconscious Testimony of Bad Men to Truth.* Pilate, the vacillating, the superstitious, the cowardly, the cruel, causes a statement to be written about Christ, which no apostle's argument or angel's song could be more truthful. It speaks of the kingship of the carpenter's son and the royalty of the peasant teacher of Nazareth. Similarly, Balaam, Caiaphas, and all who caviled at Christ because He received sinners, were all unconsciously testifying to various great truths; for example, Balaam to the moral fascination of a godly nation (see Numbers 24:1–19); Caiaphas to the necessity of vicarious sacrifice; the cavilers to the philanthropy and mercy of the Good Shepherd who *"came to save the lost."*

2. *The Failure of Mere Culture to Effect the Highest Ends.* The common, the vagrant, and the unlettered could not understand this language. We find from their record of the events of Calvary that the evangelists did not know what each part of the inscription meant. But here we find the possessor of the knowledge of these three languages using the knowledge in the service of the grossest ingratitude, meanest cowardice, and deadliest murder which the world has ever known. It is in view of this principle in the history of nations that Bunsen wrote: "Culture without religion is but civilized barbarianism and disguised animalism." And Scripture teaches, *"not by might, nor by power, but by my Spirit"* (Zechariah 4:6).

3. *The Omniscient Arrangements of God's Providence.* The fact that these three languages were thus then and there employed, reminds us of the historic marvel that the lifetime of the incarnate Christ

was just the epoch when most naturally Hebrew faith, Greek eloquence, and Latin empire could combine to serve the propagation of the new evangel. Surely the Lord came *"in the fulness of the time"* (Galatians 4:4).

4. *The Universal Availableness of Calvary.* The fact that most concerns the population of all centuries and climes is not obscure, metaphysical, or transcendental. No. It was an event that all can understand. It was a death—and the death of a Man. Its availableness is illustrated in its relation to the population of the city then. For it happened not at the distance of a long pilgrimage, but *"near the city."* And it was explained in three languages, one or other of which all the motley group that passed by could understand. So it is with the spiritual meaning of the fact. *"Say not in thy heart, Who shall ascend"*; *"the word is nigh thee,"* etc.

5. *The Worldwide Victories of the Cross.* Jerusalem, Athens, Rome, and all of which those several cities were the metropolis, has known, or is gradually knowing, the victory of Christianity. And its wondrous biography, infallible teaching, and redeeming power is now proclaimed not in three, but in hundreds of languages, and *"every tongue shall confess that Christ is Lord"* (Philippians 2:7).

The Uniqueness of the Shed Blood

"Made peace through the blood of his cross" (Colossians 1:20).
"The blood of Jesus Christ his Son cleanseth us from all sin" (1 John 1:7).
"Whoso...drinketh my blood, hath eternal life" (John 6:54).
"Redeemed us to God by thy blood" (Revelation 5:9).
"Made them white in the blood of the Lamb" (Revelation 7:14).
"Overcame him by the blood of the Lamb" (Revelation 12:11).
"Made nigh by the blood of Christ" (Ephesians 2:13).
"Purchased with his own blood" (Acts 20:28).

The expression, *"blood of Christ,"* is used by millions who have no accurate idea concerning its import. Blood is life; and the essential idea is centered on Christ's self-sacrificed life. The passages at the head of this article, which are the chief references to the blood of Christ in the New Testament, suggest two general remarks:

1. *That it is something sublimely unique in its nature.* Things are said of it here that could not possibly be said with propriety of the blood

of any other man, in any age or time, who has sacrificed his life. Millions of men have been sacrificed; they have lost their lives, but not in the way in which Christ was sacrificed. Some have been sacrificed by assassination, some by war, some by capital punishment, some by accident; most against their will, although some voluntarily, either by suicide or superstitious fanaticism. But in the case of Christ's sacrificed life, there was nothing like this. There are two facts which make Christ's sacrifice unique from all others.

First: It was in accordance with the eternal plan of God. He was the *"Lamb slain from the foundation of the world"* (Revelation 13:8). There was nothing accidental about it, nothing out of keeping with the eternal order of things.

Second: It was voluntary in the sense in which no other man's death was voluntary. Amongst the millions of men who have died most freely, not one has felt that he need not die at all if he chose, that he could continue here forever. But this Christ felt. There was no law in heaven or earth to force Him to the fate. *"I have power to lay it [my life] down, and I have power to take it again"* (John 10:18).

Third: The life He sacrificed was absolutely free from imperfection. Not one of all the teeming myriads who have departed this life has been entirely free from sin. All have had on them, to a greater or lesser extent, the common stain. But Christ was immaculate. His greatest enemies could not convince Him of sin. Pilate and all his judges could not find fault in Him. He was *"holy, harmless, undefiled, separate from sinners"* (Hebrews 7:26).

2. *That it is something sublimely unique in its effects.* In the passages above, results are ascribed to this blood which could not, with any propriety or the slightest approach to truth, be ascribed to the blood of any other man.

First: These effects are variously represented. It is represented as reconciliation: His sacrificed life was the atonement. It is represented as purifying: *"it cleanseth from all sin"* (1 John 1:7), and men are made white through it. *"Unto him that loved us and washed us"* (Revelation 1:5). It is represented as an essential element of soul life. *"Whoso drinketh my blood hath eternal life"* (John 6:54): something that has not only to be applied to the soul, but taken into it. It is represented as a ransom: *"redeemed us to God by his blood;"* *"purchased by his blood."* It is the power to deliver from the guilt and dominion of sin. It is represented as a conquering force: *"overcame him by the blood of the Lamb"* (Revelation 12:11). Of whose blood have these results ever been predicated or can ever be?

Second: These effects are universal in their influence. It *"cleanseth from all sin"* (1 John 1:7), it makes the great *"multitudes that no man can number...white"* (Revelation 7:9). How extensive has been its beneficent influence on humanity already! But its present area of influence, as compared with its future, is less than a little lake to the ocean.

Third: These effects are eternal in their blessings. *"Whoso drinketh my blood hath eternal life"* (John 6:54).

> Dear dying Lamb, Thy precious blood
> Shall never lose its power,
> Till all the ransomed Church of God
> Be saved to sin no more.[30]

Conclusion

First, the subject serves to explain both the essence of the gospel and the essence of personal holiness. Christ's sacrificed life is the gospel, and hence the very effects that are here ascribed to His blood are elsewhere ascribed to the gospel, to the truth of the gospel, to the grace of the gospel, to the word of the Gospel. All these are said to cleanse, redeem, conquer, and make white. Not only does it serve to explain the essence of the gospel, but also the essence of personal holiness. That principle of love which led Christ to sacrifice His life must be appropriated by us as a vital ruling element if we would be holy. His sacrifice upon the cross will be worthless to us unless we sacrifice ourselves in love. Hence we must become conformable unto His death.

Second, the subject serves to correct the mischievous way in which the blood of Christ is popularly represented. Men talk of Christ's blood as if it were the crimson fluid that coursed through His veins that saves, washes, cleanses, etc., or at any rate that which qualified Him to be a Savior. It was not His blood. The blood was nothing only as it expressed His self-sacrificing love. Supposing that the criminal law of Rome at the time in which Christ lived had required that capital offenders should be put to death by hanging, or strangling, or suffocating, or by taking poison like Socrates. Had Christ been sacrificed in any of these ways, would the power of His self-sacrifice to save

---

30. William Cowper, "There Is a Fountain Filled with Blood," 1772.

humanity be one whit the less? Not so. It was His self-sacrificing love, not the form of His mortal agonies that made Him the Savior of the world.

◡

A Meditation for Easter Day

"Come, see the place where the Lord lay" (Matthew 28:6).

Easter has well been called the "Queen of Festivals." No language can adequately describe the joyfulness and value of the event which the Christian church brings now to remembrance. Newman says, "At Christmas we joy with the natural, unmixed joy of children; but at Easter our joy is highly wrought and refined in its character." From the event of the first Easter Day dates the very commencement of the Christian church. The existence and history of the church can alone be understood by the light of the resurrection of the Lord. The text is an Easter invitation. It is full of meaning and interest if we consider: (1) the speaker, *"An angel of the Lord"* (Luke 2:9; See Luke 24:4; John 20:12); (2) the occasion, the visit of Mary Magdalene and "the other Mary" to Christ's sepulcher; and (3), the purpose, to convince these women that their Lord had risen from the dead. Let us accept this same invitation and visit the "empty tomb." If we do this, we will find:

1. *A Fact Worthy of Profound Study.* We call it a fact. Certainly it has been, and is still, doubted by many skeptics. The entire question of "miracles" hangs upon this, but we take it as a fact that is vouched for by most competent and candid witnesses. (See Westcott's *Gospel of the Resurrection,* and Milligan's *Resurrection of our Lord.*) It is a grave we visit. That fact alone starts many solemn thoughts, but still more so does the fact that it is a grave of One risen from the dead. Whose grave was it? What a strange occupant it held! In the roll of ages, how many millions of the children have died any found a grave, but none like unto Him whose empty tomb we visit. He was perfect, holy, and sinless. He was the first of that kind that death ever touched; the first sinless Being ever buried. There are, therefore, some things in this that identify, yet separate Christ from all men. (A) The fact that Christ died identifies Him closely with men. He slept "the last sleep." He shared the "common lot." He was an actual man. (B) The fact that Christ rose separates Him from men. He was the first One who rose by His own inherent power. Death could have no lasting dominion over Him.

2. *A Doctrine Worthy of Devout Acceptance.* This doctrine dominates in all the teachings of the early apostles. It is impossible to understand the drift of the apostolic speeches and writings without bearing this in mind. Mark (a) the significance of this doctrine. It becomes the pledge that all men shall rise again; that *"Death himself shall die."* It becomes the pattern of the human resurrection. Mark (b) the influence of this doctrine. Upon the early disciples, this influence is readily seen. How great was the mental transformation of Christ's followers. What enlarged and ennobled conceptions had they of Christ's character after His death. How great was the moral transformation. What bravery and self-sacrifice. (See Westcott's *Gospel of the Resurrection*.) What influence still does this doctrine exert on all the faithful. It becomes a principle of (a) spiritual life; (b) aim; and (c), energy. *"If ye be risen with Christ"* (Colossians 3:1).

3. *A Mystery Prompting to Thankful Adoration.* The whole story of Christ's life is "ringed round with mystery." The beginning was heralded by signs of the supernatural, and the end is marked by the same harmonious signs. For whose sake was this wonderful life, death, and resurrection voluntarily taken? It was for our sakes who today praise Him, *"for His mercy endures for ever"* (Psalm 107:1). We adore Him because we now realize that (a) our spiritual redemption and salvation is certain and complete; that (b), our religious faith has an immutable foundation; and that (c), all the promises of the Master and Teacher are certain of fulfillment.

4. *A Theme for Joyful Proclamation.* *"Taste and see,"* (Psalm 34:8). We, too, may join in uttering the same invitation. Accepting such invitation will be the best method for (a) solving mental doubts. Do doubts arise concerning the faith that "has turned the world upside down"? Here is an invincible proof of the truth of that faith. It is also the best method for (b) consoling the heart's bereavement and sorrow. Those we have loved and lost are not gone forever; we shall see them again, and be with them in a higher and nobler state. What rich and full consolation for us...

When tears are spent
And we are left alone with ghosts of blessings gone.

Lastly, it is the best method for (c) calming in the prospect of death. We, too, shall be victors over death and the grave. Our graves shall be "emptied." With enlarged and emphatic meaning, we can use the words—*"Yea, though I walk"* (Psalm 23:4).

> So buried with our Lord we'll close our eyes
> To the decaying world 'till angels bid us rise.

~

Glad Tidings of Easter

"Then were the disciples glad, when they saw the Lord" (John 20:20).

Eventide. The day was one of strange tidings and great excitement. The disciples were now together—their hopes, their fears; their belief, their unbelief. The appearance of Christ—how He completely conquered their doubts and gave them peace and joy!

1. Joy

Reasons for it:

a. *They were assured they had not really lost their best friend.* Notice their brokenhearted sorrow on the day of crucifixion, and the awful gloom on the day that followed. Their thoughts of Him— His looks, words, and deeds; what He had been to each of them personally; what each and all had lost; how if He had not risen, they would have gone through the world disappointed and crushed. Additional causes of fear were their cowardly fear, disloyalty, and desertion. How all was changed when He appeared back from the grave to be their friend— unfailing and forgiving!

b. *His resurrection was the assurance that injustice and iniquity had not conquered.* The death of Christ was a sore trial for the apostles' faith. John the Baptist had already fallen. Sin seemed triumphant. They had centered their hopes in Christ, their belief firm that He would conquer the enemies of truth and righteousness. They too took joy in praising Him during the triumphal procession when the people shouted *"Hosanna."* They were stunned in amazement as well as sorrow when they heard of the death sentence. What a triumph of iniquity, and defeat of innocence, purity, gentleness, love. What hope of the triumph of goodness did they have now that they thought He had failed? But when He appeared, all these thoughts of failure changed to the certainty of success. Therefore, their joy.

c. *His resurrection was the assurance of the truth of His words.* Notice the various occasions of foretelling His suffering death and resurrection; also notice the refusal of the disciples to believe, and the reasons for their disbelief. Their remembrance of His words was all too vivid after His death. His words in part were only too true; but they would not believe the other part; it seemed incredible that He should rise. But when He appeared before them, they knew that all that He had promised would be fulfilled. Endless life, the Father's house, their everlasting peace and joy was certain news; and therefore they *"were glad when they saw the Lord"* (John 20:20).

d. *And so His resurrection was the assurance that His work was not a failure.* Their opinions were partly erroneous and their desires, to some extent, were worldly. But their knowledge was clear that He had come to do a great and blessed work in the world—that they were to share in it and in its triumph. They understood the impossibility of success without Him and that His death meant the burial of their hopes. But see the disheartened warriors at their King and Leader's return. The battle is not lost now; the victory is sure. The cry, *"The Lord has risen indeed"* (Luke 24:34), gives new life to the despairing little army, and a thrill of rapture to each loyal heart. *"Then were the disciples glad when they saw the Lord"* (John 20:20).

2. Our Joy

a. *A risen Christ.* This is a constant joy through our Christian year. "An Easter Day in every week," and on our working days. (See Philippians 4:4; 1 Thessalonians 5:6.) Only if this is the joy of the whole life can Easter Day be one of real joy. Our commemoration of that, without which Christianity had been a failure, is because Easter is a success. Notice Luther's assertion that "The doctrine of justification by faith is the doctrine of a standing or falling church." This also is true of the resurrection of Christ. A powerless creed ending with "crucified, dead, and buried," is followed by a creed of inspiration, power, and victory: *"the third day he rose again."* The empty tomb is the joy of the church.

b. *A present Christ.* Explain how we, too, see the Lord; how He comes now as friend, teacher, and deliverer stronger than death

and all our foes; He is too strong for us, for our doubts and fears—
the great conqueror of all. We have this, not the hallucination of
the weak or the fever diseases of troubled brains. This is not mere
opinion, but fact. Notice the testimony of the earnest church from
age to age, and the proof of what men have been and are who have
believed.

Conclusion

Exhortation to great joy in worship, in work, in life, in death.
Source: J. Morell Blackie, LL.B.
Cheltenham, A.D. 1885

Mystical Transfusion

"The life of the flesh is in the blood" (Leviticus 17:11).

The transfusion of blood from one person to another is a wonderful dis-
covery of science, whereby the fresh life of a healthy body is imparted to a
dying person in order to restore expiring life. The weak, diseased, impoverished blood of a sufferer is vivified and strengthened by the impartation of
the pure, vigorous blood of the One with a sound body. And hospitals report
no lack of blood donors who are willing to pour their life-stream into a blood
bank for use in critical cases.

Years ago, I witnessed a noble sacrifice of blood. A friend of mine saw his
wife languishing in pain. She gradually grew worse, necessitating an imme-
diate and serious operation. After the operation, she seemed to be slipping
through the fingers of the surgeons who battled for her life. Blood transfusion was the last resort, and the devoted, anxious husband took a bed in a
neighboring ward of the hospital and gave his blood until fresh strength shot
through the weak frame of the woman he loved. And such an incident and fact
of surgical science suggests one or two helpful spiritual parallels as we come to
think about the efficacy of the blood of Jesus.

The Need of the Sufferer

That dear woman was in a weak and dying state, unable to resist the death
throes battling for supremacy. What a picture this is of the sinner who is weak,
helpless, and about to die! Unless help reaches him from an outside source, he
must perish in his sins, for he does not have strength to save himself.

The Sacrifice of the Friend

That loving husband could not bear to see his wife suffer. She needed fresh blood, so he allowed his own veins to be opened that healthy blood might be pumped into the wasted form of the sufferer. Thus, he gave part of himself to save his wife, for the life of the flesh is in the blood. And the blood Christ shed for our redemption was the blood of a dear friend—the lover of our souls.

It is clearly evident that all blood transfusions are not successful. If transfusions are successful, the blood given and imparted must be pure and untainted by disease, giving strong, active cells. This is the secret of Christ's efficacious blood shed on the shameful tree for our sins—it was pure, holy, warm, and powerful. It was the blood of God's beloved Son.

The Nature of the Blood

John's rich statement about the blood of Jesus Christ, God's Son, having power to cleanse from all sin has become so commonplace that its deep significance is lost upon us.

The Blood

Blood is the symbol of life. The difference between a corpse and a living person is that one has living blood coursing through his veins and the other does not. And out poured blood is a symbol of life given. The blood Jesus spilled at the cross, then, signified the outpouring of His life. He had power to lay down His life; He willingly sacrificed it that we might live. And now when we speak and sing about being washed in the blood of the Lamb, we do not mean that the blood as a possession still exists, but that God can receive the sinner in virtue of Calvary. The blood represents the abiding efficacy of the cross. If only those who find the preaching and teaching of the blood repugnant would realize this fact, they would come to value the finished work of Calvary in a new way.

a. The Blood of Jesus. Jesus, the human One! Surely this thought has a tender appeal. He sacrificed rich, warm, human blood. It was blood of the One who was kind, sympathetic, and compassionate. It was blood poured out for friend and foe alike. *"My blood, which is shed for you"* (Luke 22:20). What an offering to make—that unworthy sinners might be saved!

b. The Blood of Jesus Christ. Christ, the Anointed One! So the blood was not only real, human blood but also royal blood. It was the blood of the Messiah, of the King. We talk about those of a royal house as being of the "blood royal." Well, Christ has "royal blood," seeing that He was the eternal King. Thus, when He died, He shed the blood as the sent One of God, not a despised Jew or Nazarene. And if there is power where the word *King* is, then what greater power must the blood of a King have?

c.   The Blood of Jesus Christ, His Son. His Son! The blood shed was the blood of the Divine One. And it is this fact that adds efficacy to the blood. Had it been the blood of an ordinary man, it would never have availed for men. But there is power in Christ's shed blood, seeing that it was the blood of God. (See Acts 20:28.) The blood of the God-man! Yes, but here we enter a mystery too deep and profound for words. The great miracle of the virgin birth was the fusion of deity and humanity, the wedding of godhead and manhood into one personality. Thus, when Jesus died, He shed the blood of the God-man created by the Holy Spirit within Mary's womb. This, then, is the reason why the blood can cleanse from all sin, and why Satan strives to thwart the preaching of the cross.

d.   The Blood of Jesus Christ, His Son, Cleanseth from All Sin! Cleanseth from *all* sin. Yes, from all kinds and acts of sin. Oh, the countless victories of the blood! May we never tire of exalting its glorious triumphs! The blood, as we have seen, represents the finished work of Christ at Calvary for sinners everywhere, and John sings of three glorious virtues of the blood of God's dear Son.

These are the three notes in this blood-glorifying song:

1.   It Has Perpetual Cleansing. The word "cleanseth" in the present tense implies that the blood keeps on cleansing. Its efficacy is continuous; it never loses its power to save and deliver. Age after age it retains its capacity of cleansing. The crimson stream never ceases to function as a channel of pardon. In the hour of our salvation we experienced deliverance from the guilt of sin as the Spirit applied the blood to our hearts, but every hour of every day since then, the healing virtue of the blood has been pleaded on our behalf. We need its washing and loosing power every minute of every day. (See Revelation 1:5.)

> Dear dying Lamb, Thy precious blood
> Shall never lose its pow'r,
> Till all the ransomed Church of God
> Be saved, to sin no more.[31]

2. It Has Personal Cleansing. Whatever our need may be, we can lay a finger on this verse and claim it as our own. Martin Luther has told us to watch the pronouns of Scripture. And here is one for us to appropriate. May we learn how to translate *us* into *me!*

   John, of course, is writing to saints; therefore, his message about the cleansing blood has a direct application to believers, all of whom need a daily cleansing from sin. The apostle has the practice of sin in mind rather than its principle; fruit rather than root; sins, rather than sin. And the blood of Jesus Christ keeps on cleansing us from all the association of sin as we endeavor to abide in unbroken fellowship with God.

3. It Has Perfect Cleansing. John declares that the blood of God's Son is able to cleanse from all sin! It is a tremendous but blessedly true fact. And all means all—secret sins or presumptuous sins; sins of youth and age; sins against others; sins against ourselves; or darker sins against God. Yes, the blood can deal with all kinds and degrees of sin because of its royal, rich nature. Shed over 1900 years ago, its abiding efficacy is experienced the moment a sinner turns to the Savior. The miracle happens immediately—the red blood of Jesus makes the black heart white as snow.

The Act of Transfusion

Reverting to the incident told at the beginning of this study, there is a further truth to be emphasized concerning the act of transfusion made possible by surgery. There came the exact moment when the blood of the husband was drained from him and entered the suffering wife. The Holy Spirit is the great transfuser, the divine Surgeon who causes the virtue and efficacy of the cross to pass into sinful, needy lives. And He applies the blood as the sinner turns toward the Savior. It would be well for us to pray, "O blessed surgeon, transfuse more of the precious, priceless, powerful blood of Jesus into my poor, weak life—that life more abundant may be mine."

---

31. William Cowper, "There Is a Fountain Filled with Blood," 1772.

In his monumental study in "Genetic Theology," Dr. John B. Champion writes about a somewhat fastidious lady who always objected to Scripture lessons and hymns mentioning "the blood." When she heard a hymn such as "There Is a Fountain Filled With Blood," she was so disturbed that she would leave the worship service.

This went on for some time, until she contracted an anemic disease. The time came when only one thing could save her life—a blood transfusion. While several people volunteered to give their blood, it came about that her husband's blood was most compatible with hers. After the transfusion, which restored her health, her attitude was completely changed. Seeing that her life was saved at the cost of a blood transfusion, by her husband's sacrifice, blood became a saving, sacred, and divine thing to her. From the analogy of her experience, she could understand how Christ's saving life had entered into her own, how His sacrificial life had redeemed her. After this, she could not hear enough about the redeeming blood of Christ. Hymns telling of "the sacrifice of nobler name and richer blood" now sounded like a heavenly melody to her ears. Experience had lifted her up to the language of the blood.

Some professing to be refined may scoff at the gospel of blood, and call it a "slaughterhouse salvation." They forget, however, that animals slain in a slaughterhouse are killed so that man might have physical life. Man may reject the blood of Christ, but he is hopelessly lost without it, for it is the blood that makes atonement for the soul.

⌣

The Cross and Divine Sovereignty

"Say among the heathen that the Lord reigneth: the world also shall be established that it shall not be moved; he shall judge the people righteously" (Psalm 96:10).

It is both refreshing and inspiring in these days of crumbling earthly kingdoms to return to the Psalms, with their air of certainty regarding the present sovereignty and coming universal dominion of the Lord. Psalm 96 is one such psalm wherein God's supremacy is unchallenged in every realm.

We turn to verse 10 for a summary of this theocratic psalm presenting a trinity in unity; the threefold cord of sovereignty, security, and sanctity cannot be broken.

Sovereignty

"*Say among the nations that the Lord reigneth*" (Psalm 96:10). This is an age of proud dictatorships. Man has little room for God. Brute force would seem at times to be the world's sovereign lord, yet amid chaos and despair and godlessness, God reigns. God is not dead, as some believe. He may appear at times to be standing in the shadows. His throne, however, has not been abdicated. This guilty earth has yet to receive his reckoning.

Security

"*The world also shall be established that it shall not be moved*" (verse 10). Well, there is little semblance of this predicted settled order. We live in a changing world. Thrones, governments, and systems are changing with startling rapidity. Nothing is established. But our verse offers us a changeless world, an order of government fixed and immovable. Such will be experienced when that One is in complete control who declared Himself to be the Lord who does not change.

Sanctity

"*He shall judge the world with righteousness*" (Psalm 9:8). Here again we have a study in contrast. Righteous judgment is a scarce commodity. Deceit, bribery, graft, corruption, and unrighteous practices are associated with men and places least suspected.

Some time ago, the papers carried the report of one of the highest judges in the land who is now behind bars for dishonest transactions. Yes, the best of men are only men at the best. But a Man is coming, a glorified Man, who will judge the people righteously.

The burden of our message, however, is in the first phrase of the basic verse, "*Say among the nations that the Lord reigneth from the tree.*"

In another connection, we have indicated that Psalm 96 is a great missionary psalm revealing Israel's responsibility to make God known among the nations, with emphasis on the world empire of the heavenly Sovereign. He is declared an emperor. As we noted before, there is a distinction between a king and an emperor, the former being chief ruler in and over a nation, while emperor being the highest title of sovereignty and suggesting a ruler of nations and lesser sovereigns. And the day is coming when the kingdoms of this world will become a world-kingdom, and Christ will reign supreme over all. (See Revelation 11:15.)

Our English version ends with *"the Lord reigneth,"* but as you know, Justin Martyr accused the Jews of erasing *"from the tree"* from the original because of their intense hatred of Christ. But Jesus does reign, and the truth we are setting out, then, is that in the realm of sovereignty, Christ's cross is His throne; the dying Savior was the triumphant Lord who died as a victor, not a victim. Thus, we come to our meditation on the cross and divine sovereignty.

The Confession of Sovereignty

"Say...the Lord reigneth." Divine sovereignty is a truth we need to experience personally and proclaim nationally. On every hand there is a tendency to deify man and humanize God. Let us therefore say, and utter it loudly, that God reigns!

Say that God reigns to Russia, with its blatant godlessness, its bloody rule, and its strongly-expressed desire to rule the world, and will yet laugh at those who try to exterminate Him.

Say that God reigns to the nations like Germany, who have brutally and inhumanly treated the Jews, and will yet empty His curse upon those who curse His own.

Say that God reigns to Rome, proud nationally, corrupt religiously— Rome, with its sensuous and paganized form of Christianity, and will yet see to it that His Son will be fully worshiped and adored.

Say that God reigns to Britain, concerning her past dealings with Palestine, and will yet have His ancient people in full possession of the land which is theirs by divine gift and right.

Say that God reigns to America, with its self-complacency, extreme worldliness, and gross materialism, and will yet exact the uttermost farthing in judgment.

Yea, verily, and say it to our own hearts when depressed by hostile forces arrayed against us, that God reigns! He rules and overrules! Glory to His name! The Lord God omnipotent reigneth. Let the earth tremble, and tremble it will—tremble and crumble when His power is unleashed.

The Circumference of Sovereignty

"Among the nations." Divine sovereignty is not limited to the angelic realm. God's will is accomplished among the inhabitants of the earth as well as with the armies of heaven. All power is His in heaven and on earth.

God reigns among the nations! Well, apparently the world bears no semblance of a divine rule. No matter where you look, truth is on the scaffold and wrong is on the throne. Strife, suspicion, hatred, chaos, and bloodshed are all around us, and the world is an armed camp.

And what kind of a world can we expect when Satan is its god? At present the world is satanically controlled. Behind destructive and horrible modern engines of war, there is a destroyer. Evil forces are inspired by a figure; godless influences emanate from an individual. Chaos, anguish, blasted lives and hopes are caused by Satan, who has been a murderer from the beginning. The struggle is not against flesh and blood. One nation rises in the flesh and tries to conquer another nation prepared to fight back in the flesh. But earth's conflict is not human; it is superhuman and super terrestrial. We wrestle not against flesh and blood, but against the potentates of the dark present, the spiritual forces of evil in the heavenly sphere. Yet we are to say among the nations, torn as they are by war, that God reigns! No matter how the agony of the world may contradict the truth of divine sovereignty, God is still able to make the wrath of men and demons to praise Him. Whether it be satanic or universal, God is supreme. Hellish forces may appear to have the ascendancy, but the devil who commands them is a dog on a leash and cannot go beyond divine permission.

Our responsibility, then, is to tell it out among the nations that God's day is coming. Perplexed hearts feel that He is a little inactive, but He can afford to wait. He is never before His time, and never behind. God is coming to give the warring earth peace. He will yet reign without a rival. The uttermost parts of the earth will be His possession when He fashions the nations into His own world kingdom.

The Center of Sovereignty

"From the tree." Such a pregnant phrase from ancient translations brings us to the secret and source of sovereignty. The cross provided Christ with crown rights. Limiting the benefits of the cross to the initial work of cleansing a sinner from the penalty and guilt of sin, we err, not knowing the Scriptures. Calvary gave the Savior power over spheres as well as souls. In virtue of the anguish, shame, and sacrifice, Jesus will reign from shore to shore. The nail-pierced hand is to wield the scepter of universal dominion. John, in his apocalyptic vision, saw a slain Lamb conquering all hostile powers and establishing His worldwide reign.

Calvary, then, was a grim battlefield where Satan met his "Waterloo." The cross was the bloody arena where Jesus laid hold of principalities, powers, world-rulers, satanic potentates and robbed them of their authority. When He cried, "*It is finished,*" our Lord not only had in mind our redemption, but also the deliverance of a groaning world from Satan's dominion. The cross, then, was a throne. Jesus reigns over His own from the tree, and will yet reign over the world. The cross transcends all human and hellish power. The blood of the Lamb made the sovereignty of the Lamb possible. The motto of an ancient Scottish house is a cross with the words, "By this sign we conquer." A cruel cross, then, will yet turn spears into pruning hooks, and swords into plowshares.

Yes, our adorable Lord reigns from His tree, and such is the truth we must proclaim to the nations magnifying brute force. Jesus revealed how love can triumph over hate; unselfishness over greed; holiness over sin; truth over falsehood; gentleness over force; and sacrifice over sordid gain.

⤳

The Magnetism of Calvary

"*And I, if I be lifted up from the earth, will draw all men unto me*" (John 12:32).

There are at least two thoughts within the narrative leading up to the unique verse before us, describing as it does the magnetism of the cross.

The Greek's Request

"*Sir, we would see Jesus*" (John 12:21).

One cannot say what it was that actually drew these Gentiles to Christ. Perhaps it was curiosity which is often the mother of wonder, or the minister of deathless devotion as it was in the case of Zacchaeus. Or, possibly, hunger compelled the searchers to seek out Jesus. Grecian art, music, and philosophy supplied bread for their dissatisfied souls; therefore, they found their way to Him who came as the Bread of Life. If the latter is true, that unsatisfied craving brought these Greeks to Jesus, then we have a foreshadowing of the participation of the great Gentile world in the redemptive work of the cross.

The Master's Response

"*Except a corn of wheat…die*" (John 12:24).

If the love of the Greeks for the beautiful led them to the beautiful One, then these Greeks must learn that Jesus cannot be known after the flesh. It is only as the Crucified One that He can be received and admired. And as a result of Calvary, He came to draw both Jew and Gentile unto Himself. As the corn of wheat He fell into the ground and died, but what a rich and plentiful harvest is the outcome of His death and resurrection!

His Magnetic Person

I, if I! Such personal pronouns suggest His adorable person, so let us think in the first place of "the Christ of the Cross." Christ Himself is the most magnetic of all forces. *"Draw me, we will run after Thee"* (Song of Solomon 1:4).

It is profitable to note the recurring "I" in our Lord's teaching. Here the pronoun is emphatic, "I and I alone." What a stupendous claim to make! But as the great I Am, He could make it without assumption. Repulsive when used by others, the "I" is quite natural when Jesus uses it. Constant usage of "I" strengthens egotism when we use it. With Him, however, it is different. Leaving His lips, it carries divine authority. He could say and do all that He uttered and accomplished because of who and what He was. Deity is wrapped in the pronoun.

Furthermore, the "I" is used in opposition to *"the prince of this world"* (John 12:31). What a contrast of character: the Light of the World; the Prince of Darkness. The one draws to death; the other to life. Jesus draws us to Himself with the cords of love; Satan draws us by deceit and crafty subtlety.

His Magnetic Passion

Lifted up from the earth! So, we are led to His passion from His person; from His deity to His death; from His character to His cross; from the Christ of the cross to Christ on the cross.

Three times the phrase *"lifted up"* is employed by Jesus in John's gospel, and each reference carries a different aspect of Calvary with it. For example:

1. The Reason of the Cross (John 3:14). *"Even so...lifted up."* There we have the basis of regeneration. There can be no salvation without sacrifice.

2. The Revelation of the Cross (John 8:28). *"When lifted up...know that I am he."* Even the dying thief came to know that the dying One near him was the Son of God with the power to save.

3. The Reign of the Cross (John 12:32). *"Lifted up...will draw."* And the cross is still the greatest draw. Thus, the prophecy of Scripture, the ministry of the Holy Spirit, and the perpetual ministry and power of the Crucified One are happily blended.

The twofold aspect of Calvary is emphasized in the narrative we are considering. First of all, there is the fact of Christ's death, and then its form. The fact—"*The death he should die*" (verse 33)—indicates that the shadow was ever before Him. Man is born to live; Christ was born to die. He was actually slain before He left the glory. The form of His death is implied in the phrase "*lifted up*" (verse 32). One version says, "*lifted out of the earth*"! Crucifixion was the Roman form of death meted out to malefactors, meaning our Lord was treated as a felon when cruel hands nailed Him to a wooden gibbet. He was lifted up on the earth at His death, lifted out of the earth at His resurrection, lifted up from the earth altogether at His ascension. And it takes all that is wrapped up in Christ's death, resurrection, and ascension to complete His drawing power. The fact that He died and lives constitutes the saving gospel.

His Magnetic Power

"*I will draw all men after me.*" A threefold cord is not quickly broken. Thus we have our Lord's person, passion, and power, as well as deity, death, and dynamic. The death of deified humanity is all implied in Christ's declaration. So we have the Christ of the cross: "*I, if I*"; the Christ on the cross: "*lifted up*"; and the Christ through the cross: "*draw all men unto me.*" And truly, there is no other way by which we can reach Him.

A gifted writer has pointed out that the magnetism of Christ is seen in that He lifts men up and unites them to God by revelation, by the gift of the Spirit of divine light whereby the reign of night is ended; unites them to God by redemption by the gift of divine life whereby the reign of death is ended; unites them to God by inspiration and the gift of divine liberty whereby the reign of infirmity is ended.

Several precious truths can be gleaned from this record of Christ's magnetic Calvary power. For example, we have...

1. The uplifted Lord is the only magnetic power.

No other truth can awaken men to a life of surrender and devotion like that of the cross. They realize that love so amazing demands the best they have to give. Yes and the preaching of Christ crucified breaks up the frozen indifference of some hearts, delivering them from inertia. The cross disturbs the conscience, awakens moral pains, accomplishes a spiritual resurrection, and draws souls to a life of undying love.

Sacrifice is always strangely majestic. In common life it never fails to allure one's interest and admiration. Some time ago in an "In Memoriam" column of a daily paper, the following notice occurred: "In memory of a lovely little lady, who made the supreme sacrifice of motherhood, leaving sweet memories but a brokenhearted hubby." Yet somehow the vast majority of people are unresponsive to the supreme sacrifice of all. They can hear and read about the sufferings of Christ and remain untouched and unmoved. A trashy novel can move them to tears, but Calvary in all its horror and anguish has not appeal to their cold, dead hearts.

Furthermore, if Christ is proclaimed as an ethical teacher, such an aspect may arrest the mind, but it will never generate heat in a cold heart. If He is presented as a fiery reformer, one may gain signatures of those who are willing to join in a crusade against glaring sins. As a young prophet, He may draw the cheap, blind worship and mental asset of those who are out for hero worship. If exalted as a lowly Galilean peasant, He may draw the sympathy of humble souls who never reach higher than human feelings.

If, however, Christ is to deliver men from the penalty and pollution of sin, then He must be lifted up as the sacrificial Savior. He may win the plaudits of men as a beautiful teacher, ardent reformer, and zealous prophet, but as the Son of God, crucified for sinners, He captivates the souls and moves men to holier living. Therefore, let us make much of the cross, seeing that it has been the theme of all who have been used by God. Persuaded that their only magnet was the Lord Jesus in the wonderful energies of His transcendent sacrifice and not in His beautiful teachings and incomparably lovely life, they lived to extol Him.

2. Being above, He can draw from beneath.

Lifted up from the earth, Christ can draw men out of it! The Christ some men preach can never draw, for they keep Him on the earth. They declare that He was only a man and no higher than others. He is relegated to the level of ordinary humanity; such a perverted gospel has no magnetism whatsoever. Had Christ remained on the earth, He would not have had the power to save the world. Crucified, however, He can conquer the world. A church or a Christian living on the level of the world can never draw souls nearer the Savior. We must be raised from earth like Him if we would lift it up to God. Let us therefore exalt the cross both by lip and life.

3. The uplifted Christ possesses a universal magnetism.

The cross draws all men. This truly foreshadows the universality of the Gospel with all nations, clans, and conditions participating in the fruits of Calvary.

But some hearts may argue that "if Christ has power to draw all men, why are not all men saved?" Well, it is evident that the cross has sufficient efficacy to save all men. Universal attraction is focused in the sacrificial energy of His death: *"the last fragrant syllable of God's utterance of love."* Freedom of will and moral power, however, can resist the charm of the cross. It should be noticed that Christ "draws," not "drags." He strives to win souls, not worry them. But his overtures can be rejected. *"I would...ye would not."*

Thus, the drawing and the coming are united. The magnet says "come," but "draws" as it speaks. (See Matthew 11:28; John 12:32.) Can your heart sing,

> He drew me, and I followed on,
> Charmed to confess the voice divine.[32]

And, blessed be His name, the day is coming fast when the Master will appear in the air and, as a magnet, draw all the blood-sheltered ones up to Himself. They will rise to Him as filings to a magnet.

4. *The magnetic power of Christ is concentric.*

If a standard were placed in the center of a building and people urged to get as near to it as possible, what would happen? Why, the nearer they found themselves to the standard, the nearer they would be to one another. And the nearer we live to the cross, the more we find ourselves drawn together. But somehow we have forgotten the center. The church has created centers of her own, and if men do not travel to her center, judgment and expulsion ensues.

Christianity ought to be the expression of brotherly love, but has become an avenue of strife and isolation. Journeying from the cross, so-called Christians have separated from one another. And whenever we plant our feet on a self-chosen, self-created center, fighting only for particular interpretations of a creed, forgetting to keep our eyes fixed on the uplifted Lord, we miss the superlative sacrifice of His cross. A return to the Crucified One would quickly heal the church's lamentable division.

5. *The magnetic power of the cross is christocentric.*

Christ on the cross is the center and circumference of all things. As the Crucified One, He draws all men to Himself. He will not give His glory to another. There is a modern tendency to bring men to His works, His words, and His ways, rather than to Himself. And it is sadly possible to draw men

---

32. Philip Doddridge, "O Happy Day, That Fixed my Choice," 1755.

to a church and yet not to Christ! Nothing, however, must obscure His adorable person. Our ultimate goal must always be to attract souls to the Master Himself.

May it always be that our passion is strong to present the Savior in all the fullness of His grace and charm and that in seeing Him, all hearts would be lost in the contemplation of His majesty! Because He has power to lift men out of the cold prison house of guilt, delivering them thereby from the bitterness of a Christless death with its awful doom of abiding wrath, let us extol His virtue.

Martyrs like Stephen were forced into death. Christ, however, walked deliberately to His bitter end. He descended the slope of sacrifice from grade to grade until He tore out death's sting; and in one supreme victory, He triumphed over sin, death, and hell. Hallelujah, what a Savior!

The question is, have you allowed the uplifted Christ to draw you? Can you sing,

> Drawn to the Cross which Thou hast blessed,
> With healing gifts for souls distressed,
> To find in Thee my life, my rest,
> Christ crucified, I come.
>
> To be what Thou wouldst have me be,
> Accepted, sanctified in Thee,
> Through what Thy grace shall work in me,
> Christ Crucified, I come.[33]

We read of those who came to Him from every quarter. If you do not know Him, may you come to Him out of your need. May God enable you to yield to the charm of the cross!

～

The Easter Evangel

"God was in Christ, reconciling the world unto himself" (2 Corinthians 5:19).

It used to be said a generation ago that "the heart of the world is Britain—the heart of Britain is London—the heart of London is Westminster." It is truer to say that the heart of Christianity is the Bible—the heart of the Bible is the cross—the heart of the cross is the very heart of God Himself. *"God was in Christ reconciling the world unto himself"* (2 Corinthians 5:19). And

33. Genevieve Irons, "Drawn to the Cross, Which Thou Hast Blessed," 1880.

such a divine heart is full of the most tender compassion for a sinning, erring humanity.

It would seem as if Paul is the greatest exponent of Calvary's Evangel, for all his writings drip with the blood of the Redeemer, whom the apostle so dearly loved. What an incomplete, partial revelation we would have if Paul's epistles were removed from the New Testament. "The Lamb, the Lamb, the bleeding Lamb" was Paul's preeminent theme. The cross was the center of his theology:

Corinth received the declaration, "*I determined not to know anything among you, save Jesus Christ, and him crucified*" (1 Corinthians 2:2).

Galatia read the Pauline utterance, "*who gave himself for our sins;*" "*the Son of God, who loved me, and gave himself for me;*" and "*God forbid that I should glory, save in the cross of our Lord Jesus Christ*" (Galatians 1:4; 2:20; 6:14).

Rome, proud mistress of Paul's world, was reminded that "*in due time Christ died for the ungodly*" (Romans 5:6).

Thessalonica had those who, through the apostle's ministry, believed that "*Jesus died and rose again*" (1 Thessalonians 4:14).

Ephesus, too, was reminded that there were those within the city who had been far off from God, but were "*made nigh by the blood of Christ*" (Ephesians 2:13).

Philippi had its saints who were exhorted to share the apostolic ambition of knowing Christ "*and the power of his resurrection, and the fellowship of his sufferings*" (Philippians 3:10).

Colosse also was enjoined to remember that redemption was only "*through his blood*" (Colossians 1:14).

The Revelation of the Evangel

Paul was not the author of the Easter Evangel. It came upon him as a distinct revelation from God. "*That which I also received*" (1 Corinthians 15:3), he said. He was merely the recipient of such a truth, as he is careful to emphasize. "*I neither received it of men, neither was I taught it, but by the revelation of Jesus Christ*" (Galatians 1:12).

"*By revelation he made known unto me the mystery*" (Ephesians 3:3, 5). And it is here that Paul's gospel differs from all man-made gospels which originate in the human mind. While the gospel of redeeming grace is for the earth, it is not earthly. It ever remains a revelation. The Spirit of God must reveal the need of the sinner, and the ability of God to meet that need through the cross.

The Foundation of the Evangel

Although the great fundamental foundation of such an Evangel is the death of God's beloved Son at Calvary, it would seem as if there are three aspects of the glorious theme which Easter proclaims.

First of all, there is the "Prophetic Witness," for, as Paul states it, *"Christ died for our sins according to the scriptures"* (1 Corinthians 15:3–4). Thus Paul, like his Master, set his seal to the Old Testament. Drenched as he was in Old Testament literature, Paul was ever thrilled as he traced the cross in these Old Testament books.

"Prophetic Scriptures" revolve around the cross. Passages like Psalm 22 and Isaiah 53 are clearly related to the Crucified One.

"Prophetic Symbols" of the cross are before us in the Red Sea, Isaac, and Jonah (Hebrews 9:19; Matthew 12:42).

"Prophetic Ordinances" associated with the tabernacle provide us with a picture book of the cross (Hebrews 9:12, 14).

Second, we have the "Messianic Works." There are three parts to Paul's first creed of Christendom, which must always remain the substance of the gospel, delivering from the penalty and power of sin.

1. "Christ died for our sins."

The fact and the purpose of the cross are here proclaimed—*"Christ died."* Here is an indisputable fact directly mentioned some one hundred seventy-five times in the New Testament. And being an historical fact as well as a biblical one, it cannot be contradicted. *"Christ suffered under Pontius Pilate, was crucified, dead, and buried."*

Dying for "our sins" constituted the purpose of the cross. Jesus did not die as a martyr or a hero may die. The incontestable testimony of all the Scriptures is that Christ was manifested to destroy the works of the devil. We see Jesus as the sinless One on the cross dying for sinners.

2. "...was buried,,,"

John Bunyan saw in his dream "Christian" trudging with his load of sin to the cross where it fell off and tumbled into the sepulcher nearby. And, to be buried in a grave was the depth of humiliation for Christ. Think of it! He came from the highest heaven into the heart of the earth.

<blockquote>
Low in the grave He lay,
Jesus, my Savior.[34]
</blockquote>

---

34. Robert Lowry, "Low in the Grave He Lay," 1874.

But as He made His grave with the wicked and the rich in His death, He carried our sins far away.

3. *"…rose again the third day…"*

Some of the old saints used to say that the resurrection was God's receipt for Calvary. How true! The empty tomb declares that the debt has been paid and that God is completely satisfied with the death and work of the cross. Christ's resurrection is also the seal of the perfection of His life and labors.

Furthermore, it was necessary for Christ to rise again for our justification. The cross certainly delivers the sinner from the guilt of sin, but by rising again from the dead, Christ is now able to make the cross alive in our lives. This is what Paul meant when he wrote, *"We shall be saved by His life"* (Romans 5:10); that is, Christ's risen, glorified, throne-life. Thus, it is wrong to worship a crucifix with its limp form of a dead Christ. Both the cross and the tomb are empty.

In his great resurrection sermon, Paul is combating false theories of this fundamental doctrine and cites historic evidence of the resurrection. He gives us the chronological order of Christ's appearance to His own. There were a total of five hundred fourteen people who saw him. And, as if to clinch his argument, Paul declares that *"last of all he was seen of me also"* (1 Corinthians 15:8).

The Description of the Evangel

In the introduction to his resurrection discourse, Paul refers to such the message as "the gospel" he had received to preach. And a "gospel" is the glad announcement of good news. Gospel is "God's spell," spell being the Saxon word for "story." Thus, the "gospel" before us is "God's Story." And what a story to tell to the nations! It is a story from God, for it originated with Him in a past eternity. Before the foundation of the world, "Love drew salvation's plan." It is also a story about God, seeing it reveals His love and grace.

The Proclamation of the Evangel

Studying the context of 1 Corinthians 15, we find a combination of terms, all related to our declaration of the gospel which the death and the resurrection of Christ made possible.

It is a Preeminent Message

"*…first of all*" (1 Corinthians 15: 3).

Paul's principal message was the cross. And in all our preaching and evangelization such a gospel must be prominent. What the apostle unfolds in this great chapter is primary because all else stands or falls by it. The same is first, seeing that the death and resurrection of Christ are indispensable when it comes to the forgiveness of sins. Obliterate these cardinal truths and we have no gospel to preach.

It is a Proclaimed Message

"...I preached unto you..." (1 Corinthians 15:1).

Going back to the Acts, we find that the church at Corinth was founded as the result of such preaching. (See Acts 18:1–11.) Paul determined to know nothing among the Corinthians save Christ and Him crucified. The word "preach" Paul uses here is related to the word "evangelist," that is, one who announces glad tidings. And truly, there is no story as joyful as the one Paul never tired of telling.

It is a Persistent Message

"...I declare..." (1 Corinthians 15:1).

"Tell me the story often." Well, Paul reiterated it! He was forever reminding his hearers and readers of "the old, old story of Jesus and His love." And, without a doubt, Calvary's gospel bears repetition. It can never grow old through telling, though told a thousand times over. We must persistently fling the cross into the race of a godless world.

It is a Proved Message

"...I delivered...which I also received..." (1 Corinthians 15:3).

The word "deliver" here means "alongside of" and infers that Paul only preached to others what he himself had proved. Having experienced the regenerating and transforming power of such an Evangel, the apostle persuades others to receive it. Knowing whom he had believed, Paul had no hesitation in beseeching those around him to be reconciled to God. (See verses 8–9.) Coming to ourselves, let us realize that it is only the truth which we have experienced that can influence others to heed it as we proclaim it.

The Application of the Evangel

Another cluster of phrases gathered from Paul's resurrection sermon indicates that the work of Christ and His cross is only effectual as applied by the Spirit on the basis of faith.

We have **Reception**

"…ye have received…" (1 Corinthians 15:1).

While Christ died, and by dying made our salvation possible, it is only our reception that can make this actual in our experience. We can only become children of God as we receive the Crucified One as our personal Savior. (See John 1:11–12.)

We have **Foundation**

"…wherein ye stand…" (verse 1).

The cross is the center and circumference of everything. It is not only our starting point, but also our way of life. And John's Apocalypse makes it plain that ultimate triumph will be Christ's as the Lamb. Modernism is out to destroy this foundation. It despises all preaching about the blood. This "slaughterhouse gospel," as it has been called, is repugnant to cultured minds. But…

> We have no other argument, we have no other plea,
> It is enough that Jesus died, and that He died for me.[35]

We have **Salvation**

"…ye are saved…" (1 Corinthians 15:2).

This phrase is actually cast in the present tense—*"ye are being saved"*— which implies not only initial deliverance from the penalty of sin, but also a daily, perpetual emancipation from the power and the practice of sin.

We have **Retention**

"…ye keep in memory…" (1 Corinthians 15:2).

In instituting the Memorial Feast, Jesus urged His disciples to use the bread and wine not only as symbols of His sacrifice, but also as incentives for remembrance. *"This do in remembrance of me."* One version has it, *"If ye hold fast."* Once we lose grip of the cross, our spiritual life is impoverished. Like Mary, we must always stand by the cross.

We have **Rejection**

"…believing in vain" (1 Corinthians 15:2).

How can one believe in vain? Well, he can believe in an historical Christ and yet remain ignorant of His efficacious death on their behalf. Later on, Paul

---

35. Charles Wesley, "We Have No Other Argument," 1749.

speaks of grace being in vain. (See verse 10.) Alas, it would seem as if all the anguish of Calvary was in vain, when we see how Christ is blatantly rejected! May grace be ours always to rejoice in the shed blood of the Redeemer, and to exhibit the spirit of the cross in all our ways, thereby enabling Jesus to see of the travail of His soul and be satisfied!

~

The Victory Sign

"*...triumphing over them in it...*" (Colossians 2:15).

During the dark and dismal days of World War II, the "V" sign became the symbol of the faith of free people everywhere. In countries where tyranny reigns, the "V" is plastered on walls in public places, much to the chagrin of cruel occupying forces. We are accustomed to seeing two triumphant fingers held up defiantly, making a "V" shape as the token of ultimate victory. It is the favorite pose of Sir Winston Churchill, former Prime Minister of Britain, as he indicated the brave assurance he inspired that the Allies would carry to a successful conclusion the grim task to which they were committed.

It is somewhat surprising to discover that God also employs the same sign of victory. A noted commentator, referring to the incident of Christ bearing His cross remarks: "The condemned were usually obliged to carry their crosses, the crossbeams fastened together like the letter V, their arms bound to the projecting ends." And what does the fastening of those crossbeams like a V suggest but that the cross, in fact and even in form, is God's victory sign. A somewhat suggestive translation of "*triumphing over them in it*" (Colossians 2:15) reads "winning the victory through the cross." And without a doubt, the cross is the symbol of present and ultimate victory over all the forces of Satan and sin.

The question is: Is a triumph ours? Are we more than conquerors? Have we proved the Pauline challenging assertion that "*sin shall not have dominion over you*"? (Romans 6:14). Young Christopher Benn of the British Army remarked before his death in a plane crash, "Victory is not only a national affair, it is a personal matter too." It is commendable and right to fight and suffer for the preservation of the renowned "Four Freedoms," but can we have all four and yet not experience freedom from sin's guilt and power? Have we participated in the blood-bought emancipation?

He is the freeman, whom the truth sets free,
And all are slaves beside.[36]

---

36. William Cowper, *The Task*, 1785.

Napoleon, that brilliant dictator, confessed, "For myself, nature has doomed me to win but outward victories." Yes, in military triumphs he was conspicuous, but in his moral triumphs, Napoleon was lamentably deficient.

The glad message of Calvary is that each of us can be blessedly victorious on the inner battlefield of the soul. But is the joy of inward triumph ours? Eagerly anticipating as we did the day of complete victory for the Allies, has our day of personal victory dawned? Can each of us exultantly shout, *"thanks be to God, which giveth us the victory through our Lord Jesus Christ"* (1 Corinthians 15:57)? "A victory inside of us," Henry Ward Beecher once declared, "is ten thousand times more glorious than one outside of us." May we increasingly experience the thrill of conscious victory over sin and self!

The Cost of Conquest

There are no battles without blood. Any triumph means a terrible toll of lives. Supremacy over sinister forces can only come through sacrifice. Victory has its price. "Madam," said the Duke of Wellington in conversation with a friend, "Madam, there is nothing more terrible than a great defeat, except a great victory." And the blood-soaked battlefields, strewn with human wreckage and countless wooden crosses, testify to the fact that victories are costly to achieve. When it came to our redemption we have no conception of what it cost the Son of God to die in our room and stead.

> None of the ransomed ever knew
> How deep were the waters crossed,
> Nor how dark the night the Lord passed through
> Ere He found the sheep that was lost.[37]

Shameful indignities, physical anguish, inward groans, excruciating pain, desolation, and a broken body are all indications that our salvation was bought at a price. The question is, if the Redeemer is satisfied when He sees of the travail of His soul? Because of our thirst for likeness to Himself, does He know that His sacrifice was not in vain? As our brave fighters heard of our selfishness and complacency, perhaps they wondered whether the sacrifice of their blood on some foreign battlefield was worth it. Is it so with the Savior? Are we giving Him extreme satisfaction for all His tears and thorns? By our deliverance from the guilt of committed sin and the thralldom of controlling sin, is He being rewarded for shedding His blood?

---

37. Elizabeth C. Clephane, "The Ninety and Nine," 1868.

The Force of a Fact

To the unspiritual, cultured mind it may be repugnant to sing, "There's power in the blood." Nevertheless it is sound evangelical theology. *"They overcame him* [the devil] *by the blood of the Lamb."* All God's power is available for us in the cross of Christ. Calvary is more than a fact—it is a force. The cross is a dynamic, as well as a doctrine. John reminds us that the blood of Jesus Christ can cleanse us from all sin. Calvary can provide us with power sufficient to make victory gloriously actual in our lives. But are we winning daily victories over sin, selfishness, worry, temper, and other manifestations of the flesh, through His cross? The Crusaders, seeing the cross blazing in the heavens, cried, "By this sign we conquer!" Are we able to appreciate and apprehend the principle and power of God's victory sign? Through Calvary's victim and victor are we victorious?

The Lamb Is All the Glory

"Behold the Lamb of God which taketh away the sin of the world" (John 1:29).

The evolution of the lamb in Scripture forms a most profitable meditation. The Levitical and typical significance of the lamb dominates the Bible. Lambs were an integral part of almost every Jewish sacrifice. While the first mention of lambs is in Genesis 21:28—*"Abraham set seven ewe lambs of the flock by themselves"*—it is taken for granted that the firstling of the flock which Abel presented to God was a lamb. His was a more excellent sacrifice than Cain's, seeing that it represented the shedding of innocent blood. (See Hebrews 11:4.) Christ's offering resulted in better things than Abel's. (See Hebrews 12:24.)

Lambs that were to be used for offerings had to be faultless males and keep with the established estimate of animal perfection. (See Malachi 1:14.) They had to be less than one year old, meek, gentle, and possess a docile nature. Lambs for sacrifice had to be kept whole in order to be roasted that way. *"Not one of them* [bones] *shall be broken"* (Psalm 34:20). The lamb was the symbol of unity—the unity of the family, the unity of the nation, the unity of God with His people whom He had taken into covenant relationship with Himself.

The typical significance of the lamb is not hard to trace. It typifies:

1. Christ, the Paschal Lamb, who became the sacrifice for our sins. (See Exodus 29:38–41; John 1:29; Revelation 5:6, 8.)

2. True believers, manifesting the lamb-like qualities of humility and meekness. (See Isaiah 11:6; Luke 10:3; John 21:15.)

3. Beneficent teachers, who are not guilty of cruelty or barbarity. (See Jeremiah 11:19.)

4. Innocence, as personified by a wife. (See 2 Samuel 12:3–4.)

5. The Antichrist, who will ape the power and prerogative of Christ as the Lamb. (See Revelation 13:11.)

The offering of lambs by sinning Israelites could never grant them redemption from sin. They were accepted by God in virtue of the sacrifice of His Lamb, the Lord Jesus Christ. The question Isaac asked as he accompanied his father up Mount Moriah was unanswered all through the Old Testament, *"Where is the lamb for a burnt offering?"* (Genesis 22:7). Multitudinous lambs had been placed on bloodstained altars, but the cry for the Lamb has unanswered until we come to John's call, *"Behold the Lamb of God, which taketh away the sin of the world"* (John 1:29).

Abraham's reply to Isaac's question is significant. *"God will provide himself a lamb"* (Genesis 22:8). In His love and mercy, God did provide Himself as the Lamb. His Son, who was "very God of very God," became the Lamb through whose stripes we are healed.

> Not all the blood of beasts
> On Jewish altars slain,
> Could give the guilty conscience peace,
> Or wash away the stain.
>
> But Christ, the heavenly Lamb,
> Takes all our sins away;
> A sacrifice of nobler name
> And richer blood than they.[38]

Prophets and apostles loved to think of Christ as the sacrificial Lamb. Isaiah wrote of Him as the Lamb led to slaughter. (See Isaiah 53:7; Acts 8:32.) John had the distinction of being the forerunner of Christ as the Lamb. (See John 1:29.) John Wesley said that his whole business here was to cry, "Behold the Lamb." It is our solemn business to re-echo that cry. Peter extolled the preciousness of Christ's blood, who died as a Lamb without blemish or spot. (See 1 Peter 1:19.) John the apostle was also lost in contemplation of Christ as the Lamb as the last book of the Bible clearly proves.

---

38. Isaac Watts, "Not All the Blood of Beasts," 1709.

Let us meditate for a moment on this unique figure of the Lamb, describing as it does the Christ's person and plan.

Think of His Nature. Emphasis is laid upon the definite article. John tells us that Christ is *the* Lamb. All the lambs of the Old Testament, which were slain on Jewish altars, only typified the offering of this perfect Paschal Lamb. Jesus is the great and only Lamb whose sacrifice is efficacious to redeem and save lost sinners. And the Lamb was the most fitting figure to use, seeing that Christ completes all the hopes enshrined in the sacrifices, rites, and symbols of Jewish ritual.

Think of His Innocence. A child untried, never tested, ignorant of the great and gross sins of life, is spoken of as an innocent child. But Christ's innocence was greater. He was in innocent holiness, an innocence tested but never lost. His life remained unsoiled. As sunbeams never absorb the filth they shine through, so Jesus remained holy, harmless, and undefiled. It is true that He became sin, but never a sinner. Had He sinned, He would have forfeited the right to be our Savior; but being sinless, He can save.

Old Testament lambs remained innocent simply because they had no conscious or knowledge of evil. But God's Lamb was holy. He had at intimate acquaintance with evil, but yet refused its seductive charms.

Think of His Gentleness. Meekness is associated with a lamb; but in God's Lamb, meekness was not weakness. A lamb is a mute animal, and yet so fierce when passions are roused. And do we not read of *"the wrath of the Lamb"* (Revelation 6:16)? Silent amid suffering is God's Lamb, but His very gentleness makes Him great. The meek inherit the earth, Jesus said; and as God's meek Lamb, He will yet see the whole earth filled with His glory.

Think of His Submission. A lamb never complains as it is slain. Of course it cannot, seeing that it lacks the elements of personality. Old Testament lambs were forced, dragged to the altar. Christ, however, was not an unwilling victim. He gave Himself as our ransom. The world has witnessed many kinds of death—covenanters, heroes, martyrs; but such were liable to die. The difference with Christ is that He chose death. Death did not claim Him. He was born in order that He might die. We often say that if we had known what faced us, we could have never lived, but Jesus knew every step of the blood-red way, and walked the entire road with bleeding feet until He reached the cross. His entire life was one of voluntary sacrifices. His sacrifices began at His incarnation and culminated at Calvary.

Just as a lamb exists for others, so the whole of Christ and His work is for us. A lamb gives its wool, and we have clothing; its flesh, and we have sustenance. And from God's Lamb, we likewise receive both covering and food.

Think of His Deity. Jesus was no ordinary man. The Jews could bring any lamb to the altar, providing that it fulfilled certain conditions. But it was different with God's Lamb. No other person would atone for man's sin. "There was no other good enough to pay the price of sin."[39] Who He was gave virtue to what He did. The blood He shed was *"the blood of God"* (Acts 20:28) as well as the blood of man. God and man died at the cross, seeing that Christ was the God-man; therefore His sacrifice was efficacious, seeing that deity was joined to humanity. The blood has transcendent power owing to its unique character. The Lamb was God and of God. This is what marks the difference between Christianity and the religions of the world. In pagan religions, man provides a sacrifice for his god. In Christianity, God provides a sacrifice for man; and the mystery of mysteries is that God gave Himself! God is the source of our salvation. It was He who loved the world and reconciled it to Himself with His beloved Son.

The book of Revelation is essentially "The Book of the Lamb." Within it, Christ is only once referred to as a Lion but twenty-eight times as the Lamb. While there are various ways of approaching the book of Revelation—the most dramatic book of the Bible—it is conspicuous as the Lamb-honoring book. In the apocalypse, John uses *arnion*, meaning "the little lamb," not *amnos* as he employs in John 1:29. Over the arrogance and wickedness of the Beast, the false lamb, John places the meekness and innocence of Christ, the little Lamb. Such a title combines almightiness and invincibility necessary for the full and final subjugation of all evil forces.

The book of Revelation, then, is essentially the book of the Lamb. The entire volume revolves around Christ. He is the center and circumference of this mystic and glowing book. It is also to be noted that Christ is always presented as the Lamb that was slain. The scepter of universal sovereignty will rest in His pierced hand. His cross wins Him the crown. Government is founded upon His grief. His reign as Sovereign is His as one of His redemptive rights. His wounds, evidence of His past sufferings and token of our present unworthiness, are also precious in that they are prospective of His vengeance on His foes. His Calvary marks form the ground of coming judgment. His pierced hands and feet are ever a source of comfort for His own (see John 20:20), and are yet to strike terror in the hearts of His enemies. Those sacrificial scars declaring Christ's willingness to be slain rather than submit to

39. Cecil F. Alexander, "There Is a Green Hill Far Away," 1847.

sin cannot possibly compromise with iniquity; they are therefore alone worthy to dispense righteous judgment.

While there are many serviceable outlines of Revelation, focusing on its uses of the Lamb, we can divide it in the following way:

1. The Vision of the Lamb: 1
2. The Church of the Lamb: 2–3
3. The Adoration of the Lamb: 4–5
4. The Wrath of the Lamb: 6–19:6
5. The Marriage of the Lamb: 19:7–10
6. The Reign of the Lamb: 19:11–22.

Classifying John's references to Christ as the Lamb, we recognize the following aspects:

The Lamb and His Eternal Wounds

Two pregnant phrases call for attention, namely, *"A lamb as it had been slain"* and *"The blood of the Lamb"* (Revelation 5:6; 7:14). Here we have reminiscences of His "blood, sweat and tears" on our behalf. When Winston Churchill promised the British people this trinity of anguish, did he recall Byron's use of it in the memorable lines?

> Year after year they voted cent for cent
> Blood, sweat, and tears—wrung millions—Why? For rent?

It is interesting to note that the word John uses for *"slain"* means "newly" or "freshly slain." Furthermore, seeing Christ as the slain Lamb implies that He carries the scars of sacrifice. In heaven, those "rich wounds, yet visible above" eternally remind the saints of all they owe to Christ, who became both victim and victor. Faith has no difficulty in believing that the glorified body of Christ bears the indelible scars of the cross. (See John 20:20–27.) Memories of Calvary are treasured in heaven. On earth, we see the Lamb wounded and slain. In heaven, He is the center of power and glory.

John turned to see a Lion but beheld a Lamb, and Christ is a combination of majesty and mercy. But the Lamb John saw was not nailed to a cross or even sitting, but "standing" between the throne and the elders. He is about to assume His redemption-inheritance. He is presently seated at the Father's right hand (see Hebrews 1:3; Revelation 3:21; Psalm 110:1), but His patience has ended. The Lamb vacates the throne to take His power and reign unto Himself. Sitting is a state of rest. Standing bespeaks of readiness for action.

How we love the sight of the scarred, standing Lamb!

> Dear suffering Lamb, Thy bleeding wounds
> With cords of love divine,
> Have drawn our willing hearts to Thee
> And linked our life with Thine.

We are thrice blessed if we have the mystic robes made white by the blood of the Lamb. His scars are our only right to access into the holiest of all. His blood alone can make saints. Trials and tribulation make sacrificial sufferers of saints.

The Lamb and His Worship

All of His creation is stirred to the depths as it comes to worship the Lamb. Angels adore the Lamb, but they cannot praise Him as the redeemed of earth do, for...

> They sing the Lamb of God
> Once slain on earth for them;
> The Lamb, thro' whose atoning blood
> Each wears his diadem.

The Lamb, the bleeding Lamb, is the theme of the new song, which is the only theme worth singing about. The cross is the grandest fact of all time. Without it, Christ would have been in glory alone, and sinners would have had no deliverance from the guilt and government of sin. But the suffering, conquering Lamb of God has all intelligences ascribing praise and honor to His name. (See Revelation 5:8–14).

While on earth, the Lamb was silent before His shearers. No word of rebuke or reproach came from His lips as He willingly endured all the contradictions of sinners. He never exercised His inherent power to save Himself from those who put Him to shame. Now all is changed. He no longer stands in the midst of the godless horde. He is no longer silent and alone in His holiness and calm dignity, with spittle and blood covering His face. Universal adoration is His. He is acclaimed as the object of heaven's worship. Once patient in His agony, this is now the Lamb's supreme moment, when all are prostrate before Him.

We have the redeemed of all ages around the throne with angels forming the outer circle. Having taken the seven-sealed book, meaning the transfer of authority and government to the Lamb, He is now worthy to receive every mark of distinction one can lay on Him. He is raised for the perfection of attributes He can now manifest.(See Revelation 5:12; 7:12.)

Power—This is first named, for the Lamb is about to exercise power in its widest, most comprehensive character.

Riches—All wealth, whether material, moral or physical, is His due. As the Lamb who gave His all, He claims our best.

Wisdom—Coming as the personification of divine wisdom, and being made unto us wisdom, He will manifest highest wisdom when He comes to reign.

Strength—Here we have the quality enabling Him to carry out all He determines to do for His own, and for the earth as He comes to reign.

Honor—As the Lamb, He died dishonored. Religious leaders caused Him to die as a felon on a wooden cross. Now deserved recognition is His.

Glory—He is also worthy to receive all public glory. Now the Lamb can be glorified with the glory He had with the Father in the dateless past.

Blessing—All forms and characteristics of blessedness or happiness are to be His. Full contentment will be the Lamb's.

What exaltation is His! The tide of praise gathers force and volume until the whole universe ascribes honor to the Lamb.

> The Lamb is all the glory
> Of Immanuel's land.[40]

The Lamb and His Wrath

John writes as an eyewitness of the act of the Lamb opening the seals, containing as they do the judgments of heaven for earth. The Lamb is related to the seals; the angels with the trumpets; God with the vials or bowls. In his gospel, John reminds us that God has given His Son the necessary authority to execute judgment (see John 5:27), and now in his apocalypse, John depicts Christ as the Lamb about to exercise all governmental and civil authority. All must bow to Him when the great day of His wrath comes. (See Revelation 6:17.)

What a vivid emblem of terror the last section of chapter six presents! How staggering it is to read about *"the wrath of the Lamb."* The Lamb! The One who is noted for meekness, gentleness, and patience is now swept along by a fearsome, righteous indignation. Seldom does the lamb give way to anger or disturbed feelings. When it does, we are told it can be very ferocious, as it

---

40. Anne R. Cousin, "The Sands of Time are Sinking," 1857.

will be when the Lamb of God comes to execute judgment on the godless. The outburst of His concentrated agony will be terrible, causing the rebellious to seek somewhere to hide. How grateful we should be that through the experience of the cleansing blood of the Lamb, we will never witness the wrath of the Lamb!

Divine and satanic anger form another profitable study in the book of Revelation. Not only do we have *"the wrath of the Lamb,"* but twice over we read of *"the wrath of God"* (Revelation 14:10, 19). God and Christ are one in their determination to rid the earth of all beast-worshipers. Such a scene depicted in the fall of Babylon fulfilled the prophecy about *"the day of vengeance"* (Isaiah 63:4; see Matthew 25:31–46).

Then there is the *"great wrath"* of Satan. (See Revelation 12:12.) Exiled from his domain in the heavenlies, he realizes that his time is short and indulges in one final outburst of rage and destruction. We gather that these will be terrible days when Satan is here in person from John's warning: *"Woe to the inhabiters of the earth and of the sea!"* (Revelation 12:12). Deposed as the prince of the power of the air, the devil will be more diabolical than ever after his war with Michael and his angels.

The Lamb and His Sovereignty

Christ, as the Lamb, is often associated with a throne in this climactic book of the Bible. He is on a throne, in the midst of a throne. (See Revelation 7:10, 17; 22:1.) The sacred head once crowned with sharp cactus thorns is to bear many a diadem. Rejected by earth, He is to rule over it. Regal glory is to be His. With all his sorrows and sacrifices past, the strength and security of the throne is the Lamb's.

Exercising all dominion and power from the midst of a throne, He is able to meet every need of His own, conquer all His foes, and dispense salvation in its most comprehensive sense to Jews and Gentiles alike. This is why the throne is the prominent object in the last part of the vision granted to John. The saints also are to reign with Him. They are to be sharers of His royalty.

It must not be forgotten that it is as the Lamb that Jesus Christ is to reign. Thus, when He climbed those bloody slopes leading to His cross, He secured more than deliverance from the penalty and power of sin. Certainly He died as the sinless substitute for sinners. But He provided more than salvation through His death. With it came His sovereign rights as the King of kings. In the messianic Psalm we read, *"Say among the heathen that the LORD reigneth"* (Psalm 96:10). Yes, those scars of the Lamb mean sovereignty as well as salvation. The Redeemer will reign. In virtue of His cross, the slain Lamb will exercise His kingly prerogatives. Because of the tree, He is to have a throne. The royal diadem will adorn the brow of the One cruel men crowned with thorns. Instead of a mock coronation, unsurpassed majesty will be His, when from *"the throne of God and of the Lamb"* (Revelation 22:3), He reigns in righteousness.

The Lamb and His Register

While various names are mentioned in the book of Revelation, there are two specific references to the Lamb:

"The book of life of the Lamb" (Revelation 13:8).

"The Lamb's book of life" (Revelation 21:27).

This register contains the names of those who have been washed in the blood of the Lamb and whose names are inscribed in the sacred volume before the foundation of the world. (See Ephesians 1:4–5.) None of these names will ever be erased. Once we become the Lord's, we are His forever. *"Whatsoever God doeth, it shall be for ever"* (Ecclesiastes 3:14). It is different with the book about which we read in a previous chapter—*"I will not blot out his name out of the book of life"* (Revelation 3:5). This is a record of professors and possessors. All who make a Christian profession, true and false, make up this register. The true are those who have had their names written in the book of life from the foundation of the world. (See Revelation 17:8.) But in this particular register for the redeemed, the names of the unsaved do not appear. *"Whosoever was not found written in the book of life was cast into the lake of fire"* (Revelation 20:15). Only those whose names are written in the Lamb's book of life (see Revelation 21:27) are delivered from eternal separation from the Lamb. These are the ones who will enter into the eternal blessedness of the holy city. Thus, the question of paramount importance for each of us to ask as we think of the Lamb's register is, "Is my name written there?"

Commenting on John's solemn declaration, *"If any was not found written in the book of life, he was cast into the lake of fire"* (Revelation 20:15), William R. Newell says, "Let us mark certain facts here:

1. It is not the absence of good works in the book that dooms a person. It is the absence of his name. There are no works written in that book, only names.

2. It is not the fact of evil works. Many of earth's sinners have their names in the Book of Life.

3. All whose names do not appear in the Book are cast into the lake of fire.

4. All names there found in that day will have been written before that day. There is no record of anyone's name being written into the Book of Life on that day. *'If any man was not found written.'* How overwhelmingly solemn this is!"

The Lamb and His Firstfruits

Chapter thirteen presents the false lamb and his followers, for whom there is nothing but doom. In chapter fourteen, John brings us to the true Lamb and His followers. The 144,000 refers to the spared Jewish remnant, the tribe particularized in chapter seven. The remnant was considered loyal in their witness to God and the Lamb, and is now publicly owned by heaven. Many of these Jews are depicted as sealing their testimony with their blood. Others were spared through the sorrows of the tribulation and share the seat of royalty. They pass from tyranny under the Beast to triumph under God. From the scene of suffering they go to the seat of sovereignty.

The divine estimate of these faithful followers of the Lamb is full of spiritual instruction for our own hearts. Apart from participation in the new song, they are described as walking in virgin purity. They were also obedient to the Lamb, following Him wherever He went in spite of surrounding idolatry. Multitudes were loyal to the Beast, but this godly remnant gave the Lamb undivided heart affection. Theirs was a "magnificent obsession." We are also told that no guile was in their mouth; they were considered blameless before the divine tribunal. (See verses 14:6–8.) What a reputation to have! Beast worshipers believed a lie and were deluded by his false claims. However, no lie was found in any mouth of this godly company. They acknowledged the Messiah to be the true One, refusing to conform to the Beast's blasphemous edicts.

It is no wonder, then, that these redeemed ones are spoken of as being *"the first fruits unto God and to the Lamb"* (Revelation 14:4). Priority in time and blessing is theirs, and they form the earnest of a more glorious harvest. William R. Newell says of them, "They are the first fruits of the millennial reign. They connect the dispensations—somewhat as Noah did, who passed through the judgment of the flood into a new order of things. Therefore the Lamb is seen standing on Mount Zion (before He actually comes there, as in Revelation 19 and Psalm 2), that with Him may be seen this overcoming host, who will very shortly share His actual reign there."

The Lamb and His Victory

What jubilant overcomers are before us in the issue of the heavenly war! *"They overcome him by the blood of the Lamb"* (Revelation 12:11). Satan heads up the imperial powers on earth as the prince of this world just as he controls all evil and spiritual powers as the prince of the power of the air. All saints, however, are victorious as they seek the shelter of the blood, representing as it does the empowering virtue of Christ's death and resurrection. The cross was Satan's "Waterloo." Therefore, we conquer him in pleading that cross. We often sing about marching on to victory. Is it not truer that we are marching from victory, even the victory of Calvary? Deliverance from all diabolical machinations will be experienced by the devil-driven Jews as they plead the abiding efficacy of the blood. Along with this evidence of victory, we also have prophetic witness and willing martyrdom. Released from satanic oppression, the accused brethren rejoice. Are we among the singing victors?

Later in the book of Revelation is the victorious Lamb Himself. *"These shall make war with the Lamb, and the Lamb shall overcome them"* (Revelation 17:14). This conquest brings us to the final act of the Beast and his allies. The conflict between the Lamb and these satanically inspired forces is more fully described in chapter nineteen. Here, in chapter seventeen, the war is anticipated and the victory assured. The Lamb is the mighty conqueror, exercising all vested authority. As the Lion-Lamb, He is to reign in power and tenderness. (See Revelation 5:5–6.) The victor of Calvary is to take the throne, and when He does, earth's sighs, sobs, sin, and sorrows will cease. *"The Lord shall be king over all the earth"* (Zechariah 14:9). Inflexible righteousness will characterize His reign. There will be no more contention between right and wrong, truth and error, peace and war. *"He shall be a priest upon his throne"* (Zechariah 6:13). How glorious will be His reign as He manifests priestly grace and kingly authority. What ultimate triumph will be His! All His enemies will be routed, and His church will be entirely free from all blemishes and the antagonism of sin.

The Lamb and His Bride

As we have several glimpses of the church under the figure of the Bride, it may be profitable to gather them together under this section. There are some who affirm that Israel—not the church—is the Bride. The Scriptures, however, are explicit on the fact that Israel is the adulterous wife of Jehovah. Those who reject the church as the Bride affirm that she cannot be the Bride and the body at the same time. Why not? It is no more incongruous to think of the church as a Bride and a body than it is to speak of Christ as the Priest and the Lamb. He is both though, is He not?

First of all, we have the marriage of the Lamb (see Revelation 19:7, 9) which takes place in heaven amidst rapturous scenes of joy. Here the Bride is spoken of as "wife" for the simple reason that as soon as a marriage is completed, the bride becomes the wife. "The 'bride' speaks of her deep place in the affection of the Bridegroom," says Walter Scott. "The 'wife' intimates the established relationship existing between the Bridegroom and the Bride."

This celestial marriage precedes the assumption of the kingdom by the Lord. Because of the relationship existing between the Bridegroom and the Bride, the latter is to share the former's glory and reign with Him while occupying her special place in His heart's deep love. In Revelation 21:9, the Bride, as a city, is shown to Israel in her millennial glory. The church is the city of millennial and eternal days. A city represents an organized system of social life, united interests, and government activity—all of which the church will experience.

The bridal robes of the wife (see Revelation 19:8) are in sharp contrast to the gorgeous attire of the harlot (see Revelation 17:4). The glorious clothes of the Bride speak of character and a righteousness both provided and practiced. The deeds of the Bride are appraised at their true value in heaven; now she is clothed in pure white linen. And beautiful as her trousseau will be, the Bride will not eye her garments, but "her dear Bridegroom's face."

The guests are distinguished as friends of the Bridegroom. (See Revelation 19:9.) All of the saints who are not incorporated within the church will be among the invited guests to the marriage of the Lamb.

Presently, the Spirit and the Bride are united in their desire for the Lamb's return. (See Revelation 22:17.) It is not merely the Spirit in the Bride crying "Come!" Both cry as one. The Lamb will appear as the bright and morning star when He comes to claim His Bride. He will appear as the Sun of Righteousness to Israel, in all His noonday splendor. No one can meditate upon the revelation granted to John without realizing something of the glorious heritage awaiting both the church and Israel.

The Lamb and His Song

Two songs are united, seeing that they both celebrate redemption—one redemption by power, the other by blood. *"They sing the song of Moses the servant of God, and the song of the Lamb"* (John 15:3). The first song celebrates the marvelous deliverance God gave Israel at the Red Sea. The second song magnifies the Lamb for the redemption He provided from sin's guilt and government. The one was an earthly redemption; the other is a spiritual redemption. The song of Moses speaks of triumph over the power of evil by divine judgment. The song of the Lamb is taken up with the exaltation of the rejected Messiah. It is the song of the faithful remnant, sung in the midst of the unfaithful, apostate Israel—the song of martyred victors.

The theme of the song is the Holy One of Israel. What a tower of strength we have in the combination of the given titles. (See John 15:3–4.) He is great and marvelous, just and true and holy. As the same versions expresses, He is the King, not only of the saints, but also of the nations. When the Lamb appears on the earth, it will be as the Sovereign of His redeemed ones of Israel, and of all the nations of the earth. *"Who would not fear thee, O King of nations? For to thee doth it appertain: forasmuch as among all the wise men of the nations, and in all their kingdoms, there is none like unto thee"* (Jeremiah 10:7).

What a day that will be when the Lamb is lauded as the world-emperor! What a relief for our blood-soaked earth it will be when Christ takes the throne as King of the nations with Satan imprisoned in the pit!

Are you not grateful that if you have the assurance of being washed in the blood of the Lamb, yours will be the joyful privilege of joining in the glorious "Hallelujah Song" as Christ takes the throne?

The Lamb and His Servants

The last reference to the Lamb in the Lamb-exalting book of Revelation is in the concluding chapter. *"The servants of the Lamb shall serve him"* (Revelation 22:3). Note that which all lovers of the Lamb are found doing.

They serve Him. We are not to idle eternity away playing harps. Highest and holiest service will be ours.

They are to see Him. What soul-thrilling rapture will be ours to see His face and eternally behold it!

They are to bear His name. This means that we are to reflect His character. *"In their foreheads"* (Revelation 22:4) implies a place that is easily seen.

They are to bask in His presence. Natural and artificial illumination will no longer be necessary. The Lamb will be the Light of the world.

They are to have His eternal provision and guardianship. The Lamb who sits on the throne is to feed and lead His own forever. (See Revelation 7:15–17.) Through all eternity He will shepherd, protect, and illumine His followers. They will not be able to dispense with Him through the ageless future. They will be the Lamb's dear debtors forever. He will be their guide and glory in Immanuel's land.

〜

Easter Messages for Children

Pastors and teachers who may have occasion to include a talk for children on the Sunday before Easter or Good Friday could develop the following outline. A scarlet cord could be used to illustrate that scarlet is the color of blood and usually symbolizes "sacrifice."

1. *Scarlet Curtain.* Exodus 26:1, 31, 36; "Sacrificial Access"; blue is the heavenly color; purple is the royalty color; scarlet is the sacrifice color.
2. *Scarlet Thread.* Joshua 1:2; "Sacrificial Safety."
3. *Scarlet Clothing.* 2 Samuel 1:24; Lamentations 4:5; Daniel 5:7; Revelation 18:16; "Sacrificial Position"; no dignity apart from death.
4. *Scarlet Lips.* Song of Solomon 4:3; "Sacrificial Speech."
5. *Scarlet Sins.* Isaiah 1:18; "Sacrificial Cleansing."
6. *Scarlet Robe.* Matthew 27:28; "Sacrificial Derision"; Worn by Roman officers of distinction. This was a cast off one.
7. *Scarlet Wool.* Hebrews 9:19–22; "Sacrificial Remission."
8. *Scarlet Beast.* Revelation 17:3; "Sacrificial Blasphemy."

5

LENTEN ILLUSTRATIONS

When it comes to illustrative material applicable to the Lenten season, a preacher finds himself embarrassed by riches. History, daily life, literature, science, art, and biography can supply him with stories and illustrations he can subordinate to any aspect of the Passion Week he wants to preach about. Outstanding expositors on "The Art of Preaching" all warn preachers against compilations of illustrations, many of which have become the "wandering Jew" of the pulpit and travel ceaseless rounds of a thousand sermons from January to December. While a slavish use of such common pasturage for sermons is to be condemned, there can yet be a wise selection of the polished illustrations of masters in the art of mixing "plums in the cake," as illustrations have been called. Alexander Maclaren, Wm. L. Watkinson, George Morrison, Dinsdale Young, Robert G. Lee, and a host of other renowned pulpiteers provide preachers with unusual illustrations that truly illustrate biblical truth.

C. H. Spurgeon said that there are "no illustrations so good as those from Scripture," which is true even when it comes to the events of Easter Week. The Levitical order and Israelite history, which form God's picture book of redemption, are replete with telling parables of the cross and the resurrection; for example, there are the stories of the selection and offering of a lamb, the law of the two birds, the uplifted serpent, and Abraham's sacrifice of Isaac. As we recall the many illustrations Jesus used, we find that although His mind was saturated with Old Testament Scripture and He often used events and episodes from such to enforce His teachings, He yet employed familiar scenes and circumstances around Him to shed the light of truth on His hearers. Preachers will never go astray as long as they take Jesus as their model whose figures and parables were often drawn from His own life and the lives of His neighbors. How the lamp and the bushel, the lost coin, the hen and her brood, the wandering sheep, the wheat and tares growing up together, the net cast into the sea, the varying winds, the ruddy heavens with their promise of good weather, and the lowering sky forecasting foul weather give life and animation to our Lord's heart-gripping discourses! His teachings were ever real, fresh, and vivid; largely owing to His skill at taking the everyday, common incidents of life, and the most ordinary scenes and sounds of nature to enlighten truth. Nothing was too trivial for the Lord of glory to turn into themes for divine instruction.

While the writers of the New Testament loved to unfold and magnify the inner significance of the work of Christ, they yet manifested a commendable reticence in their accounts of the actual physical sufferings of our Lord—an example preachers should follow when they describe the crucifixion. Expository works on the life and work of our Lord abound, and the best of these, particularly those covering His last days up to His ascension, yield a rich treasure of illustrative material for the preacher. Works from masters of pulpit ministry who lived near to the cross—W. M. Clow in his volumes *The Day of the Cross* and *The Cross in Christian Experience*; James Stalker in his *Trial and Death of Christ*; and James Denny in his classic work *on The Death of Christ*—provide a bountiful fare of expository and illustrative material for Lenten messages. We, herewith, cite a selection from our reading of such literature to aid preachers as they come to preach the word of reconciliation.

His Heart of Fire Is a Heart of Flesh

Plato, in his most glorious dialogue, told of the meeting in the prison of Socrates with his friends. The sacred ship has arrived from Delos, the chains are being struck off, and Socrates is to die instantly. Xanthippe is sitting by her husband and holding his child in her arms. History has treated her ill; and perhaps—if one of two extremes must be chosen—life may, in some aspects, be a happier thing for the wives of certain fools than of certain philosophers. Xanthippe may have had provocations which a great idealistic biographer found it convenient to forget. But at all events, she had a woman's heart, a Greek woman's passionate nature. "Socrates!" she cried, "this is the last time that either you will talk with your friends, or they with you."

Then Socrates turned to a friend and said quietly, "Let someone take her home." She is led home, sobbing wildly as she goes; and Socrates, relieved of her presence, frigidly begins a disquisition on pleasure and pain, suggested by the blended sensations in his limb when a chain was removed—possibly not without bitter sarcasm about the loving, if not imperfect, wife who mourned him so bitterly. Which presents the more tender, the most exquisitely human ideal—Socrates or Christ? Let us thank God that the Savior's heart of fire is also a heart of flesh. *"Father, forgive them; for they know not what they do!"*

(Luke 23:34). From the cross He rained down legacies. No showers were ever so rich in harvests as the red drop of Calvary.

You Must Die

John Tauler, the greatest preacher of the fourteenth century, preached one day in Strasbourg Cathedral on the highest degree of Christian perfection attainable in this life. Although his theology was sound as he eloquently discoursed on the necessity of a dying to self out of which springs a wholehearted love for God and man, he had not experienced such truth in his own life. A saintly man, Nicholas of Basle, heard Tauler preach six times went to him after detecting the defection, saying,

"Master Tauler, you must die!"

"Die?" said the popular cathedral preacher. "What do you mean?"

"John Tauler, you must die to live," he replied.

"What do you mean?" asked Tauler.

Nicholas replied, "Get alone with God. Leave your crowded church, your admiring congregation, your hold on this city. Go aside to your cell. Be alone, and you will see what I mean."

At first Tauler was offended and irritated, but he eventually followed the advice of the old saint. He took leave of his church and went alone with God to face the un-crucified foe within him—self. The battle was long and fierce, but determined to know the secret of self-abdication, Tauler came to the place where he was willing to let go and let God. He came to a believing recognition and experimental understanding of his oneness with his crucified Savior. The old John Tauler had died, and out of that death blossomed a red and more abundant life. Meeting Nicholas, Tauler related his experience with him to which the aged saint said, "Now one of thy sermons will bring forth more fruit than a hundred aforetime," which it inevitably did. Identification with Christ in His humiliation, death, burial, and resurrection is surely one of the greatest aspects of His cross we must not neglect.

Shadow of the Cross

In one of the earliest pictures of the nativity, Jesus is represented as lying in the manger, while just above Him on the wall of the stable is the shadow of a cross. Holman Hunt, who gave the world his masterpiece, *The Light of the World*, also painted Jesus in the carpenter's shop at Nazareth. The day's work is over. The spent toiler lifts His arms in an attitude of utter weariness, and the level rays of the setting sun cast on the wall reveal the shadow of a cross. How true was the artist's suggestion! Jesus was born under, and lived under, the shadow of the cross. He was born to die. The penalty had been passed upon the race, *"The soul that sinneth, it shall die"* (Ezekiel 18:4), and knowing that there could be no deliverance from sin but by death, He tasted death for every man.

That's What I Want

A renowned missionary relates that among those converted by his preaching at the sacred city of Benares was a devotee who had dragged himself many miles on his knees and elbows to bathe in the so-called "sacred" Ganges. Deep within there was a conviction of sin and a desire for deliverance from its bondage. "If I can but reach the Ganges," he thought, "this shame and burden and fear will be washed away." Weak and emaciated from his long pilgrimage, he dragged himself down to the river's edge and, praying to Gunga, crept into it; then withdrawing, he laid on the river's bank and moaned: "The pain is still here!"

At that moment he heard a voice from the shadow of a banyan tree nearby, the voice of a missionary telling the old, old story of Jesus and His love. Rising from his knees, and unable to restrain himself, he clapped his hands and cried, "That's what I want! That's what I want!" Is this not what all men need; what the whole creation has groaned and travailed for? Let us tell it out among the nations that His red blood is able to make the black heart of the sinner whiter than snow!

A Monument to Substitution

Reverend W. E. Sutterfield, pastor of the First Baptist Church in Palmyra, Missouri, gives us this telling incident:

Many times I have heard ministers, when discussing the doctrine of substitution in the Bible, give as an illustration the story about a man during the war between the States who offered himself as a "substitute" for another man who had been condemned to death by a military court. One such incident happened here in Palmyra on October 17, 1862. During the war both the North and the South had troops in this area. At the time this incident happened Palmyra was practically under military law and in a state of siege. Many acts of violence, no doubt, were committed on both sides. It happened that an informer for the military power in the town at the time disappeared and the commander in charge, in order to bring about the return of the missing man and to prevent the recurrence of such incidents, ordered ten men to be shot in reprisal.

Several men were being detained in Palmyra jail as prisoners of war at that time, and ten men were selected from among them. Of this number one was Wm. T. Humphrey, the father of several children, whose wife pleaded for his release. Because of her physical condition and because Humphrey was the father of several children, the commanding officer struck his name from the list and chose the name of Hiram Smith, a young man without a family. However, it cannot be said that Smith volunteered to take the place of Humphrey, but it is known that he did give his consent and stated that perhaps it were better for a single man to die rather than a man with a family.

The ten men were shot on 17 October, 1862 in what has come to be known as the "Palmyra Massacre". At Mount Pleasant Church cemetery in Mount Salem Association is a stone erected to the grave of Hiram Smith by G. W. Humphrey, the son of the reprieved man, and an inscription on it which reads:

This monument is dedicated to the memory of
HIRAM SMITH
The Hero that sleeps beneath the sod here
Who was shot at Palmyra, Oct. 17, 1862, as a substitute for
Wm. T. Humphrey, my father.—G. W. Humphrey"

Spurgeon declared that his theology could be condensed into four words: "He died for me!"

Richer Blood

In his book entitled *Modern Illustrations for Public Speakers*, Robert G. Lee, the eloquent Baptist orator, tells how the New York Regional Red Cross Blood Program received eight hundred twenty-five pints of blood on a Tuesday in August, 1953. The collection included two hundred eighty-seven pints taken aboard the aircraft carrier *Antietam*, which was tied up for repairs at the New York Naval Shipyard in Brooklyn and aboard which a five-day mass collection of blood began on Monday; one hundred forty-four pints at the Lederle Laboratories, Pearl River, N.Y.; one hundred twenty-eight at the

Railway Express Agency, 278 East Forty-fourth Street, N.Y.; and one hundred thirty in a community collection at Middleton, N.Y. But while all that blood was doubtless efficacious in saving physical human lives, not one drop of it had the power to remove a single sin from any human heart. All the blood stored up in blood banks cannot cleanse a sinful soul from all unrighteousness. At the dedication of the glorious and costly temple in Jerusalem, King Solomon offered a sacrifice of 22,000 oxen and 120,000 sheep. (See 2 Chronicles 7:5.) But the stark fact is that...

> Not all the blood of beasts,
> On Jewish altars slain,
> Could give the guilty conscience peace,
> Or wash away the stain.
> But Christ, the heavenly Lamb,
> Takes all our sins away;
> A sacrifice of nobler name,
> And richer blood than they.[41]

Easter reminds us that "the blood of the cross" is eternally efficacious because of its intrinsic nature; it was *"the blood of God"* (Acts 20:28).

Divine Wrath Against Sin

William A. Clow reminds us that...

...the darkest line in a human face is the line of an anger which is shot through with grief. It is not otherwise with the face of God. We have seen so many human faces in which love has been grieved and heated to a stern anger that we shall not wonder at this line in God's dear face.

Professor Clow goes on to say that Sir Walter Scott has pictured this truth of divine wrath against sin in the *Heart of Midlothian*, the novel drawing on the austere features of David Deans, grave and solemn as those of a man who speaks much with God. When the news of his daughter is brought to him, the rugged lines of his face stand out in anguish. He still hopes that she is guiltless of the crime with which she is charged. But when the convicting evidence seems complete, the lines of a holy and solemn wrath appear in the strong face. David Deans said to his other daughter in his vexed indignation: "She went out from us because she was not of us; let her gang the gate. The

---

41. Isaac Watts, "Not All the Blood of Beasts," 1709.

Lord kens His time. She was the bairn of prayers, and may not prove a castaway. But never more let her name be spoken between you and me."

But no human anger against sin, however noble be the heart which feels it, can perfectly image the wrath of God which His beloved Son bore on our behalf. Both of human and divine anger, at their highest, there is this to be said, that it can by no means clear the guilty, even though the guilty be its own.

> Jehovah lifted up His rod
> O Christ, it fell on Thee!
> Thou waist sore stricken of the God
> There's not a stroke for me.
> Thy tears, Thy blood beneath it flowed
> Thy bruising health me.[42]

The Test of Love

According to Professor Clow, the true test of love, accurately and permanently, is to what length it will go. He illustrated this point in the following way:

I can remember a widowed mother left with a family of little children. Their father was little more than a memory to most of them. I saw the mother toil and stint and starve herself, robbing herself of comfort and joy, and even of restoring sleep. I was given her confidences as her troubled mind thought about the future of her children. Her pale cheek turned paler at the thought of evil befalling them. I marked her strength failing, her step growing feebler, the pallor of weakness upon her face. At length the whole self-denying tragedy of her life was played out to the last scene, and she was laid in her grave. Then, at last, as her sons stood at her place of burial, did they awake to the fact that hers was a love which had stood the test of death. So it is always. From the soldiers who died for Greece in unquestioning calm at Marathon, to the obscure girl who gave her life in the fire in a mean London street for the little child who had fastened on her heart; the one test of love is the length to which it will go.

In order to fully comprehend the limit of the love of God for a sinning race, we must come and stand below the cross of Christ, and learn anew that

---

42. Anne R. Cousin, "O Christ, What Burdens Bowed Thy Head."

He so loved a guilty world as to empty heaven of its very best that the worst of earth might be saved. We will never be able to plumb the depth of God's love in the phrase, *"He gave his only begotten son"* (John 3:16).

What Is a Mediator?

A colporteur, when visiting a quiet English village, chanced to meet a man to whom he had sold a New Testament on a previous visit. After inquiring as to how he was getting on with the Book, the man said there was one word he could not understand, the word *mediator*.

"See that bridge?" said the colporteur, pointing toward it. "Let's walk over it and I'll explain the meaning of this important word."

As they crossed the bridge together, the colporteur said: "This bridge is the means whereby you are able to cross the gap. That is just what a mediator does. The Lord Jesus became that for us so that the mighty gap which lay between sinful man and a holy God might be bridged. In virtue of His atoning death and glorious resurrection, it has been accomplished for us."

This illustration made the problem so clear that the man thereupon asked the Savior to enter his life and become his Mediator and Redeemer, and, as he did, so may all.

Shrinking from the Cross

Although in the light of centuries of Christian experience, Christian history, and Christian thought, we view the cross as a glorious triumph over the forces of darkness and death, we shall never know the extent of our Lord's mental anguish and physical suffering as He faced the cross and died upon it. Was there no other way for God to save the world? Was the way of the cross the only way to deliver sin-bound prisoners? On that memorable evening, September 22, 1862, Abraham Lincoln—"Honest Abe"—sat with the proclamation of the emancipation of the slaves before him. He had dedicated his life to the liberty of Negro slaves, throwing himself into such a cause with all the vehement energy of his nature. He had prophesied the abolition of slavery with a fervent hope. All through the years as the President of the United States, he had cherished the high ambition that his might be the hand to break the fetters of the slave. Yet when faced with actual power to proclaim freedom, he hesitated. We are told that he took up his pen and laid it down again and again throughout the long hours of that sleepless night. He knew how holy and necessary and inevitable the deed was, and how thousands of hearts would swell in tumult of thanksgiving to God. But with quivering lips he said, "Is this the hour?"; "Is this the will of God?"; "Is there no other way, gentler, more patient, less violent than this?" Through the long night he pondered the situation, and as the gray of the morning light broke in upon his room, he signed his name.

None of the ransomed will ever know how deep the waters Jesus had crossed in Gethsemane causing Him to cry out, *"Father, if this cup may not pass away from me, except I drink it, thy will be done"* (Matthew 26:42). But He saw the cross as God's only way of emancipating the slaves of sin, and He went forward with animation of spirit. His calm resignation to the divine will is manifest in His call to His disciples, *"Rise up, let us be going"* (Mark 14:42). Out He went to die not as a victim, but as glorious victor over hell's dark foes.

The Victory of Love over Betrayal

The deepest wound Jesus endured was inflicted by the hand of His own familiar friend in whom He had trusted and eaten His bread with. (See Psalm 41:9.) Those long and heavy hours of that night in which Judas sat by Christ's side make the darkest background against which any character was ever set. For the figure of Jesus as Paul sees Him is that of one who is spreading a table of forgiveness and cleansing in the very hour when malice and greed and hate are compassing His death.

A modern writer tells the story of a woman whose husband, to whom she had given her loyal love, had been unfaithful in every way. He broke every vow, bought her to poverty, and made their common name a byword. He had become an idle, shiftless scoundrel, and left her for weeks at a time. Driven by want, he returned home but made no profession of repentance. He had only a sick and helpless brute's whine for relief, and as his long-suffering wife looked on him, a strong revulsion against him rose within her. Yet, somehow, as she saw his degradation and misery, her pity was stirred. The memory of a better past rose up within her to cover his misdeeds, as a rising tide will cover a foul stretch of beach. Her love broke out as a fresh spring prompting her to take her hard-earned savings to relieve his wants. As she overcame evil with good, a gleam of beauty rested on her worn face, a soft love light filled her eyes, and she came to experience what it was to walk in heavenly places with Him whose grace triumphed over grief. *"In the same night in which Christ was betrayed he took bread"* (1 Corinthians 11:23)— He found nourishment. That dark night of betrayal gave His grace its widest opportunity. Trust overcame treachery and love conquered hate. May we be kept from a betrayer's heart, and traitor thoughts! The heaviest and most awful sin we can commit is to persist in our evil purposes while we are putting our hand in the same dish with the One whose love is breathing on our hearts.

Accepting the Atonement

To receive the atonement is to perceive and accept its meaning. Those who have not received it (see Romans 5:11) have not entered into Christ's secret. Another illustration from Professor Clow's rich treasure tells of a man that he met while preaching on the east coast of Scotland. As a retired naval officer, he entertained the preacher who found him genial, downright, and nobly simple in his faith as some sea-going men usually are. When it came time for family worship, the naval officer handed Dr. Clow the English church prayer book he used, and asked him to read because he could not pray before others. Turning over the pages of the prayer book, Dr. Clow found that the officer had marked through, with two red firm lines, the words "for Christ's sake." These words closed most of the prayers. Noticing that the preacher had discovered this crimson obliteration, the sailor explained that his idea of God was that He did not need to be coaxed to forgive sinners. To him the matter was simple. He went to God, owned up to his wrong-doing and God forgave him; that was the beginning and the end of it. After worship, Dr. Clow and his host talked late into the night about sin, the love and holiness of God, and His willingness to receive sinners and cleanse them. As the old man listened to the old story of Jesus and His love, he meekly said, "That is a better Gospel than mine." Repenting, he believed that God, for Christ's sake, had forgiven him, and became one with God. Atone, divided into two words spells—at one—which is what happened when the atonement is believed and received and the repentant sinner is made into one with God.

Christ has for sin atonement made,
What a wonderful Savior![43]

The Shafts of Judgment

Biblical types of Christ's redemptive work, as we have indicated, are most effective. The provision of the scapegoat, for instance, is a most clear exposition of the truth of substitution. One of the most tender scenes of the Old Testament is that of Judah's heart-shaking address, in which he makes his appeal to Joseph to spare Benjamin in whose sack the cup had been placed. It appeared as if the youth was a willful, ungrateful, and pitifully foolish thief. There seemed to be no reason why he, and only he, should not suffer the full penalty of his crime. But Judah had given surety to his father for him, so he steps forward and declares Jacob's love and longing for Benjamin, and offers himself as a bondman in his

---

43. Elisha A. Hoffman, "What A Wonderful Savior," 1891.

room and stead. Who cries out on the injustice of that proffered sacrifice? Who does not feel that had Joseph been unwilling to accept Judah's bond-service for Benjamin, he would read his bond with the merciless eyes of a shylock? Does not Jesus, our brother, stand to bear our sin and do homage to God's broken law? Did He not stand in the judgment hall of God for us? As the chief may die for His clan, as the king may die for his people, as the true priest, whether he bear an outward consecration or not, is always dying for men, so Jesus met the shafts of judgment for us and quenched them in His death.

O Christ, what burdens bow'd Thy head!
Our load was laid on Thee;
Thou stoodest in the sinner's stead,
Didst bear all ill for me.
A Victim led, Thy blood was shed;
Now there's no load for me.[44]

Awaking to Newness of Life

Many years ago when the ground in central London was being cleared of the old buildings to make the new Kingsway, the cleared site laid exposed to light and air for a year and a strange sight drew naturalists to the area. In some cases, the soil had not felt the touch of spring since the day when the Romans sailed up the Thames and beached upon its strand. When the sunlight poured its light and life upon this uncovered soil, a host of flowers sprang up, many of which were unknown in England. They were the plants the Romans had brought with them. Hidden away in the darkness, lying dormant under the mass of bricks and mortar, they seemed to have died. But under the new conditions, obeying the law of life, they escaped from death and blossomed into beauty. So, after years of wrongdoing, after all that is pure and holy in a man's heart seems to be lost, the simplicities and sanctities of his innocent youth arise from the dead. The truth that Christ does not deal with us after our sins, begets penitence and surrender, and the believing one awakes to newness of life.

Down in the human heart, crushed by the tempter,
Feelings lie buried that grace can restore;
Touch'd by a loving heart, Waken'd by kindness,
Chords that are broken will vibrate once more.[45]

---

44. Anne R. Cousin, "O Christ, What Burdens Bowed Thy Head."
45. Fanny Crosby, "Rescue the Perishing," 1869.

6

LENTEN PRAYERS

The preacher who is careful regarding the preservation of his own personal prayer life, fostering in every way unbroken contact with heaven, will have little difficulty in expressing himself publicly in prayer and intercession, no matter what the nature of the church service may be. When it comes to any special day on the church calendar, the preacher should drench his mind with as many Bible verses as he can, and use them as fuel for public prayer. For instance, as he approaches the Lenten season, if he stores his memory with the words of Jesus and the events crowding in upon His last days, he will experience much liberty of thought and speech as he weaves truth into prayer. Another avenue of inspiration and expression is that of meditation on the prayers of renowned saints—ancient and modern. Such a phase of spiritual inspiration is extensive. Methuen's *Library of Devotion* provides a list of great souls at prayer. Then we have *The Christian Year* by John Keble; *Holy Living and Holy Dying*, by Jeremy Taylor; *A Chain of Prayer Across the Ages*, compiled by Selina Fox; *The Temple*, by Dr. W. E. Orchard; *Divine Service for Public Worship*, by Trowde; *Pulpit Prayers of Spurgeon* and a similar volume made up of Alexander Maclaren prayers; *Prayers of the Social Awakening*, by Walter Rauschenbusch, and *The Prayers of Peter Marshall*, compiled by his wife. Every faithful pastor of a flock longs for the same experience in public prayer—praying as if on intimate terms with God and in such a way as to express the deepest needs of his listeners. (Other prayers can be found in Chapters 3 and 4.) Likewise, manuals for ministers, and the *Anglican Prayer Book* and hymn books are helpful aids. Here is a collection gathered from various sources for preachers. For those who keep Lent from Ash Wednesday on with the days of penitence and preparation, we have the prayer of King Manasseh from 700 B.C.:

> O Lord, Almighty God of our Fathers, we have sinned above the number of the sands of the sea. We have done evil before Thee; we have not done Thy will. Now therefore we bow the knee of our heart and beseech Thee to forgive us, O Lord. Thou art its God, even the

God of them that repent, and in us Thou wilt show all Thy goodness, for Thou wilt save us that are unworthy according to Thy great
mercy. Therefore we will praise Thee for ever all the days of our life;
for all the powers of the heavens to praise Thee, and Thine is the
glory forever and ever. Amen.

The renowned Anglican preacher, Dean Goulburn (1818), voiced his confession and desire the following was as the Lenten period began.

O God, our Heavenly Father, we humbly pray Thee for Thy dear
Son's sake, to bless abundantly at this time whatever efforts may be
made to turn the hearts of Thy children to more sincere repentance
and more living faith. Give a double portion of Thy Holy Spirit to all
who minister and work for others. Prepare all hearts to receive the
seed of Thy Word. Grant that it may take deep root, and bring forth
fruit to Thy glory. Alarm the careless, humble the self-righteous,
kindle the lukewarm, soften the hardened, encourage the fearful,
relieve the doubting, and bring many souls in loving faith to Thyself.
Remember us, O Lord, according to the favor that Thou bearest unto
Thy people. O visit us with Thy salvation. Give more than we can
desire or deserve: for the sake of Thy Son, Jesus Christ our Lord.
Amen.

Another prayer from Dean Goulburn at a later period, reads...

Almighty God and heavenly Father, who by Thy divine providence
hast appointed for each of us our work in life, and hast commanded
that we should not be slothful in business, but fervent in spirit, serving Thee, help us always to remember that our work is Thy appoint-
ment, and make us to live with loins girded and lamp burning that,
whensoever our Lord may come, we may be found striving earnestly
to perfect the work that Thou hast given us to do; through the same
Jesus Christ our Savior. Amen.

Throughout the Lenten days, and all the days of the year we have need to
constantly pray,

Grant, O Lord, that we may carefully watch over our tempers and
every unholy feeling that by conforming to Thy will in small things,
we may hope, by Thy protection and help, to pass safely through the
dangers and trials to which we may be exposed. In the Redeemer's
name. Amen.

Then there is the prayer for the spirit of sacrifice which Ignatius Loyola left for our use—

Teach us, good Lord, to serve Thee as Thou deservest; to give and not to count the cost; to fight and not to heed the wounds; to toil and not to seek for rest; to labor and not to ask for reward, save that of knowing that we do Thy will. For Christ's sake. Amen.

That we might be brought into the fellowship of the cross as we journey through the days leading up to and culminating in the Savior's death, this prayer teaches us to cultivate the spirit of the cross.

Almighty God, who hast shown us in the life and teaching of Thy Son, the true way of blessedness, Thou hast also shown us in His suffering and death that the path of love may lead to the cross, and the reward of faithfulness may be a crown of thorns. Give us grace to learn these hard lessons. May we take up our cross and follow Christ in the strength of patience and the constancy of faith; and may we have such fellowship with Him in His sorrow that we may know the secret of His strength and peace, and see even in our darkest hour of trial and anguish the shining of the eternal light. In the name of Him who is worthy of all blessing, honor, glory, and dominion, Thy Son and our Savior. Amen.

Bishop Ridley, who was martyred for Christ's sake in 1555, has taught us to pray in these words:

Heavenly Father, the Father of all wisdom, understanding, and true strength, we beseech Thee look mercifully upon Thy servants and send Thy Holy Spirit into their hearts, that when they must join the fight in the field for the glory of Thy holy name, then they, strengthened with the defense of Thy faith and of Thy truth, can continue in the same unto the end of their lives, through Jesus Christ our Lord. Amen.

With the repentance, humility, and self-discipline associated with Lent, one could use this entreaty from the *The Treasury of Devotion*, published in 1892 A.D.:

O gracious Savior, we beseech Thee of Thy love and goodness to remember our manifold infirmities; give us full pardon of our sins and a new spirit. Give us grace, that we may always imitate Thy humility, resignation, purity, patience, charity, and all virtues, that we may be well-pleasing to Thee, may become daily more like Thee, and may hereafter dwell with Thee forever. For Thine own name's sake we ask it. Amen.

Another prayer for Lent was offered by Thomas a Kempis in 1379 A.D.:

We beseech Thee, our most gracious God, preserve us from the cares of this life, lest we should be too much entangled therein; also from the many necessities of the body, lest we should be ensnared by pleasure; and from whatsoever is an obstacle to the soul, lest, being broken with troubles, we should be overthrown. Give us strength to resist, patience to endure, and constancy to persevere; for the sake of Jesus Christ our Lord and Savior. Amen.

Seeing that confessing sin and praying for forgiveness are Lenten exercises of the soul, the prayer of Bishop Thomas Wilson, 1663 A.D., is worthy of a heartfelt repetition.

O Father of mercies and God of all comforts, who by Thy blessed Son hast declared that all sins shall be forgiven unto the sons of men upon their true repentance, let this most comfortable word support us Thy servants against the temptations of the devil. Though our sins are great, they cannot be too great for Thy mercy, which is infinite. O give us true repentance for the errors of our life past, and steadfast faith in Thy Son Jesus Christ, that our sins may be done away by Thy mercy, through the merits of the same Jesus Christ our Lord. Amen.

When it comes to Holy Week itself covering the period between Palm Sunday and Easter, we have an abundance of prayers and supplications from saintly preachers of the past whose ministry was so dynamic because of their personal traffic with heaven. In 1841, the saintly Bishop Handley C. S. Moule prayed the following prayer on Palm Sunday:

As on this day we keep the special memory of our Redeemer's entry into the city, so grant, O Lord, that now and ever He may triumph in our hearts. Let the King of grace and glory enter in, and let us lay ourselves and all we are in full and joyful homage before Him; through the same Jesus Christ our Lord. Amen.

The revised Anglican prayer book of 1928 contains this prayer for use on the Sunday before Easter:

O God, who by the passion of Thy blessed Son hast made the instrument of shameful death to be unto us the means of life and peace: grant us so to glory in the cross of Christ that we may gladly suffer shame and loss; for the sake of the same Thy Son our Lord. Amen.

As it is the custom of churches to plan for special week night services during Passiontide, sometimes culminating with a united three-hour service on Friday, these suggested prayers for each night of the week may prove suggestive. From the nineteenth century, we have gathered two petitions for use on Monday:

O God who hast brought us to this Holy Week, wherein we renew the memory of our Redeemer's passion, hear us we beseech, and enable us to observe it in the spirit of holiness and piety, of humility and penitence, of love, and adoration and gratitude. Grant that His sufferings may show us the grievousness of sin, and the punishment due to it, while they give us comfort in showing to us the ground of hope. That so, putting our whole trust in Him, who is the sacrifice and ransom for our sin, we may enter into the fellowship of His sufferings, and dying unto the world, may live evermore with Him, our Savior and Redeemer, even Jesus Christ Thy Son our Lord. Amen.

O Lord God, who didst give Thine only Son as at this time to suffer and die for us, give us grace to humble ourselves before Thee in heartfelt sorrow for sin. Help us to deny ourselves, and to take up our cross and follow our Lord. Have mercy on all men and draw them to Thyself by the power of the cross. Bless all the services of this week, and grant us that we may have such trust and confidence in Thy mercy toward us in Christ, our Lord, that we have found in Him all pardon and peace. Prepare our hearts for the joyful worship of the coming Easter Day; for His merits, who died, was buried, and rose again for us, Thy Son Jesus Christ our Lord. Amen.

For the Tuesday of Holy Week, we have selected the two following supplications. This prayer arose to heaven by Archbishop Cranmer who was cruelly martyred in 1489 A.D.

O Thou who art almighty power but meek, and in perfect excellency wast lowly, grant unto us the same mind, that we may mourn over our evil will. Our bodies are frail and fading; our minds are blind and forward; all that we have which is our own is naught; if we have any good in us it is wholly Thy gift. O Savior, since Thou, the Lord of heaven and earth, didst humble Thyself, grant unto us true humility, and make us like Thyself; and then, of Thine infinite goodness, raise us to Thine everlasting glory; who livest and reignest with the Father and the Holy Ghost forever and forever. Amen.

Roman Catholic literature related to Lent, particularly to Easter Week, can provide the discerning, evangelical preacher with most rewarding material both for his own devotional use and public petitions. From Pope Innocent III, who died in 1216, we have the prayer:

Lord Jesus Christ, Son of the living God, who for our redemption willedst to be born, and on the cross to die the most shameful of deaths, do Thou by Thy death and passion deliver us from all sins and penalties, and by Thy holy cross bring us, miserable sinners, to that place where Thou livest and reignest with the Father and the Holy Spirit, ever one God, world without end. Amen.

Wednesday is usually the mid-week night service in many churches, and they invariably have a special Easter program for the evening. These prayer selections might guide the pastor or leader through the gathering.

O God, our heavenly Father, who to redeem us didst deliver up Thine only Son to be betrayed by one of His disciples and sold to His enemies, take from us, we beseech Thee, all covetousness and hypocrisy, and so help us, that loving Thee and Thy truth above all things, we may remain steadfast in our faith even unto the end, and cleaving to Thee with all our hearts may at last attain to the inheritance of the saints in light; through Him who ever liveth to make intercession for us, Jesus Christ, our Lord. Amen.

A female saint of the nineteenth century, the honorable Mrs. Lyttelton Gell, would have us repeat her petition:

By all the sufferings of Thine early years, Thy fasting and temptation, Thy nameless wanderings, Thy lonely vigils on the mount, by the weariness and painfulness of Thy ministry among men—good Lord deliver us!

By Thine unknown sorrows, by the mysterious burden of the spiritual cross, by Thine agony and bloody sweat—good Lord deliver us!

O Lord Jesus Christ, who wast lifted up from the earth that Thou mightest draw all men unto Thee, draw us also unto Thyself, for Thine own name's sake. Amen.

Interceding that the world in general may pause and think of the true significance of Easter for all nations, a prayer like this could be adapted:

O Lord, who hast made of one blood all nations of men, mercifully receive the prayers that we offer for our anxious, troubled, and Christless world. Send Thy light into our darkness, and guide the nations as one family into the ways of peace.

From all prejudice and hatred and fear…

From deafness to Thy call and preoccupation with self-chosen ends…

From slackness in seeking Thy will for ourselves and others…

From self-seeking and indifference to others in the work of earning a living…

From conformity to the world, and contentment with less than the best…

From negligence to hallow the common life of business…

From pride of clan or race, from carelessness of speech and action, and from contempt of others…

From unscrupulous ambition, selfish rivalries, and false judgments…

Good Lord, deliver us!

Amen.

As Thursday has a deep significance as the eve of our Lord's anguish and death, the preacher, in public ministry, will approach it with much solemnity. From a true pastor's heart, W. E. Scudamore, we have this appropriate supplication from 1813 A.D.

O Lord Jesus Christ, who, when about to suffer, didst institute the Holy Sacrament of Thy body and blood, and bid us observe it as a memorial of Thy death, and as a means of union and communion with Thyself, grant, we beseech Thee, that neither Thy great love, nor this last command, may ever fade from our forgetful hearts, that in all things following Thee, and ever hasting unto Thy coming, we may at last be found of Thee in peace; Who livest and reignest with the Father and the Holy Ghost one God forever and ever. Amen.

A godly Bishop of the Anglican Church, Walsham How, in 1823 A.D., left us this further fitting petition for use as Calvary approached:

O Lord Jesus Christ, the Son of God, and Savior of the world, who didst foretell to Thine apostles that at the time of Thy sufferings they should weep and lament, while the world rejoiced, and that they should be sorrowful, but their sorrow should be turned to joy, grant that, during this time wherein Thou didst suffer and wast afflicted for the sins of the whole world, we Thine unworthy servants may so weep and lament and be sorrowful for our sins, the cause of all Thy sorrows and sufferings, that on the day of Thy triumphant resurrection we may rejoice with that joy which no man can take from us: grant this, O blessed Lord and Savior, who didst die for our sins, rise again for our justification, and now livest and reignest with the Father, in the unity of the Holy Ghost, world without end. Amen.

Having come to Easter proper, with its good yet grim Friday; its Saturday, with Jesus low in His grave; its Sunday, when He rose a victor over the dark domain, the preacher has an abundance of suitable prayers and devotional literature to meditate on as he prepares his own heart to lead worshipers in the prayer periods of public service.

Going back to the fifteenth century, we have an intercessory prayer, offered by Bishop Hamilton at Easter;

Lord God, who didst send down Thine only Son to redeem the world by His obedience unto death; grant, we humbly beseech thee, that the continual memory of His bitter cross and passion may teach us so to crucify the flesh with the affections and lusts thereof that, dying unto sin and living unto Thee, we may, in the union and merits of His cross and passion, die with Him, and rest with Him, and rise again with Him, and live with Him forever; to whom with Thee and the Holy Ghost be all honor and glory, world without end. Amen.

Charles Kingsley, in 1819 A.D., left us this brief petition:

O Christ, give us patience, and faith, and hope as we kneel at the foot of Thy cross, and hold fast to it. Teach us by Thy cross, that however ill the world may go, the Father so loved us that He spared not Thee. Amen.

Reaching Saturday, we think of Jesus buried in Joseph's new tomb. Dying for our sins, He was buried, and as the Easter hymn puts it…

> Dying He saved me,
> Buried He carried my sins far away.[46]

---

46. L. Wilbur Chapman, "Living, He Loved Me; Dying, He Saved Me."

As we remember the hours Jesus was taken by death we pray...

Gracious God, give us a living faith in our Redeemer and a thankful remembrance of His death. Help us to love Him better for His exceeding love to us, and grant that our sins may be put away, and nailed to His cross and buried in His grave, that they may be remembered no more against us; through the same, Thy Son, Jesus Christ our Lord. Amen.

An ancient prayer reminds us of the load of our sins Jesus took to and left at the grave...

O Lord, we implore Thee, by the memory of Thy cross's hallowed and most bitter anguish, make us fear Thee, make us love Thee. Wash out our offenses, comfort us as we faithfully call upon Thee; and, we beseech Thee to restore us from death to the land of the living, through Him who rose again from the grave. Amen.

The miracle upon which the reality of Christianity rests, and which made the church Jesus bought with His own blood, such a dynamic force in the old Roman Empire, was the truth Easter Sunday proclaims, namely the resurrection of Him who was crucified and buried. The glad and glorious evangel of His triumph over death and the grave has found expression in myriads of prayers of gratitude. An adaptation of Peter's benediction reads thus:

Blessed be the God and Father of our Lord Jesus Christ, which, according to His abundant mercy, hath begotten us again unto a lively hope, by the resurrection of Jesus Christ from the dead, to an inheritance incorruptible and undefiled, and that fadeth not away, reserved in heaven for us. Keep us this day, O God, by Thy power unto salvation, through Jesus Christ our Savior. Fill us with all joy and peace in believing that we may abound in hope through the power of Thy Spirit. Amen.

From St. Anselm, whose fragrant ministry was so blessed of the Lord in the tenth century, we have the prayer of praise:

O Lord Jesus Christ, our redemption and our salvation, we praise Thee and give Thee thanks; and though we be unworthy of Thy benefits, and cannot offer unto Thee due devotion, yet let Thy lovingkindness fill up that which our weakness endeavoreth. Before Thee, O Lord, is all our desire, and whatsoever our hearts rightly willeth, it is of Thy gift. Grant that we may attain to love Thee even as Thou commandest. Let not Thy gift be unfruitful in us. Perfect that Thou hast begun, give that which Thou hast made us to long after; convert Thou our lukewarmness into fervent love of Thee; for the glory of Thy holy name. Amen.

St. Gregory, 590 A.D., is credited with the petition...

O God, who for our redemption didst give Thine only begotten Son to the death of the cross, and by His glorious resurrection hast delivered us from the power of the enemy, grant us to die daily to sin, that we may evermore live with Him, in the joy of His resurrection: through the same Jesus Christ our Lord. Amen.

The great apostolic benediction is so full of the message of Easter.

Now the God of peace, that brought again from the dead our Lord Jesus, that great shepherd of the sheep, through the blood of the everlasting covenant, make you perfect in every good work to do His will, working in you that which is well-pleasing in his sight, through Jesus Christ: to whom be glory forever and ever. Amen.

Dr. F. Schleiermacher, pastor and professor in Berlin (1768–1834), was the most illustrious and prominent preacher and theologian of his time. In a Good Friday service that he conducted in his Berlin church, he prefaced his sermon with this prayer:

Heavenly Father! look graciously down upon all who meet this day to celebrate the death of the Holy One in whom Thou wert well pleased! Grant that none may leave the cross of Thy Beloved without exclaiming, in new and living faith "Truly this was the Son of God!" that the tear of sensibility may continue to flow until everyone is seized with the intense desire that the end of this Righteous One may be his also! Oh, let not the feeling of holy reverence and wonder which must take possession of every heart at the remembrance of the dying Christ—let it not remain here fruitless within these walls, but let it accompany us all out into life, that that life may become ever increasingly consecrated to Thee, and more like His, until at length we also follow Him in cheerful ascension unto Thee. Amen.

There are many other prayers to be found in the chapter of "Lenten Preaching" that can be added to this section for the pastor's consideration.

7

LENTEN POEMS

Inspirational poets are among the best teachers of the wise and discerning preacher, who treats good poetry as an effective handmaid. Those in possession of a noble poetic gift see the analogies of external nature to moral and spiritual truth as most of us cannot, and open up to us unknown depths in our own nature. When the poetic art is subordinate to spiritual profit, the poet kindles our imagination, gives it general direction, and brings us to appreciate the many facets of God, nature, and man. As to the use of poetry in a sermon, quotations should be used sparingly, and hackneyed couplets and verses should be avoided. "If the poetry is poor it should not be quoted at all. If it is good you can trust the congregation not to credit you with a gift which you do not possess."

There is no poetry comparable to that which the Bible contains. Well over a century ago, George Gilfillan wrote a remarkable book on *The Bards of the Bible* in which he proved that much of Scripture is written in the language of poetry—a fact emphasizing the genuineness, power, and divinity of the oracles of our faith. Poetic language has the greatest power of permanent impression, and, as the language of the imagination, is the highest language of man.

The Bible is, on the whole, a mass of beautiful figures—its words and its thoughts are alike poetical—it has gathered around its central truths all natural beauty and interest—it is a temple, with one altar and one God, but illuminated by a thousand varied lights, and studded with a thousand ornaments…The living Spirit of the Book has ransacked creation to lay its treasures on Jehovah's altar—thus the innumerable rays of a far-streaming glory have been condensed on the little hill Calvary and a garland has been woven for the bleeding brow of Immanuel, the flowers of which have been culled from the gardens of a universe.

Among those who displayed matchless merit as masters of the lyre, we have Job, David, and Solomon, all of who are conspicuous as the rightful poetic rulers of the belief and the heart of man. Professor R. G. Moulton in *The Modern Reader's Bible* brings the Psalms, Lamentations, and the Song of Songs under the section of "Bible Poetry," and sets these books out in an impressive poetic form. Without a doubt, David is the most conspicuous poet of the Bible whose poetic Psalms were no fancy pieces or the elaboration of his mind alone, but which, in the main, were founded upon episodes and events of his varied career. Whether meditating upon praise, prayer, or penitence, David, the sweet psalmist of Israel, blossomed into poetry. "Each flower stands rooted in truth; and the poetry is just fact on fire." In the Psalms, David reveals a more exceeding simplicity and artlessness than in the rest of Scripture poetry. Although he lived hundreds of years before Christ, he takes a prophetic leap and graphically depicts in a poetic form many of the incidents in our Lord's last week. We have the Calvary Psalm (see Psalm 22) which Jesus quoted on the cross; the Resurrection Psalm (Psalm 16); the Betrayal Psalm (Psalm 41)—all of which supply the preacher with sufficient expository material for Holy Week.

Besides the Bible, we have numerous poets and hymnists who have enriched us with forceful and unforgettable poems on almost every incident in the life of Jesus during the Via Dolorosa. Isaac Watts, the poet of the passion, gave the church some of its most memorable hymns on Redeemer's cross. There is nothing comparable in poetic literature to the heart-moving poem:

> When I survey the wondrous cross
> On which the young Prince of glory died,
> My richest gain I count but loss,
> And pour contempt on all my pride.

Watts also gave us the great poetic impositions *Join All the Glorious Names* and *Not All the Blood of Beasts*. Another remarkable poem on the cross came from the gifted pen of Thomas Kelly:

> We sing the praise of Him Who died,
> Of Him who died upon the cross:
> The sinner's hope let men deride:
> For this we count the world but loss.

My favorite Easter poem or hymn is by Sir J. Bowring:

> In the cross of Christ I glory,
> Towering o'er the wrecks of time,
> All the light of sacred story
> Gathers 'round its head sublime.

During his services of Passion Week, the preacher might find it profitable to devote an evening to the "Poetry of the Passion." In order to help him develop such a profitable theme, we cite a few treasures our reading has brought to light. On Lenten week as a whole, there is the following comprehensive poem by Henry Beer taken from *My Garden of Verses*, which could be memorized and then recited either it a women's group or during an evening service.

His Last Week

From peaceful Galilee up to Jerusalem
The Savior turned His face and thither went His way.
The vision of a cross upon a lonely hill
Stood out in bold relief against that coming day.

Up to the sacrificial feast He needs must go,
For heaven will a Paschal Lamb provide.
Farewell to kindred ties in pleasant Galilee,
For He must keep this feast whatever may betide.

The Jesus with the loved disciple band
Descended from the Mount of Olives on the way.
Steadfastly to Jerusalem He set His face,
And rode upon a colt in lowly, meek array,

The loved disciples, children, people all
Cried out with waving palms, "Hosanna to the King.
Hosanna to the King who cometh in God's name,
Hosanna in the highest." His praises they did sing.

Though oft He went unto the Paschal feast,
Yet now He went e'en as the Lord had willed.
The altar is prepared, the sacred hour draws nigh;
How is He straightened till it all shall be fulfilled!

And as the time drew nigh He showed His power divine:
The fig tree is accursed and withered in one day;
For henceforth shall no fruit on thee be borne.
They all marvel, all who chance to pass that way.

Straight to the temple where He oft had taught,
He entered in, and as He looked about

The money changers who did buy and sell
Were by His words and power put to rout.

He told them by what power He did His works,
And with authority He did expound
The holy truths which we embrace today,
Which in the blessed Book of Life are found.

Sweet parables of truth: The wicked husbandman,
And the two sons, and tribute we must give;
The marriage of the son, and the true vine
Are words of truth He spoke which evermore shall live.

In this eventful week rare gems of love He spoke;
How love fulfills the law, and is the great command.
The widow's humble mite, the resurrection quest.
And how the pure in heart shall in God's favor stand.

The Jews for whom He came from heaven's realm
Could not perceive His love, His power divine.
For they who say they see, their blindness shall remain,
To such as seek me not my heavenly light shall shine.

Then to the upper room which was for them prepared
The Savior with the twelve sat round the festal board.
How sacred, holy was the evening hour,
As they did eat the farewell supper with their Lord.

What pain and sorrow filled the Master's heart,
For one who sits in fellowship near by
Shall by the morn betray me to my foes.
Then answered they the Master, "Is it I?"

How sad the thought, we fain would call the name,
'Twas Judas who betrayed his friend and Lord.
Then to the priests he went with soul bowed down with guilt,
And thirty silver pieces was his deed's reward.

Then Jesus with His true disciples there,
The holy sacrament did then ordain.
The bread I break, the wine I share with you,
I give in memory of my suffering and pain.

And then to prove His love and deep humility
The Savior washed the loved disciples' feet.
What I do now ye neither can perceive,
But afterward will follow blessings full and sweet.

Before they left the holy upper room,
Before He needs must go into the depths of woe,
They sang a hymn with loving sweet accord,
Then Jesus said, "Arise, and let us go."

And then the holy band went over Cedron's brook
Into the garden of Gethsemane,
For it was hither where He often did resort
There with His own in fellowship to be.

It was in Eden's garden where man first did sin,
His innocence and first estate were lost.
The gate to paradise to men was closed,
And they were driven out at awful cost.

So in this garden of Gethsemane
Our Savior sought the help of power divine,
And won the victory o'er self and Satan's power,
And prayed submissively, "Thy will be done, not mine."

Then the disciples whom He asked to watch
And share with Him the sorrow and distress
Fell into slumber there. Their help could not suffice.
Then angels came the sorrowing Christ to bless.

Then the betrayer with the soldier band,
The priests and scribes with torches all aglow
Came forth from out the midnight darkness deep,
And Judas went before the way to show.

Here heaven oft had blessed the Son of God,
But now the powers of darkness did prevail.
O woeful night of sin and wretchedness,
When sinful men the Prince of Peace assail!

Then Judas gave a token to the soldiers there
And with a kiss he did the Lord betray.
Then they came forth with swords and staves and all
And led the Savior, Christ, the Lord away.

Then came the judgment of the only just.
The Judge supreme, was judged by mortal man.
And false accusers rose in wrath and scorn,
Which did fulfil prophetic word and plan.

False witnesses came in to testify,
And every justice was the Lord denied,
By envy moved to wrath and vile contempt,
Then they cried out, "Let Him be crucified!"

What if the Christ would deal with men on earth
As they had done and sentence us to die?
What if He had no mercy or regard
When men for justice and for mercy cry?

It was a custom on that noted day
A prisoner from the city to set free.
Barabbas, vile and sinful, was their choice,
But Christ, the pure, must die, was their decree.

O sinner as you walk this earthly vale,
What is your choice, the sinful, or the pure?
Do you prefer the vile whose wage is death,
Or will you choose the Christ, whose wage shall e'er endure?

Then from the judgment hall condemned to die
Out to Golgotha's hill they led the way.
There Jesus fainting 'neath the cross He bore,
The cross on Simon of Cyrene they lay.

The surging multitude that followed on that morn
With soldiers, priests, and scribes in one accord
Went on, it seemed, by some satanic power moved,
As out to Calvary they led the loving Lord.

O well for men who can this day perceive,
And feel the debt of love to Christ we owe.
And keep the vision of His passion in our hearts;
It was for sinful men that Christ this way must go.

The vision of the cross which Christ had long foreseen,
Whichever stood before His heart and eye,
Was now the sacrificial altar for the Lamb,
On which the Christ for fallen man must die.

The world will once be judged by Calvary's cross.
It is the crowning act of holy, sacred page.
Herein the hope of every nation lies,
By it men come to God in every clime and age.

'Twas there on Calvary's brow the Savior died.
O spot despised by all who go that way!
Into the depths of darkness Christ did go
To lift men up unto eternal day.

To you who do not know the power of the blood,
Let it by faith to your heart applied.
Draw nigh to Christ in prayer and penitence,
And by His healing power be wholly sanctified.

Then Nicodemus, ruler of the Jews,
With Joseph of Arimathea on that day
Went forth to Pilate—begged the body from the cross.
They were disciples of the Lord, but in a secret way.

And Joseph took the body from the cross,
Now openly he did the Lord confess.
And Nicodemus came with spices rare
The body to anoint—to prove his faithfulness.

And near the place where He was crucified
They laid the Lord in Joseph's own new tomb.
They rolled a stone before the sepulchre,
And sadly parted in the evening gloom.

Is there a soul who truly loves the Lord,
Who keeps it secret, locked within his heart?
Now Jesus on the cross revealed His love for you,
Will thou not openly thy love to Him impart?

There was a hush—a silence in Jerusalem,
As thoughts returned to Calvary on the Sabbath day.
The quaking earth, the darkness o'er the land,
How Jesus suffered there, in anguish passed away.

And when the next day dawned of this eventful week
The earth did quake and Christ the Lord arose.
The grave could not retain the sinless Son of God.
Triumphantly He came from out His death's repose.

O who alone but Christ, the sinless one,
The Prince of Peace, the hero of the cross,
Could rob death of its sting, the grave of victory,
And save us from eternal wrath and loss?

O wondrous thought—the resurrected Christ still lives.
He lives all glorious in the realms above!
He sheds abroad His spirit into hearts of men.
'Tis He who lives, and reigns, and intercedes and loves.

O seek not for Him in an earthly tomb,
Where now the kings and nobles of all ages lie.
No grave can keep the sinless, matchless One.
All glorious Prince, He lives again on high!

Awake my soul! The Lord will come! Awake!
The rapture of the saints is drawing near.
O consecrate yourself to Him anew,
Be wholly sanctified and live in Godly fear!

Robert Herrick (1591–1694) wrote these unusual lines:

To Keep a True Lent

Is this a fast, to keep
The larder lean
And clean?
No, 'tis a fast to dole
Thy sheaf of wheat
And meat
Unto the hungry soul.
It is to fast from strife,
From old debate
And hate;
To circumcise thy life.
To show a heart grief-rent
To starve thy sin,
Not bin.
And that's to keep thy Lent.

As the period of Lent is supposed to be the time when we draw aside
from the world to examine our hearts in the light of the cross and discard that

which is alien to the holy mind and purpose of the Savior, the verses of the venerated George Herbert are moss apt:

Self-Examination

By all means use sometime to be alone,
Salute thyself: see what thy soul doth wear,
Dare to look in thy chest; for 'tis thine own;
And tumble up and down what thou findst there.
Who cannot rest till he good fellows find,
He breaks up homes, turns out of doors his mind.

Sum up by night what thou hast done by day;
And in the morning, what thou hast to do.
Dress and undress thy soul; mark the decay
And growth of it; if, with thy watch, that too
Be down, then wind up both; since we shall be
Most surely judged, make thy accounts agree.

And ancient Lent carol reads:

To bow the head
In sackcloth or in ashes
Or rend the soul,
Such grief is not Lent's goal;
But to be led
To where God's glory flashes
His beauty to come nigh,
To fly, to fly.
Arise, arise,
Arise, and make a paradise.

Reviewing the life and labors of Jesus during His public ministry until He finally sealed His witness with His life's blood, the following poem could be effectively used in a message of such a theme during Holy Week:

The Cross Was His Own

They borrowed a bed to lay His head,
When Christ the Lord came down;
They borrowed an ass in the mountain pass
For Him to ride to town.

But the crown that He wore
And the cross that He bore
Were His own.

He borrowed the bread when the crowd He fed
On the grassy mountain side;
He borrowed the dish of broken fish
With which He satisfied.
But the crown that He wore
And the cross that He bore
Were His own.

He borrowed the ship in which to sit
To teach the multitude;
He borrowed the nest in which to rest,
He had never a home as rude;
But the crown that He wore
And the cross that He bore
Were His own.

He borrowed a room on the way to the tomb,
The Passover lamb to eat.
They borrowed a cave, for Him a grave,
They borrowed a winding sheet.
But the crown that He wore
And the cross that He bore
Were His own.

The thorns on His head were worn in my stead,
For me the Savior died.
For guilt of my sin the nails drove in
When Him they crucified.
Though the crown that He wore
And the cross that He bore
Were His own,
They rightly were mine—instead.

Mary Brainerd Smith has given us a similar poem emphasizing the voluntary poverty of Him who left nothing but His peace.

Poor for Our Sakes
The earth, with all its fullness, is the Lord's:

He made it, and 'tis His alone for aye;
Yet in a borrowed bed in Bethlehem
They laid Him, when He came to earth one day.

The sea is His, and all its mighty waves
He holds within the hollow of His hand;
Yet 'tis a borrowed boat He needs must use
To put out from that thronged Gennesaret strand.

The cattle o'er a thousand hills are His,
The fruitage too that countless valleys yield;
Yet He must borrow bread and fish to feed
The hungry people in Bethsaida's field.

And all the silver and the gold are His,
With all earth holds of treasures rich and vast;
Yet in a borrowed room He spread a feast,
And in a borrowed tomb was laid at last.

Yea, for our sake, He laid His wealth aside;
Yet from His poverty such blessing streams,
That we, the very poorest of the poor,
Are rich beyond all counting and all dreams.

The institution of the Last Supper, the night before Jesus died, is usually recognized during Lent with the observance of the Supper, with a message on its spiritual significance, the Master's question, *"Where is the guest chamber?"* (Luke 22:11) gave Frank J. Exley the inspiration for these lines:

The Guest Chamber

And dost Thou ask to be my Guest,
Lord of the myriad worlds that wheel in space?
Is this poor heart of mine fit dwelling place
For Thee to rest?

Yet unworthy room doth most
Call for the transformation of Thy grace;
Then come, but not as Guest, to this mean place,
Come, Lord, as Host.

Bring Thy provisions with Thee, lest
My empty board should mock Thee: Pierce my gloom

With Thine own light, and furnish all the room—
I'll be Thy guest.

Discoursing upon the Master's experiences in the garden of Gethsemane, the messenger of the Lord finds many solemn truths to preach about in the blood, sweat, and tears associated with the garden. Among fitting poetical material for such a phase of His anguish, we have the expressive poem by William L. Stidger:

Resignation

He prayed by the stone,
Where they left Him all alone;
And He watched for the light
Of the torches through the night.

He bowed His head and wept
While the three disciples slept
Where He watched for the light
Of the torches through the night.

And there came the gift of calm
Like some heavenly peace and balm
As He watched for the light
Of the torches through the night.

Then a surge of strength and power
Came to Him that tragic hour
Where He watched for the light
Of the torches through the night.

In his volume *The Call to Lent*, Bishop Handley Moule quotes the two closing stanzas of a heart-moving war poem which appeared in the *Spectator* on September 11, 1915, under the signature "L. W." It was part of a soldier's address to...

Christ in Flanders

We think about You kneeling in the garden—
Ah God! the agony of that dread garden—
We know You prayed for us upon the cross.
If anything could make us glad to bear it—
'Twould be the knowledge that You willed to bear it—
Pain—death—the uttermost of human loss.

Though we forget You—You will not forget us—
We feel so sure that You will not forget us—
But stay with us until this dream is past,
And so we ask for courage, strength, and pardon
Especially, I think, we ask for pardon—
And that You'll stand beside us to the last.

To the making of poems on Easter there is no end. What a rich store-house of applicable compositions there are on almost every aspect of the death and resurrection of Christ! Preachers may find our selection profitable for his Easter messages. The mystery and meaning of Calvary are condensed for us in this captivating poem:

Under an Eastern sky,
Amid a rabble cry,
A man went forth to die,
For me!

Thorn-crowned His blessed head,
Blood-stained His every tread,
Cross-laden on He sped,
For me!

Pierced glow His hands and feet,
Three hours o'er Him did beat,
Fierce rays of noon-tide heat,
For me!

Thus wert Thou made of mine,
Lord make me wholly Thine,
Give grace and strength divine
To me!

In thought and word and deed,
Thy will to do: oh, lead my feet,
E'en though they bleed,
To Thee!

Dealing with the approach to the cross, the preacher can use with much profit the incident of Simon of Cyrene who was commandeered to carry Christ's cross. Suggestions for such a message on cross-bearing can be found in Clow's volume on *The Cross in Christian Experience*, under the title of "The

Mark of the Disciple." An apt lyric is this anonymous one which Dr. Harry Rimmer quotes in his book, *Voices from Calvary:*

> Simon of Cyrene bore
> The cross of Jesus—nothing more.
> His name is never heard again,
> Nor honored by historic pen;
> Nor on the pedestal of fame
> His image courts the loud acclaim:
> Simon of Cyrene bore
> The cross of Jesus—nothing more.
>
> And yet, when all our work is done,
> And golden beams the western sun
> Upon a life of wealth and fame,
> A thousand echoes ring our name;
> Perhaps our hearts will humbly pray
> "Good Master, let my record say
> Upon the page Divine, 'He bore
> The cross of Jesus'"; nothing more.

Then there is also this further delineation of Him whom cruel men crowned with thorns:

> I see His blood upon the rose
> And in the stars the glory of His eyes.
> His body gleams amid eternal snows
> His tears fall from the skies.
> I see His face in every flower
> The thunder and the singing of the birds
> Are but His voice, and carven by His power
> Rocks are His written words.
> All pathways by His feet are worn,
> His strong heart stirs the ever-beating sea,
> His crown of thorns is twined with every thorn
> His cross on every tree.

The Loneliness of Christ
(Matthew 4:1)

> Alone! Yes, Jesus was alone
> In that great stretch of sand and stone,

And later in earth's noise and din
Alone, since He was free from sin.
And men who gathered to be taught,
Oft failed to reach His inmost thought;
Still later 'neath a darkened sky,
They listened to a lonely cry,
From One upon th' accursed tree.
"O, why hast Thou forsaken Me?"—
We pause, and pray, "Lord help us guess
The depth of that great loneliness."

—E. E. Trusted

The two following brief poems from William E. Stidger's book, *I Saw God Wash the World*, are complementary. The first bears the title...

Integrity

He made honest doors,
Did Christ, the Nazarene;
He laid honest floors—
His work was fine and clean.

He made crosses too,
Did Christ the Crucified;
Straight and strong, and true—
And on a cross He died!

The second one is named...

The Cross and the Tree

A tree is such a sacred thing;
I never knew just why
Until I saw my Savior, Christ
Stretched on a tree to die;
And heard Him lift His pleading voice
In one great, tender cry!

And now I know why poets sing
About a common tree
As if it were a sacred thing
Of God-like destiny

As if each stalwart oak had roots
That reached to Calvary!

Dr. Robert G. Lee, the Southern Baptist orator, in a graphic message on the cross said that, "Our sins were the palms that smote Jesus, the fists that beat Him, the scourge that cut Him, the thorns that crowned Him, the nails that transfixed Him," and recited the telling poem by John Trowbridge to enforce his message:

A crown of thorns
And a purple robe—
Somebody fashioned them both.
Somebody platted the bloody crown,
Somebody fitted the gaudy gown,
Somebody fashioned them both.

A crown of thorns
And a purple robe—
And was it so long ago
They made that vesture our Savior wore,
And wove that crown that He meekly bore?
And was it so long ago?

A crown of thorns
And a purple robe—
I read the words with a sigh:
But when I remember my own misdeeds,
My soul awakes, and my conscience pleads,
And I say to myself, "Is it I?"

Dr. William Alexander, Archbishop of Armagh, in his remarkable volume *Verbum Crucis*, to which we made previous mention, concludes his chapter dealing with the "Seven Words of the Cross" with the following poem of his own composition:

O kingly silence of our Lord!
O wordless wonder of the Word!
O hush, that while all heaven is awed,
Makes music in the ear of God!
Silence—yet with a sevenfold stroke
Seven times a wondrous bell there broke
Upon the cross, when Jesus spoke.

One word, one priestly word, He saith—
The advocacy of the death,
The intercession by the throne,
Wordless beginneth with that tone.
All the long music of the plea
That ever mediates for me
Is set upon the selfsame key.

One royal word—though love prevails
To hold Him faster than the nails,
And though the dying lips are white
As foam seen through a dusky night:
That hand doth paradise unbar,
Those pale lips tell of a world afar,
Where perfect absolutions are.

One word, one human word—we lift
Our adoration for the gift
Which proves that, dying, well He knew
Our very nature through and through.
Silver the Lord hath not, nor gold,
Yet His great legacy behold
The virgin to the virgin-soul'd.

Three hours of an unfathom'd pain,
Of drops falling like summer rain,
Earth's sympathy and heaven's eclipse—
Three hours the pale and dying lips
By their mysterious silence teach
Things far more beautiful than speech
In depth or height can ever reach.

One word, the Elitwice wailed o'er—
'Tis anguish, but 'tis something more
Mysteriously the whole world's sin,
His and not His, is blended in.
It is a broken heart whose prayer
Cryeth as from an altar-stair
To One who is, and is not, there.

One word, one gentle word.
In pain He condescendeth to complain

Burning, from whose sweet will are born
The dewinesses of the morn.
The Fountain which is last and first,
The Fountain whence life's river burst,
The Fountain waileth out, "I thirst."

One royal word of glorious thought,
A hundred threads are inter wrought
In it—the thirty years and three,
The bitter travail of the tree,
Are finished—finished, too, we scan
All types and prophecies—the plan
Of the long history of man.

One word, one happy word—we note
The clouds over Calvary float
In distances, till fleck or spot
In the immaculate sky is not;
And on the cross peace falls like balm;
And the Lord's soul is yet more calm
Than the commendoof His psalm.

When it comes to the glad and glorious Easter day and the preacher heralds forth the triumph of Christ over the grave, and expounds Paul's Magna Carta of the resurrection, namely 1 Corinthians 15, he has a plethora of hymns and poems to choose from to adorn his message. One of the most effective is that by Dr. H. H. Barstow titled,

If Easter Be Not True

If Easter be not true
Then all the lilies low must lie;
The Flanders poppies fade and die;
The spring must lose her fairest bloom
For Christ were still within the tomb—
If Easter be not true.

If Easter be not true,
Then faith must mount on broken wing;
Then hope no more immortal spring;
Then hope must lose her mighty urge;

Life prove a phantom, death a dirge—
If Easter be not true.

If Easter be not true,
'Twere foolishness the cross to bear;
He died in vain who suffered there;
What matter though we laugh or cry,
Be good or evil, live or die,
If Easter be not true?

If Easter be not true—
But it is true, and Christ is risen!
And mortal spirit from its prison
Of sin and death within him may rise!
Worthwhile the struggle, sure the prize,
Since Easter, aye, is true!

The peace of the world is to come from the pierced hands of Christ:

And those hands hold,
Though pierced with nails
They hold on still,
Through power and pain.
And they shall hold
'Till Satan fails
And love comes to its own to reign.

In his excellent poem "The Everlasting Mercy," John Masefield, poet laureate of Britain, describes the thrill that came to Saul Kane after opening the avenues of his being to the Savior:

The station brook to my new eyes
Was babbling out of paradise,
The waters rushing from the rain
Were singing Christ was risen again.
I thought all earthly creatures knelt
From rapture of the joy I felt.

The narrow station wall's brick ledge,
The wild hop withering in the hedge,
The lights in huntsman's upper story
Were parts of an eternal glory

Were God's eternal garden flowers,
I stood in bliss at this for hours.

There are several pearls of poetic appeal the preacher can use to adorn the necklace of truth when applying all that the Lenten season implies to our Christian character and conduct, particularly the sufferings and victory of the Savior. In this category we give the preference to the spiritual masterpiece by E. C. Clephane, which is found in old hymn books.

Beneath the cross of Jesus,
I fain would take my stand,
The shadow of a mighty rock,
Within a weary land:
A home within the wilderness,
A rest upon the way,
From the burning of the noontide heat,
And the burden of the day.

George Matheson's moving lyric, "O Love That Wilt Not Let Me Go," is another composition after the same order. Not many of us dare to say that "the solemn shadow of Thy cross is better than the sun." Fewer still can accept with meek content all that full identification with the cross entails. Is not one of the lessons of the cross implied in these lines?

Just to give up, and trust
All to a fate unknown,
Plodding along life's road in the dust,
Bounded by walls of stone;
Never to have a heart at peace,
Never to see when care will cease;
Just to be still when sorrows fall
This is the bitterest lesson of all.

All through the ages martyrs and saints have found consolation in their last hours by meditating upon the final agonies of the Savior.

"Hold Thou Thy cross before my closing eyes." It is remarkable how the thought of Calvary pervades the majority of the dying sayings from the ones who sealed their testimony with their blood.

Is it not strange, the darkest hour
That ever dawned on sinful earth,
Should touch the heart with softer power

To comfort than an angel's mirth?
That to the cross the mourner's eyes should turn,
Sooner than where the stars of Christmas burn.

Yet so it is, for duly there
The bitter herbs of earth are set,
Till, tempered by the Savior's prayer,
And with the Savior's lifeblood wet,
They turn to sweetness, and deep holy balm,
Soft as imprisoned martyrs' deathbed calm.

The Poets of the Atonement

Isaac Watts was a consecrated Christian man apart from his quality as a writer of sacred song.

It is difficult to realize how comparatively small a part actual hymn writing played in his life-work in viewing him, as we do now, almost exclusively as a hymnologist. His capacious and virile mind engaged ably in several studies, including logic, education, ontology, geography, astronomy, philosophy, psychology (in *The Improvement of the Mind*), and theology; and, in them all, he had something to present which tended "to promote the glory of God, and the benefit of the human race."

No one, except a specialist in each of these fields, could now judge whether or not Watts added a permanent fragment to the structure of human knowledge in the sciences, but the average man is at least able to judge that religion and the arts profited materially by his contributions.

The Cradle Hymn

Johnson, as we have said, decried Watts' quality as a hymn writer though he was prepared to allow some virtues to the secular verses. Hasty modern critics have decided, with almost uniform agreement, to dismiss the name of Watts from the roll of English poets. He remains securely in the company of the great, however, through the fine critical discernment of Sir Arthur Quiller-Couch, whose *Oxford Book of English Verse* contains two of Watts' poems—"The Day of Judgment" and the beautiful "Cradle Hymn." Although Watts was a contemporary of Alexander Pope, he maintained an individual freedom in poetic form which is at pleasing variance with the norm of most eighteenth century verse. "The Day of Judgment" is almost a precursor (within ordered limits) of the "free verse" which is used in the present time. And our own age, which prides itself upon its intimate concern for the welfare of children, can show very few lyrics more beautiful than the "Cradle Hymn."

> Hush, my dear, lie still and slumber!
> Holy angels guard thy bed!
> Heavenly blessings without number
> Gently falling on thy head.
>
> How much better thou'rt attended
> Than the Son of God could be,
> When from heaven He descended,
> And became a Child like thee!
>
> Soft and easy is thy cradle;
> Coarse and hard thy Savior lay;
> When His birthplace was a stable,
> And His softest bed was hay.

The "Cradle Hymn" is one of the pieces from Watts' *Divine and Moral Songs for Children*, which have added a great number of proverbial phrases to the English language. Hundreds of thousands who know nothing more of Watts than his name make almost daily use of such lines as:

> For Satan finds some mischief still
> For idle hands to do.

> One sickly sheep infects the flock.

> Birds in their little nests agree.

> Let dogs delight to bark and bite.

> 'Tis the voice of the sluggard; I heard him complain,
> "You have waked me too soon, I must slumber again."

More than one descriptive title has been applied to Isaac Watts, and although it is as "The Poet of the Sanctuary" that he is best known, a more definite indication of his evangelical position is afforded by Paxton Hood, who called him "The Poet of the Atonement." It is in this character that Watts appears with full power in what many agree to regard as his finest hymn—that "masterpiece of impassioned contemplation"—"When I Survey the Wondrous Cross." As we sing this hymn—and it can be sung only in prayerful humility—we are led to the utmost negation of self as the poet draws aside the veil of delusive earthly sufficiency that too often hangs between mankind and the vision of the cross. He does not spare us any of the agony of that sacrifice, nor does he mitigate by one single heartthrob the boundless love that prompted the sacrifice:

> Sorrow and love flow mingled down

And in the last stanza there is the culminating utterance, with its tones of ringing anthem-music, in which we are led to see that it is not only all we have that must be yielded, but all we could have in any conceivable circumstances. We must be suffused by the abstract spirit of giving—the sacrificial spirit which not merely "gives something," and which is not satisfied even when it "gives everything," but which embraces the whole unmeasured impulse to "give utterly":

> Were the whole realm of nature mine,
> That were a present far too small;
> Love so amazing, so divine,
> Demands my soul, my life, my all.

Another of his Calvary hymns is, "Not All the Blood of Beasts."

Several of the hymns provide evidence of the evangelical fervor of Watt's regard for the Bible. He cries, in the hymn beginning, "Great God, with wonder and with praise":

> Here are my choicest treasures hid,
> Here my best comfort lies...
> Then may I love my Bible more,
> And take a fresh delight
> By day to read those wonders o'er,
> And meditate by night.

The Bible is his "lasting heritage," as he proclaims in another hymn— "a broad land of wealth unknown, where springs of life arise"; while, in yet another place, is found an equally eloquent testimony:

That sacred stream—Thy holy Word—
Supports our faith, our fears controls.

More than Theory

None of these utterances is the product of mere theory or theological reasoning—every one is the outcome of personal testing and experience of the unique value of the whole Bible in Christian life and practice.

When it is considered that his life was founded upon the "Unshakable Rock," fewer occasions arises for wonder that the hymns of Isaac Watts should have been so marvelously blessed in the lives of others, both in the exalted as well as the obscure. Wesley's last hours were filled with the remembrance of the hymn he never ceased to love—"I'll Praise My Maker While I've Breath"; and, "I'm Not Ashamed to Own My Lord," sustained Henry Drummond on his deathbed. That latter scene is worthy of recalling:

On the last Sunday evening of Drummond's life, March 7, 1897, his friend and physician, Dr. Barbour, played hymn-tunes to him, like he usually did. There was no response to "Lead, Kindly Light" or "Peace, Perfect Peace," so he tried "Martyrdom," an old favorite of Drummond's, and before many bars had been played he was beating time on the couch with his fingers. When Dr. Barbour began singing the fifty-fourth paraphrase, "I'm not ashamed to own my Lord" (as modified in the Scottish version of Watts' rendering), his friend's voice joined in, clear and strong, through the verse, "I know that safe with Him remains," to the end. When it was finished, he said, "Nothing can beat that, Hugh!" Then he was weary and quiet.

On Mount Calvary

Beneath a great banyan tree on Whitsunday, 1862, the king of Tonga held a service to celebrate the day on which Christian government was instituted in the land. One of the hymns sung on that occasion was "Jesus shall reign where'er the sun," and "as the people remembered how they had been saved from cannibal horrors, one after another broke down in sobs over the bitter past from which the Gospel had rescued them." A more recent incident in connection with this hymn comes from a story in the magazine *The Foreign Field*. On the Sunday morning following General Allenby's entrance into Jerusalem, Watts' great prophetic song was sung on Mount Calvary by a gathering of Lancashire Fusiliers. What an inspiring occasion that must have been!—as a little company of British soldiers sang "Jesus shall reign" over the very city that rejected and crucified Him!

In sickness and despondency, or even in the sad day when it might seem that we are laid aside for the rest of our earthly pilgrimage, can we fail to be uplifted and renewed in faith when we recall that the One who spoke of himself as "a calendar of diseases" was to have the future unspeakable joy of knowing that his words had ascended from the hill of atonement, whence "peoples and realms of every tongue" draw their assurance of salvation and their hope of eternity?

The bulk of our hymns, it will be found, are rich in their Calvary content.

It is interesting to note, as Bishop D. A. Thompson points out, that, whenever the Lord has been pleased to visit His people in a special way and on a wide scale, there has been prolific composing and singing of sacred songs, whereas the dominance of religious rationalism, higher criticism, and modernism has dispelled such fruit of the lips and heart. At such seasons of refreshment from the presence of the Lord, the love of God toward the undeserving and hell-deserving people with the other leading elements of the Gospel, occupy a prominent place in hymnology. It is instructive to observe that in these bursts of holy activity, the "precious blood of Christ" is as much stressed as it is in Holy Writ. The writers are only giving expression to their own deep spiritual conviction that nothing but that particular love of the Father, and that special grace of the Lord Jesus Christ which led Him to shed His blood and die for them, effected the great change in their lives, making the things of heaven real and joyful to them.

At the beginning of the fifth century, the church was given "The Hymn of the Holy Trinity," or as it is better known from its first two Latin words, the "Te Deum." At the close of the section dealing with the person and the work of Christ is the petition: "We therefore pray Thee, help Thy servants, whom Thou hast redeemed with Thy precious blood."

During the Dark Ages, and the long night of worldliness and error, the voice of spontaneous and joyous singing was well-nigh hushed, but with the dawn of the Reformation, true believers once again had their mouths filled with laughter and their tongues were singing. (See Psalm 126:2.) At first the composing and singing of sacred songs was largely confined to Europe. Germany led the way in this respect. Luther (1483–1546) gave his countrymen the first German hymn book and composed thirty-seven hymns himself. It was not until the seventeenth century that hymns for congregational use appeared in England and in English. In this brief study, references must be restricted almost entirely to selections from those first written in our mother tongue and which are familiar to most regular churchgoers.

Isaac Watts (1674–1748) wrote,

> Not all the blood of beasts
> On Jewish altars slain,
> Could give the guilty conscience peace,
> Or wash away the stain.

> But Christ the heavenly Lamb
> Takes all our sins away,
> A sacrifice of nobler name
> And richer blood than they.

In his hymn, "When I Survey the Wondrous Cross," the second stanza reads:

> Forbid it, Lord, that I should boast,
> Save in the death of Christ my God;
> All the vain things that charm me most,
> I sacrifice them to His blood.

Philip Doddridge (1702–1751), who composed "My God, and Is Thy Table Spread?" for use at the administration of the Lord's Supper, concludes with the lines:

> Revive Thy dying churches, Lord,
> And bid our drooping graces live;
> And more, that energy afford,
> A Savior's blood alone can give.

John Wesley (1703–1791) wrote,

> Jesus, Thy blood and righteousness,
> My beauty are, my glorious dress.

Wesley's brother Charles (1707–1788) penned these lines:

> O for a heart to praise my God,
> A heart from sin set free,
> A heart that always feels Thy blood
> So freely shed for me!

In his companion hymn, "Oh, For Thousand Tongues to Sing," is the verse:

> His blood can make the foulest clean,
> His blood availed for me.

Joseph Hart (1712–1768), in his prayer to the Holy Spirit beginning with the words, "Come Holy Spirit, Come," pleads,

> Convince us of our sin,
> Then lead to Jesus' blood,
> And to our wondering view reveal
> The secret love of God.

John Bakewell (1721–1819) in his "Hail, Thou Once Despised Jesus," declares,

> Paschal Lamb, by God appointed,
> All our sins on Thee were laid:
> By almighty love anointed,
> Thou hast full atonement made.
> All Thy people are forgiven,
> Through the virtue of Thy blood;
> Opened is the gate of heaven;
> Peace is made 'twixt man and God.

John Newton (1725–1807), in his "Come, My Soul, Thy Suit Prepare," petitions,

> With my burden I begin;
> Lord, remove this load of sin;
> Let Thy blood for sinners spilt
> Set my conscience free from guilt.

In his hymn, "Let us Love and Sing and Wonder," he concludes each verse with the lines (or a variant):

> He has washed us with His blood,
> He has brought us nigh to God.

At Olney, where he enjoyed Newton's close friendship, William Cowper (1731–1800) composed the lines:

> There is a fountain filled with blood,
> Drawn from Immanuel's veins,
> And sinners plunged beneath that flood
> Lose all their guilty stains.

Some thoroughly orthodox theological critics have not been satisfied with this verse. They have felt that the poet had failed in this particular case to give a true and consistent picture of the figure of speech used by the Hebrew prophet. (See Zechariah 13:1.) A fountain, it was objected, should be associated with "springing up," not with being "filled." Moreover, in the Levitical ceremonies, the blood of the sacrifice was applied by sprinkling (see Leviticus 14), so "plunging" was the wrong word to use. But the criticisms never extended to the term "blood" per se. Some other verses were wholeheartedly endorsed...

> Dear dying Lamb, Thy precious blood
> Shall never lose its power,
> Till all the ransomed church of God
> Be saved to sin no more.
>
> Lord, I believe, Thou hast prepared,
> Unworthy though I be,
> For me a blood-bought free reward,
> A golden harp for me.

Robert Robinson (1735–1790), author of "Come, Thou Fount of Every Blessing," concludes one of his stanzas with...

> Jesus sought me when a stranger,
> Wandering from the fold of God;
> He, to rescue me from danger,
> Interposed His precious blood.

August Toplady (1740–1778) wrote:

> Rock of Ages! cleft for me,
> Let me hide myself in Thee;
> Let the water and the blood,
> From Thy riven side which flowed,
> Be of sin the double cure,
> Save from wrath and make me pure.

Michael Bruce (1746–1767), in his "Where High the Heavenly Temple Stands," has, as the first lines of his second verse:

> He who for men their Surety stood,
> And poured on earth His precious blood.

Charlotte Elliott (1789–1871), the granddaughter of the famous preacher Henry Venn, penned the lines:

Just as I am, without one plea
But that Thy blood was shed for me,
And that Thou bidd'st me come to Thee,
O Lamb of God, I come.

Just as I am, and waiting not
To rid my soul of one dark blot,
To Thee, whose blood can cleanse each spot,
O Lamb of God, I come.

Hugh Stowell (1799–1865) wrote,

There is a place where Jesus sheds
The oil of gladness on our heads;
A place than all beside more sweet:
It is the blood-bought mercy seat.

And also...

Jesus is our Shepherd, for the sheep He bled;
Every lamb is sprinkled with the blood He shed.

An old Italian hymn concerning the blood of the Savior was translated into English by Edward Caswall (1814–1878) and began...

Glory be to Jesus,
Who, in bitter pains,
Poured for me the life-blood
From His sacred veins.

Grace and life eternal
In that blood I find;
Blest be His compassion,
Infinitely kind.

Dr. Horatius Bonar (1808–1889) places the same emphasis on "the blood" in his hymns. Every verse of "A Few More Years Shall Roll" ends with the refrain...

O wash me in Thy precious blood,
And take my sins away.

His communion hymn, "Here, O my Lord, I see Thee face to face," lead: to the central fact...

Mine is the sin, but Thine the righteousness;
Mine is the guilt, but Thine the cleansing blood;

Here is my robe, my refuge, and my peace,
Thy blood, Thy righteousness, O Lord my God!

In "I Lay My Sins on Jesus," there are the lines:

I bring my guilt to Jesus,
To wash my crimson stains
White in His blood most precious,
Till not a spot remains.

His familiar "I Was a Wandering Sheep" contains the stanza...

Jesus my Shepherd is;
'Twas He that loved my soul,
'Twas He that washed me in His blood,
'Twas He that made me whole.

In "No, Not Despairingly Come I to Thee," there is...

Faithful and just art Thou,
Forgiving all;
Loving and kind art Thou
When poor ones call,
Lord, let the cleansing blood,
Blood of the Lamb of God,
Pass o'er my soul.

A concluding sample from the Scottish theologian's sacred poetry is taken from "Not What These Hands Have Done, Can Save this Guilty Soul," in which is found:

Thy blood alone, O Lamb of God.
Can give me peace within.

Amongst the many hymns of Dr. Christopher Wordsworth (1807–1885), Bishop of Lincoln and nephew of William Wordsworth, the Lakeland poet, is that beginning, "Hark! the Sound of Holy Voices, Chanting at the Crystal Sea," whose third verse runs:

They have come from tribulation,
they have washed their robes in blood,
Washed them in the blood of Jesus;
tried they were and firm they stood.

The gifts of several deeply spiritual ladies in the last century found expression in sacred song, and they, too, made much of the precious blood of Jesus through the same Holy Spirit. Mrs. Cecil Frances Alexander (1823–1895), whose husband became the Archbishop of Armagh, in her hymn, beginning "When, wounded sore, the stricken heart, Lies bleeding and unbound," concludes with the verses:

> When penitence has wept in vain
> Over some foul, dark spot,
> One only stream, a stream of blood,
> Can wash away the blot.

> Jesus, Thy blood can wash us white;
> Thy hand brings sure relief;
> Thy heart is touched with all our joys,
> And feeleth for our grief.

> Uplift Thy bleeding hand, O Lord,
> Unseal that cleansing tide;
> We have no shelter from our sin
> But in Thy wounded side.

Amongst the hymns she wrote for children, one of the best known is that beginning "Around the throne of God in Heaven, Thousands of children stand," with its inquiry as to the cause of their presence there. The answer is given in the verse which supplies the climax of the hymn:

> Because the Savior shed His blood
> To wash away their sin;
> Bathed in that pure and precious flood,
> Behold them white and clean,
> Singing: Glory, glory, glory!

The hymns of Frances Ridley Havergal (1836–1879) abound in references to the blood of Christ. That beginning "I Am Trusting Thee, Lord Jesus," has the verse…

> I am trusting Thee for cleansing,
> In the crimson blood,
> Trusting Thee to make me holy
> By Thy blood.

Another of her compositions begins…

> I could not do without Thee,
> O Savior of the lost,

Whose precious blood redeemed me
At such tremendous cost;
Thy righteousness, Thy pardon,
Thy precious blood must be
My only hope and comfort,
My glory and my plea.

And yet another:

Thy life was given for me!
Thy blood, O Lord, was shed,
That I might ransomed be,
And quickened from the dead,
Thy life was given for me
What have I given for Thee?

In one of her hymns for children are the lines…

Jesus, Holy Savior, only Thou canst tell
How we often stumbled, how we often fell!
All our sins so many, Savior, Thou dost know;
In Thy blood most precious, wash us white as snow.

In the much-used hymn, "Who Is on the Lord's Side?" there is the
testimony:

Jesus, Thou hast bought us,
Not with gold or gem,
But with Thine own life-blood,
For Thy diadem.

To this daughter of a rectory this theme was of such surpassing importance that she devoted some seven or eight verses exclusively to it.

Precious, precious blood of Jesus,
Shed on Calvary,
Shed for rebels, shed for sinners,
Shed for me!

Precious, precious blood of Jesus,
Ever flowing free;
Oh, believe it; oh, receive it,
'Tis for thee.

Precious, precious blood of Jesus
Let it make thee whole!
Let it flow in mighty cleansing
O'er thy soul!

Though thy sins are red like crimson,
Deep in scarlet glow,
Jesus' precious blood shall wash thee
White as snow.

Precious blood that hath redeemed us!
All the price is paid!
Perfect pardon now is offered,
Peace is made.

Now the holiest with boldness
We may enter in;
For the open fountain cleanseth
From all sin.

Precious blood, by this we conquer
In the fiercest fight,
Sin and Satan overcoming
By its might.

Precious blood, whose full atonement
Makes us nigh to God!
Precious blood, our way to glory,
Praise and laud.

Mrs. A. R. Cousin (1834–1906), that lover of the writings of the Scottish Puritan, Samuel Rutherford, takes worshipers to the very heart of the Christian faith in her hymn:

O Christ, what burdens bowed Thy head!
Our load was laid on Thee;
Thou stoodest in the sinner's stead,
Didst bear all ill for me.
A victim led, Thy blood was shed,
Now there's no load for me.

Jehovah lifted up His rod—
O Christ, it fell on Thee.

Thou wast sore stricken of Thy God;
There's not one stroke for me.
Thy tears, Thy blood, beneath it flowed;
Thy bruising healeth me.

Another lady, Lucy A. Benne (1850–1927), in her plea, "O Teach Me What It Meaneth," breathes the same great truth:

O teach me what it meaneth—
That sacred crimson tide
The blood and water flowing
From Thine own wounded side
Teach me that if none other
Had sinned, but I alone,
Yet still Thy blood, Lord Jesus,
Thine only, must atone.

Mary J. Walker (1816–1878) who composed "Jesus, I Will Trust Thee," concluded with the verse...

Jesus, I will trust Thee, trust Thee without doubt;
Whosoever cometh, Thou wilt not cast out.
Faithful is Thy promise, precious is Thy blood,
These my soul's salvation, Thou my Savior God!

We turn again from the poetesses to the poets. Edward Mote (1797–1874) wrote in 1836 what Bishop Bickersteth called that "grand hymn of faith"—"My Hope Is Built."

Bishop W. Walsham How (1823–1897), for pure rhythm and for comprehensive grasp of the sacred subject to be committed to verse, has attained to a prominent place amongst hymn-writers. In his hymn beginning with the question, "Who is this?" and in which he stresses the deity and atoning work of the blessed Savior, the third verse runs...

Who is this?—behold Him shedding
Drops of blood upon the ground!
Who is this—despised, rejected,
Mocked, insulted, beaten, bound?
'Tis our God, who gifts and graces
On His church now poureth down,
Who shall smite in righteous judgment
All His foes beneath His throne.

The heart experience and theology of the Rev. Frederick Whitfield (1829–1904) was the same, as expressed in the lines…

> I need Thee, precious Jesus!
> For I am full of sin;
> My soul is dark and guilty,
> My heart is dead within.
>
> I need the cleansing fountain,
> Where I can always flee,
> The blood of Christ most precious,
> The sinner's perfect plea.

Bishop Edward H. Bickersteth (1825–1906) blazed abroad the same doctrine when he penned the verse:

> Peace, perfect peace, in this dark world of sin?
> The blood of Jesus whispers peace within.

And…

> Pray, always pray; beneath sin's heaviest load
> Prayer sees the blood from Jesus' side that flowed.

From Bristol came the hymn-writer of no mean rank, William C. Dix (1837–1898). Hear him burst into song:

> Alleluia! Sing to Jesus!
> His the scepter, His the throne;
> Alleluia! His the triumph, His the victory alone.
> Hark! the songs of peaceful Zion
> Thunder like a mighty flood:
> Jesus, out of every nation,
> Hath redeemed us by His blood.

As a final testimony to this cardinal doctrine of the Christian faith perhaps no better hymn could be cited than that written in 1877, especially for Sunday school children, by the Rev. Robert Lowry (1826–1899):

> What can wash away my sin?
> Nothing but the blood of Jesus!
> What can make me whole again?
> Nothing but the blood of Jesus!

This anthology, drawn from composers representing almost all the branches of the Christian church, and sincerely sung by countless thousands of devout worshipers over many centuries, bears witness to the fact that when the Spirit of God has brought souls under conviction of sin, and has led them to read the Word of God or to listen to its exposition to learn the way of salvation, they have found it in "the blood of Jesus." The complete absence of that phrase would indicate a sad lack of understanding, or the deliberate rejection of the gospel.

The term itself and its variants, found in the Scriptures and embodied in the hymns, lies at the very center of Christian theology and covers much that a Holy Writ reveals concerning the Person and the saving work of Christ. It implies, *inter alia*, that the second person of the Holy Trinity became man— *"the man Christ Jesus"* (1 Timothy 2:5)—without ceasing to be God; that His incarnation was effected supernaturally by birth without a human father— of the Virgin Mary; that the Holy One born of her was sinless and did no sin; that this God-man lived an altogether righteous life, that the merit of it might be imputed to all who repent and believe (see Romans 4:1–8; 5:12–21); that He died on Calvary's tree as the substitute of the people of God, bearing there those sufferings justly due to them for their sinfulness and sins (see Isaiah 53:5–6; 2 Corinthians 5:21), so that for them, after death, instead of the pains of hell, there should be bliss of heaven; and that this Jesus rose from the dead, ascended into heaven, from whence He will *"appear the second time, without sin unto salvation"* (Hebrews 9:28).

May writer and readers in their spiritual experience, by the grace of God, find their hearts touched and warmed as they meditate on this theme, and rely increasingly on that "precious blood" for present salvation and future glory.

Hymns on the Resurrection

Hymns on the resurrection have witnessed to that loyalty of heart and life to a risen, living Christ. The first leaders of the Christian church were content to be *"witnesses of the resurrection of the Lord Jesus"* (Acts 4:33). They proclaimed the resurrection as a fact; they reasoned from it as evidence; they unfolded it as vital doctrine. They taught, as Jesus Himself did, that the present life, no matter how great its opportunities, was to the believer the vestibule to a new and larger life beyond the grave. If we would secure the joy and confidence of that springtime of faith, we must give proper emphasis to the realities of the Easter message—the risen life, the life everlasting.

Christ's Guarantee

It is a question that comes home to everyone. Sometime or other we sigh for "the touch of a vanished hand, and the sound of a voice that is still."[47] Desire and reason alike point to the existence of life after death—the life of the world to come. When a man seriously sets himself to study the subject, the person of Jesus Christ rises upon him in lovely grandeur. Many have spoken doubtfully, or based their hopes on instinct or reason. Jesus alone speaks with conviction of the other world—*"because I live, ye shall live also"* (John 14:29).

Next to the New Testament, it is the great Christian poets and hymnists who support our faith and interpret the longings and aspirations of the soul for a future life. Great Christian hymns, which are popular as well as great, bear witness to the faith of the people who sing them, as well as of the men who wrote them. For the benefit of preachers and teachers, we offer this selection as a basis of a message on "Resurrection Hymns."

The first poet who deserves mention is St. John of Damascus, born about the eight century. He is generally considered the greatest of the Greek hymn-poets. John M. Neale, the translator of hymns, has described him as "the greatest of the poets of the Greek Church." His *Golden Canon* is admitted to be the grandest piece in Greek sacred poetry. He sings with a trumpet note of the keystone doctrine of Christianity, the beautiful Easter hymn:

> The day of resurrection!
> Earth, tell it out abroad,
> The Passover of gladness,
> The Passover of God!

Another of St. John's Easter hymns is notable for the poetic beauty of the symbolism which pervades it. "'Tis the spring of souls today: Christ hath burst His prison." The choicest and most-loved Latin Easter hymn is by Venantius Fortunatus. After his conversion, he became a monk, and was able to turn to use his gift of poetry for the church. He wrote the magnificent hymn, "The Royal Banners Forward Go," which Dante adopted in the *Inferno*. He composed a processional hymn for Easter, a long poem of one hundred ten lines, said to have been sung by Jerome of Prague at the stake in 1416 A.D. The best-known translation is the following with its appropriate note for Easter. The English hymn is a paraphrase made by Rev. John Ellerton in 1868:

> Welcome, happy morning! age to age shall say:
> Hell today is vanquished, Heaven is won today;

---

47. Alfred Tennyson, *Break, Break, Break*, 1835.

Lo! the dead is living, God for evermore!
Him, their true Creator, all His works adore.

In this six-stanza version is a remarkable array of the names or descriptions of Christ—God, Creator, King, Vanquisher of Darkness, Maker, Redeemer, Life, Health, Son, Author of Life, Lord. The theologian Dr. Philip Schaff delighted in this hymn, saying, "In this sweet poem the whole nature, born anew in the spring, and arrayed in the bridal garment of hope and promise, welcomes the risen Savior, the Prince of spiritual and eternal life."

Inspiration of Easter

The supreme attraction of Christianity for the heart of mankind is the hope it offers of the life of a world to come. The belief that Christ rose from the dead carries with it the Christian confidence in the future life. *"If we be dead with Christ, we believe that we shall also live with Him"* (Romans 6:8). A celebrated hymn based on this text was written by Christian F. Gellert, the son of a German pastor. He wrote many books and sacred poetry. His finest and most well-known hymn is the one beginning with...

Jesus lives! thy terrors now
Can no longer, death appall us;
Jesus lives! by this we know
Thou, O grave, canst not enthrall us.

It is not in the tombs of departed hopes or buried theories that we can find spiritual satisfaction. To meet the Master of life, we must make our way back again from these dwellings of the dead. It is the resurrection, the victory of Easter, that identifies the Jesus of the Gospels with the Christ whom the soul seeks and finds—*"That I may know him, and the power of his resurrection"* (Philippians 3:10), is the desire of every earnest Christian heart. So the hymn proceeds:

Jesus lives! for us He died;
Then, alone to Jesus living,
Pure in heart may we abide,
Glory to our Savior giving.

Philip Doddridge, a friend of Isaac Watts, was one of the founders of English hymnody and one of the greater religious personalities in the first half of the eighteenth century. Some of his hymns are among the best known in every hymnal, such as, "O Happy Day," "O God of Bethel" (Livingstone's favorite hymn), "My God, and Is Thy Table Spread?", and a few others which rank among the noblest for melody, style, and substance. His Easter hymn is based on Matthew 28:6:

> Ye humble souls, that seek the Lord,
> Chase all your fears away;
> And bow with rapture down to see
> The place where Jesus lay.

In quite a different strain, much richer in thought but less pathetic in expression is Montgomery's hymn (on the same text), "Come, See the Place Where Jesus Lay."

The personal appeal of Easter is surely a strong one, for our own good—and for the good of the community—to show that we are risen with Christ, and therefore that we seek those things which are above; and that Easter is rousing us out of our self-complacency to a fuller and higher spiritual life.

Bishop Wordsworth, nephew of the great poet, was one of our greatest modern hymn-writers. He sings of the cardinal doctrine of Christianity, the resurrection:

> Christ is risen; we are risen;
> Shed upon us heavenly grace,
> Rain and dew, and gleams of glory
> From the brightness of Thy face.

The reason why the Easter message and its corresponding faith have such a mighty and noble influence is obvious. It makes the life that now is to be an anteroom—a foretaste of glory. The suffering incidental to human life, with the inequalities that characterize it, lose their perplexity: Good Friday is succeeded by Easter Sunday. The pledge of immortality is given in the spiritual life which is now pulsing in the Christian soul; that life of faith and hope, and sublime thirst after perfection with which the decay of the body has nothing to do. The assurance grows stronger and clearer when we turn to the risen Lord. He traveled beyond the sunset, and He has come back again to tell us that beyond the grave and the gate of death:

> There is a land of pure delight,
> Where saints immortal reign;
> Eternal day excludes the night,
> And pleasures banish pain.

The resurrection of Jesus Christ is the supreme proof of the authenticity of the Gospel. It held a predominant place in the preaching of the apostles. The apostolic message was *"that Christ died for our sins according to the scriptures…and that he rose again the third day according to the scriptures"* (1 Corinthians 15:3–4). The message that Christ had died on the cross was not alone sufficient, for other religious teachers had been put to death. The resurrection was the supernatural event that marked the Christian faith as uniquely divine. It was the seal of God upon the finished work of Christ.

Easter Once the Supreme Festival

The church of the early centuries paid little or no attention to Christmas. Easter was the supreme festival, calling forth the church's utmost in ceremony, art, poetry, and music. For this reason, most of Christmas hymns are of comparatively recent origin, while many of the hymns of the resurrection have their roots deep in antiquity.

In the British Museum may be seen the only known copy of a rare volume titled *Lyra Davidica,* or a "Collection of Divine Songs and Hymns," partly new composed, partly translated from the High German and Latin Hymns: and set to easy and pleasant tunes, for more General Use (London, 1708). The unknown compiler stated that it had been his desire to introduce "a little freer air than the grave movement of the psalm tunes, as being both seasonable and acceptable."

A Tune Universally Sung

The hymn brought to the church a splendid new tune, for its "easy and pleasant tune"—from an anonymous composer—was the jubilant "Easter Hymn." James Lightwood, the eminent English authority on hymn tunes, has said, "There is probably no tune in Christendom so universally sung on any festal day as is the 'Easter Hymn,' with its rolling 'Hallelujah,' on Easter morning."

The same ringing tune is now wedded indissolubly to Charles Wesley's great resurrection hymn, "Christ the Lord Is Risen Today." If universal use is to be the criterion, this is the greatest Easter hymn of all. In both England and America, it is sung more frequently than any other on Easter Sunday. In one American city, examination of the published Easter programs of twenty-nine churches disclosed that it had been used in all but three, and usually as the opening selection.

Charles Wesley wrote "Christ the Lord Is Risen Today" in 1739 during that first year of *"joy unspeakable and full of glory"* (1 Peter 1:8), after he had come into the assurance of faith. He was a poet by talent and training; by the divine touch of conversion, his poetry flamed into sacred song. Within a year or two, he had written scores of hymns, among them being "O for a Thousand Tongues to Sing," "And Can it Be That I Should Gain," "Hark, the Herald Angels Sing," and the incomparable, "Jesus, Lover of My Soul."

The hymn as Wesley wrote it did not have the "Alleluias" that occur at the end of every line. Some hymn editor, perhaps Martin Madam, fitted Wesley's poem to the tune of "Jesus Christ Is Risen Today" and added the "Alleluias" as in that hymn to complete the measure. The use of "Alleluia" after each line was an early Christian custom, for "Hallelujah!" was the usual greeting on Easter morning.

Wesley's original eleven stanzas have been reduced to four, or at the most six, for general use. The last stanza, as found in some hymnals, proclaims the glorious destiny of believers:

> Made like Him, like Him we rise;
> Ours the cross, the grave, the skies.
> Alleluia!

Another stanza—by another author—and a hymn of the exalted Christ was transformed into a hymn of the resurrection! When Matthew Bridges wrote "Crown Him with Many Crowns" in 1851, he did not have Easter in mind. Taking his theme from Revelation 19:12, "*On his head were many crowns,*" he wrote six stanzas which suggested a description of these crowns: (1) the King, (2) the Virgin's Son, (3) the Son of God, (4) the Lord of Love, (5) the Lord of Peace, (6) and the Lord of Years.

When Godfrey Thring, an English clergyman and hymn writer, later revised the hymn, he must have felt that there should be seven crowns—the "sacred number." The crown of "Life" which he added in a stanza of his own has made the hymn an Easter favorite:

> Crown Him the Lord of life,
> Who triumphed o'er the grave;
> Who rose victorious to the strife
> For those He came to save!
> His glories now we sing,
> Who died and rose on high;
> Who died eternal life to bring
> And lives that death may die.

A number of the Easter hymns describe the crucifixion and resurrection of Christ as a battle with hell. One of the best of these is "The Strife Is O'er, the Battle Done." In each of the brief stanzas the third line turns to an outburst of joy and praise, such as, "O let the song of praise be sung. Alleluia!"

This fine hymn—again by an unknown author—was first published in Latin in Cologne, Germany, about 1695, and was translated into English by the Rev. Francis Pott in 1861. The hymn's solemn and stately tune "Victory" has been largely responsible for its ever-increasing use. This music was composed by the English musician W. H. Monk in 1861, especially for the hymn, using a theme from the famous Palestrina. Words and music are simple, dramatic, and impressive.

The resurrection of the Christian on that "last and brightest Easter morn" is the theme of a comforting little hymn by the Rev. Sabine Baring-Gould, the famous author of "Onward, Christian Soldiers" and "Now the Day Is Over."

> On the resurrection morning
> Soul and body meet again;
> No more sorrow, no more weeping,
> No more pain!

When Robert Lowry, composer of both words and music of "Christ Arose," was asked how he wrote his songs, he explained: "My brain is a sort of spinning wheel, I think, for there is music running through it all the time...I do not pick out my music on the keys of an instrument. The tunes of nearly all the hymns I have written have been completed on paper before I tried them on the organ. Frequently the words of the hymn and the music have been written at the same time."

It is almost certain that Mr. Lowry followed this method when he wrote "Christ Arose." The music itself is descriptive of the burial and resurrection of the Lord. The verses are short, slow, and solemn—"Low in the grave He lay." By contrast, the chorus is lengthy, rapid, and jubilant—"Up from the grave He arose"—rising to the climax of "Hallelujah! Christ arose."

A modern-day Easter hymn of considerable beauty and dignity that merits a place with the standard hymns of the resurrection is "He Rose Triumphantly." The poem was written by Dr. Oswald J. Smith, famous preacher, author, poet, and missionary statesman. B. D. Ackley, pianist for Billy Sunday and maker of many of our best gospel songs, composed the music which so perfectly matches the words. The verses descend, as into the grave, while the chorus rises, as in the triumph of the resurrection.

He hymns of the resurrection have come from many hands over the centuries. They are the work of many poets and musicians—some famous, some unknown. They deal with different aspects of the resurrection and in various ways. Yet with one voice they give witness that Christ is risen and that He is alive forevermore.

8

LENTEN PLAYS

The ancient Greeks were the first to develop the drama with its inclination toward imitation and mimicry. In Allica, Thespis of Icaria is credited with having introduced the first actor, who was separate from the chorus, and impersonated some character or characters of the chorus (600 A.D.). The Thespian drama was largely choral lyric with a single plot and bits of broken dialogue. Greek drama became basically serious and oriented toward religious problems—the nature of the divine, man's destiny, and the relation of man to the gods and to himself. Vast open-air theaters provided accommodation for large crowds, like the one at Acropolis holding 14,000 spectators. The tragedies presented usually had some religious, moral, or ethical significance with the actors wearing clothing copied from life accompanied by exaggerated, grotesque masks.

That theaters were in vogue during apostolic days for dramas and public gatherings is evident from the one Luke describes that was large enough to receive *"the whole city"* (Acts 19:29). Paul speaks of the saints as being a "[theatrical] *spectacle"* (1 Corinthians 4:9)—a spectacle in which the world above and below is the theater, and angels and men the spectators. The word for *"gazing stock"* (Hebrews 10:33) is *theatrigomenoi*. Criminals were often exhibited to amuse the populace in the amphitheater, and *"set forth last"* (Hebrews 12:1) in the show to fight with wild beasts. It was in the theater that Herod Agrippa I gave audience to the Syrian envoys and was struck dead by God. (See Acts 12:21–23.)

The most famous of religious plays is the one associated with Oberammergau, a village in Bavaria, Germany, famous for its remarkable wood carvings as well as the renowned drama stages every ten years. In 1633 the village was smitten by the plague, and as an expression of their gratitude for the end of the devastating scourge, the villagers vowed to enact the passion of Christ every tenth year. The first performance of the play was in 1634. It usually takes eight hours to perform, which is divided into episodes beginning with Christ's entry into Jerusalem, each episode being introduced in a song by a passion chorus of fifty singers. The vast forestage for the play is an open-air platform replete with wings, shifting scenes, and an orchestra pit for musicians. The roofed auditorium holds over five thousand spectators. All the amateur actors are chosen from among the villagers, which is a task of some magnitude seeing that there are some one hundred twenty-four speaking parts with hundreds of villagers employed for crowd scenes. Through the centuries, the technique of play-acting has been perfected so that today in theater and films we seem to have reached the limit of presentation.

Since recognition of drama is on the increase in churches of different denominations, particularly during the Christmas and Easter periods, a pastor must be careful how he acts in the matter of plays and dramas in his church. Some examples of this increased activity is the new use of accouterments for staging plays that are being added to church buildings, and several theological colleges and seminaries making provisions for a course on dramatics. The tradition of church bodies varies considerably with the more conservative among them resisting any place for drama in their church program. This fact must not be forgotten that the church is not a theater for play actors and performers, but a sanctuary in which redeemed hearts draw near to worship God and prayerfully wait on the ministry of the Word. Yet more churches are making room for pageants, plays, and dramas. For some, the trappings of the stage with costumes, make-up rooms, lighting, scenery, and other necessities in the production of a play or drama are out of harmony with the purpose and religious atmosphere of a church. Christianity is not to be acted but lived. Faith in God is begotten not by a play, but by the unadorned preaching of the Gospel in the power of the Holy Spirit. Hollywood, sensing the dramatic aspect of many Biblical episodes and personalities, has produced films in dramatic form with its eye on box-office receipts. In order to make such religious films popular, they have embellished them with a sex appeal unwarranted by the sacred record itself.

What can be most effective at Eastertide is the mass singing of some of the world's great passion oratorios, such as Handel's *Messiah*. Basil Lam would have us know—

> *Messiah* is perhaps the only supreme masterpiece to satisfy Tolstoy's demand that a work of art should be universally comprehensible. It must have been performed more frequently than any other composition with resources ranging from a village choir and

harmonium to the vast forces of nineteenth-century Handel festivals. However it is done, the work's indestructible truth and integrity will reach the listener provided only that the performance is free from mundane sophistication. The modern rediscovery of Handel's operas and dramatic oratorios, combined with a natural wish to reverse the judgments of our forbears has produced a critical reaction against Messiah. There are finer things, we are told, in his other works, greater choruses, more dramatic arias, more advanced harmonic inventions. Any experienced Handelian will admit that all this is true, but I, for one, will add that Messiah remains his greatest work; we must dismiss the superficial connoisseurship which admires fine things in isolation, and cultivates a self-absorbed sensibility—as if the purpose of great art were the production of interesting sensations.

The theme of *Messiah* was for Handel at least as exalted as that of the *Aeneid* for Virgil, or *Paradise Lost* for Milton, that is, the greatest subject he could conceive for a work of art. It is the sustained level of adequacy to its theme which makes this "sacred oratorio: unlike anything else in Handel's long sequence of inspired compositions in every form known to his age.

Even among Handel's works it is notably plain in its orchestration, a chamber-music piece which, in the autograph, occupies very few staves, as Handel writes down voice parts and strings with occasional trumpets. Mozart's well-intended improvements, it must be said, are everywhere damaging to the classical economy of Handel's line; the glorious melodies of "O Thou that Tellest" or "I Know that My Redeemer Liveth" are essentially realized in three parts. Would anyone improve a Rembrandt drawing by additions? As for ornaments, although we do not know exactly what they were, to omit them is to rob the music of an integral part of its expressiveness, so much taken for granted that it was not written down. "Authentic" versions of a work so deeply rooted in our musical culture are bound to disturb some music-lovers, but this is not the intention of those of us who are responsible for them. Those three weeks in the au~ of 1741 gave us as precious a legacy as music can show; must honor Handel by trying to maintain it in the form in bequeathed it to posterity.

If there are two or three churches in a community, with good choirs willing to unite for a Passion Choral Service, their combined effort is sure of success, especially if the music of Bach is used. Johann Sebastian Bach, the renowned German musician, and reckoned to be one of the greatest composers of all time, is reported to have written five passions, although only two have survived. *St. John Passion* appeared in 1723, and *St. Matthew Passion* in 1729. Both Passions are different in character. *St. John* is more vehement in its portrayal of crowd scenes; while *St. Matthew* presents Christ as endowed with sublime calm and tenderness, and radiates love. Bach's beloved description, "O Sacred Head Now Wounded!" appears five times. The famous composer's *Gratiasagimustibi*—"We give Thee Thanks"—expresses Bach's conviction that the true believer need not pray for peace, but should thank his God for granting him His peace. Rightly and solemnly rendered such passions can not only stir the heart, but result in a fresh appreciation of all the Lord of Glory suffered, when bruised and bleeding He paid our debt. After all, there has never been a drama in the history of the world comparable to Calvary, where among "Dramatic Personae," the crucified Lord is the divine hero.

The Story of Maundy Thursday

Although there are those who affirm that "Maundy" is from *mound*, a basket, because on the day before the great fast all religious houses and good Catholics brought out their broken food in "maunds" to distribute to the poor; its exact significance is associated with the Latin, *dies manda'ti*—the day of Christ's great mandate or commandment. After He had washed His disciples' feet, He said, *"A new commandment I give unto you, that ye love one another"* (John 13:34).

The Royal Maundy is always distributed on Maundy Thursday, the Thursday during Holy Week. In preparation for last year's service, Dr. E. M. Gresford Jones, Bishop of St. Albans, England, and presently High Almoner, explained the origin and meaning of the Maundy Service for TV viewers of the ceremony:

> From the days of Edward I onward, there are continuous records of this distribution. Sovereign after Sovereign "kept his Maundy" until the reign of James II. Then, again, in 1932 for the first time since Jacobean days the Sovereign personally distributed the Maundy gifts. King George V's successors have followed his example and within the last twenty-five years interest in the service, particularly among visitors

from the Commonwealth, has steadily increased. Usually the service is held in Westminster Abbey. This year, by command of the Queen, the service is in Southwark Cathedral in recognition of the Jubilee of the Southwark Diocese. It is believed that no Maundy Service has been held south of the Thames, with a Sovereign present, since Queen Elizabeth I attended in the Great Hall at Greenwich in 1572.

Here is a full account of this day. Then, as now, the recipients numbered as many old men and old women as the Sovereign is years of age. In 1572, Queen Elizabeth I was thirty-nine. It is recorded that the thirty-nine recipients had their feet washed, first by the laundress, then by the Sub-Almoner, then by the Lord High Almoner, then by the Queen, who washed, crossed, and kissed the feet of the poor women and then distributed her gifts, which included broadcloth to make gowns, salmon, loaves of "Cheat-bred," and claret. She gave them each the towel she had used and as the sun was setting took her departure. Gentle folks bearing "sweet flowers" attended her majesty.

Today the clothing and provisions have been commuted into money payments and the Royal mint strikes special silver coins for the occasion. In 1946 silver coins ceased to be minted, but the sterling standard was maintained in Maundy money and in this coinage alone. The silver penny half groat (2d.), threepence, and groat (4d.) are struck each year, and the Queen will hand out the coins in white leather purses with red thongs. Incidentally, it is these silver pennies, first issued in the eighth century, that give the name of sterling to our currency.

The Queen and the Duke of Edinburgh will carry nosegays of sweet herbs, so will Almonry officials, who are still girded with towels though the feet-washing lapsed in the seventeenth century through fear of infection.

Those in Southwark Cathedral will see the Queen's Bodyguard of the Yeomen of the Guard in full dress, and the children of the Royal Almonry. They will watch the Queen make the distribution, attended by her officers of the Royal Almonry. They will enjoy the music and join in prayer.

How many who see or hear the service will understand its significance? Here is the Queen continuing the ancient custom of personal service; the distribution is symbolical of the whole of the charitable gifts given by the Sovereign by way of pensions, bounty, or educational allowances.

But the Royal Maundy has a deeper meaning. The service originates in the Gospel and helps us to commemorate Christ's passion. His action in washing His disciples' feet expresses the very essence of Christian authority. It is authority expressed in service that wins our love, but we are saved by the death and resurrection of Jesus the Son of God.

The Crowning Miracle
An Easter Sunrise Service

It was from an enemy of Christianity that one of the finest descriptions of the resurrection of Christ came. Friedrich Strauss spoke of it as "The Greatest Miracle—the touchstone of Christianity itself." Keim, another critic, declared that "the whole fabric of Christianity is built upon an empty tomb." All who teach others the foundations of the Christian faith are aware of the theories formulated against the cardinal truth of the New Testament, namely, that Jesus Christ actually rose again from the dead.

There is the once popular "Fraud Theory," still held by *"certain lewd follows of the baser sort"* (Acts 17:5). The disciples in order to bolster up what Jesus had said about rising again from the dead conceived the idea of His resurrection. That godly man Paul who exhorted others to *"lie not"* (Colossians 3:9), and who taught that *"all liars have their part in the lake which burneth with fire"* (Revelation 21:8), should fabricate the story of the resurrection is unthinkable. Surely the fraud lies with those who invented such a damnable theory.

The "Swoon Theory" is almost as dishonorable as the previous one. Advocates of this explanation of the resurrection affirm that Christ did not actually die, but merely swooned, and that the coolness of Joseph's new tomb and the fragrance of the spices on His body revived Him. To anyone in their right senses, it seems ridiculous to suppose that a man could hang upon a cross for six hours, lie in the tomb for two days, roll away a huge stone, take time to fold His grave clothes, slip past sixty guards, walk into the city, and declare that all power is His (see Matthew 28:18) simply came out of a swoon. Is it not easier to believe the supernatural than the ridiculous? Did Christ Himself not say, *"I was dead; behold, I am alive for evermore"* (Revelation 1:18)?

There is also the "Myth Theory." There are many religious leaders today who would have us believe that the wondrous story of the resurrection grew, such as the myths of William Tell or Robin Hood. The narratives dealing with the creation of the world and of Adam and Eve are likewise treated as being mythical. An honest reader of Acts cannot but be impressed with the dynamic witness of the apostles as the result of the resurrection. How the fact of it transformed them from cowards into martyrs! How the church grew and multiplied through the fearless preaching of Christ's dominion over death! If such mighty conquests were the result of a myth, well might we exclaim, "Roll on, majestic myth, roll on through the ages!"

The "Vision Theory" is also believed. Exponents of this treatment of Christ's victory affirm that this story was only a fantasy imagined by the disciples. Distraught as they were by the horrors of the crucifixion, their mind played a trick on them and brought to life their dead Master again. But Paul, by divine inspiration, declared that five hundred thirty-four people testified to having seen the risen Christ at one and same time—a lot of people to mistake an actual appearance as only a passing vision!

The "Spiritualist Theory" also exists. Another denial of the resurrection says that what the disciples actually saw was not the dead Jesus risen again, but some kind of a ghost or spirit such as spiritism produces. Strange is it not how some people are willing to believe in any kind of ghost except the Holy Ghost? It was the risen Lord who said to His unbelieving disciples, *"Behold my hands and my feet, that it is I myself: handle me, and see; for a spirit hath not flesh and bones, as ye see me have"* (Luke 24:39).

Turning to the positive side, there are at least three common proofs of the resurrection of Christ which it is difficult to gainsay.

1. *The Transformation of the Disciples.* It must have been a miracle that changed a band of fearful men into the most faithful; and we believe "the crowning miracle" of the risen Christ took the cowards who forsook Him and fashioned them into the most courageous heralds of the resurrection. Once they had rolled a great stone to the door of the sepulcher the disciples departed, as if to say, "Well, it's all over. He's gone!" Their despairing attitude is shown by the two sad disciples whom Jesus met on the Emmaus road. (See Luke 24:21.) But what a tremendous transformation the realization of the resurrection made. At Pentecost, only three weeks after Christ rose again, those once forlorn men stood in the midst of the very murderers of Christ and boldly condemned them with the

crime of history. (See Acts 2:14; 3:14; 4:13, 19). What had brought about such a dramatic change? Why, Christ was alive, and they had seen Him, heard Him, *"ate and drank with Him"* (Acts 10:41), and followed their time with him with turning the world upside down because they were endued with the power of their risen Lord.

2. *The Establishment and Expansion of the Church.* Soon after He entered His public ministry, Jesus informed His disciples that He would *"utter things which have been kept secret from the foundation of the world"* (Matthew 13:35), and one of those secrets was the formation of the mystic fabric He called *"My church"*; Paul spoke of this as *"the mystery hid from the ages"* (Ephesians 3:4–5). He was to build upon the foundation of Himself and His death and resurrection. (See Matthew 16:18.) With His ascension to heaven and the coming of the Holy Spirit, this spiritual structure began to visualize. Pentecost added 3,000 to the church, and then another 5,000, until there was a swelling tide of salvation during the first century. Luke the historian could write that as the outcome of Paul's labor, myriads—the Greek meaning of *"thousands"* (Acts 21:20)— became believers. Since those great days, countless millions down the centuries have been added to the church which is His body. Furthermore, there are millions throughout the world today who worship the One who died and rose again for their salvation. Then the church has the perpetual memorials of Christ's victory over death in the Lord's Day, baptism, and the Lord's Supper.

3. *The Apostolic Witness.* Perhaps the most outstanding living proof of the resurrection of Christ is the apostle Paul, whose life was completely revolutionized through a personal vision of the risen, glorified Son of God. (See Acts 9:5.) The most remarkable man of his own age, he has remained an outstanding character of the ages. His teachings and triumphs mark him out as one of the most precious witnesses Christ ever produced. Paul came to write of *"the power of his resurrection"* (Philippians 3:10), and if ever a Christian experienced such resurrection power to the limit, it was *"the chief of sinners"* (1 Timothy 1:15), as Paul described himself. No wonder he gave to the church the "Magna Carta of the Resurrection," referring to 1 Corinthians 15!

The apostle makes it clear that if Christ did not rise again, then His teachings have gone to the winds as autumn leaves before the storm; and that if His sacred dust reposes beneath a Syrian sky, we are still in our sins. But all that Christ taught, along with His death and resurrection worked miracles among multitudes, liberated slaves, captivated the hearts of the ignorant and learned alike, embraced the world, and continues to conquer. (See Revelation 6:2.) Furthermore, Paul would have us know that every born-again believer is a living witness of a living Christ at God's right hand. Believing that *"Christ is risen from the dead"* (1 Corinthians 15:20), untold numbers of evangelists, missionaries, teachers, and a vast multitude of unknown Christians have proved that Christ, because He could not be held by death, is *"able to save to the uttermost all who come to God by him"* (Hebrews 7:25).

The necessity of the resurrection is postulated on the question Paul raised, *"If Christ be not raised,"* then…

Preaching is vain. All the dynamic, faithful, transforming preaching of all the ages is wasted wind if it proclaimed a dead Christ. (See 1 Corinthians 15:14.)

Faith is vain. Belief in a dead man can never save those who are dead in sin. Emancipation from the guilt and power of sin can only come through one who is delivered for our offenses and raised again for our justification. (See 1 Corinthians 15:14; Romans 4:25; 5:1).

Assurance is vain. If Christ be not risen, Christians are yet in their sins. Instead of being in Christ, where Satan cannot touch them, they are in their sins, and thus in danger of eternal doom. (See 1 Corinthians 15:17; 2 Corinthians 5:17.)

Reunion is vain. If Christ was not raised from the dead, then none of the human race shall ever rise. The dead are dead forever. All hope of immortality has gone, and the prospect of a blissful reunion of the saints in heaven is a wishful dream. (See 1 Corinthians 15:18.) But we have the assurance of the risen One to which we cling, *"Because I live, ye shall live also"* (John 14:19). If there is no resurrection, then we are indeed of all men most miserable, duped in time, and forever lost in eternity. But, glory to His name, He lives! He is a Savior in life, a comforter in death, and a glorious Lord throughout the boundless future.

As for the present benefits of the resurrection, how they certify to its reality…

+ The Forgiveness of Sins (See Ephesians 1:7)
+ The Dominion Over Sin (See Romans 6:18; 1 John 5:4)
+ The Access to God (See Romans 5:2; Ephesians 2:18)
+ The New Nature (See 2 Corinthians 5:17)
+ The Savior Who Is the Prince of Life (See Acts 5:31)

Rejoice! the grave is overcome,
And lo! the angels sing;
The grandest triumph ever known
Has come through Christ our King;
All heaven proclaims the dawning
Of love's all glorious morning.[48]

---

48. Fanny Crosby, "Look Up! Ye Weary Ones."

BIBLIOGRAPHY

Note: the publisher has updated this bibliography to reflect the most recent publishers and printings that are available to the reader today.

Alexander, William. *Verbum Crucis: Being Ten Sermons on the Mystery and the Words of the Cross : To Which Are Added Some Other Sermons.* Charleston, SC: Nabu Press, 2012.

Babbage, Stuart Barton. *The Light of the Cross.* Grand Rapids: Zondervan, 1966.

Baxter, J. Sidlow. *Baxter's Explore the Book.* Grand Rapids: Zondervan, 1986.

Clow, William MacCallum. *The Cross in Christian Experience.* Charleston, SC: BiblioBazaar, 2009.

_____. *The Day of the Cross.* London: Hodder & Stoughton, 1908.

Criswell, W. A. *Expository Notes on the Gospel of Matthew.* Grand Rapids: Zondervan, 1973.

Denny, James. *The Death of Christ.* Wheaton, Illinois: Tyndale Press, 1970.

Ford, W. Herschel. *Seven Simple Sermons on the Savior's Last Words.* Grand Rapids: Zondervan, 1953.

Fox, Selina Fitzherbert. *Chain of Prayer Across the Ages.* London: John Murray Publishers Ltd., 1956.

Gilfillan, George. *The Bards of the Bible.* Charleston, SC: Nabu Press, 2011.

Gutzke, Manford G. *Plain Talk on Luke.* Grand Rapids: Zondervan, 1966.

_____. *Plain Talk on Matthew.* Grand Rapids: Zondervan, 1971.

Hardy, Thomas. *The Years with Christ.* London: A. R. Mowbray Co., 1935.

Henry, Matthew. *Matthew Henry's Commentary on the Whole Bible.* Peabody, MA: Hendrickson Publishers, 2008.

Hobbs, Herschel H. *The Life and Times of Jesus.* Grand Rapids: Zondervan, 1966.

Huegel, F. J. *Bone of His Bone*. Grand Rapids: Zondervan, 1960.

_____. *The Cross Through the Scriptures*. Grand Rapids: Zondervan, 1966.

Jamieson, R. *Jamieson, Fausett, and Brown's Commentary on the Whole Bible*. Grand Rapids: Zondervan, 1999.

Keble, John, *The Christian Year*. Ulan Press, 2011.

Krummacher, F. W. *The Suffering Savior*. Edinburgh: Banner of Truth 2004.

Lee, Robert Greene. *From Death to Life Through Christ*. Grand Rapids: Zondervan, 1966.

_____. *Salvation in Christ*. Grand Rapids: Zondervan, 1961.

Liddon, H. P. *Passiontide Sermons*. London: Longmans, Green, and Co.: London, 1891.

Loane, Marcus L. *Life Through the Cross*. Grand Rapids: Zondervan, 1966.

_____. *The Voice of the Cross*. Grand Rapids: Zondervan, 1963.

Marshall, Catherine. *The Prayers of Peter Marshall*. New York: McGraw-Hill, 1954.

McCarrell, William. *Christ's Seven Last Words from the Cross*. Andover, NH: Dunham Publishing Company, 1965.

Milligan, William. *The Resurrection of Our Lord*. Charleston, SC: Nabu Press, 2011.

Morison, Frank, *Who Moved the Stone?* Grand Rapids: Zondervan, 1987.

Moule, H. C. G. *The Call of Lent to Penitence, Discipline and Christ*. London: Sequor Ltd., 2012.

Mortimer, A. G., *Meditations on the Passion of Our Most Holy Redeemer*. London: Longmans, Green, and Company, 1903.

Murray, Andrew. *The Blood of the Cross*. Eastford, CT: Martino Fine Books, 2012.

Pink, Arthur W. *Exposition of the Gospel of John*. Grand Rapids: Zondervan, 1968.

Rauschenbusch, Walter, *Prayers of the Social Awakening*. Charleston, SC: Nabu Press, 2010.

Reid, S. J. *Do Not Sin Against the Cross*. Grand Rapids, Eerdmans, 1940.

Rimmer, Harry. *Voices from Calvary*. Grand Rapids, Eerdmans, 1945.

Spurgeon, Charles H. *Christ's Words from the Cross*. Grand Rapids: Baker Publishing Group, 1981.

Stalker, James, *The Trial and Death of Jesus*. Ulan Press, 2011.

Stidger, William L. *I Saw God Wash the World*. Chicago: The Rodeheaver Hall-Mack Co., 1934.

Strauss, Lehman, *The Day God Died*. Grand Rapids: Zondervan, 1974.

Westcott, Brook Foss. *The Gospel of the Resurrection*. London: Macmillan Co., 1866.

ABOUT THE AUTHOR

When Dr. Herbert Lockyer (1886–1984) was first deciding on a career, he considered becoming an actor. Tall and well-spoken, he seemed a natural for the theater. But the Lord had something better in mind. Instead of the stage, God called Herbert to the pulpit, where as a pastor, Bible teacher, and author of more than fifty books, he touched the hearts and lives of millions of people.

Dr. Lockyer held pastorates in Scotland and England for twenty-five years. As pastor of Leeds Road Baptist Church in Bradford, England, he became a leader in the Keswick Higher Life Movement, which emphasized the significance of living in the fullness of the Holy Spirit. This led to an invitation to speak at the Moody Bible Institute's fiftieth anniversary in 1936. His warm reception at that event led to his ministry in the United States. He received honorary degrees from both the Northwestern Evangelical Seminary and the International Academy in London.

In 1955, he returned to England, where he lived for many years. He then returned to the United States, where he spent the final years of his life in Colorado Springs, Colorado, with his son, the Rev. Herbert Lockyer Jr., a Presbyterian minister who became his editor.